The Tragedy of Human Development

The Tragedy of Human Development

A Genealogy of Capital as Power

Tim Di Muzio

ROWMAN & LITTLEFIELD
INTERNATIONAL

London • New York

Published by Rowman & Littlefield International Ltd
Unit A, Whitacre Mews, 26–34 Stannary Street, London SE11 4AB
www.rowmaninternational.com

Rowman & Littlefield International Ltd. is an affiliate of Rowman & Littlefield
4501 Forbes Boulevard, Suite 200, Lanham, Maryland 20706, USA
With additional offices in Boulder, New York, Toronto (Canada), and Plymouth (UK)
www.rowman.com

British Library Cataloguing in Publication Data
A catalogue record for this book is available from the British Library

ISBN: HB 978-1-7834-8713-4
         PB 978-1-7834-8714-1

Library of Congress Cataloging-in-Publication Data Is Available
Names: Di Muzio, Tim, author.
Title: The tragedy of human development : a genealogy of capital as power /
    Tim Di Muzio.
Description: London ; New York : Rowman & Littlefield International, Ltd., 2018. |
    Includes bibliographical references and index.
Identifiers: LCCN 2017041092 (print) | LCCN 2017054303 (ebook) |
    ISBN 9781783487158 (Electronic) | ISBN 9781783487134 (cloth : alk. paper) |
    ISBN 9781783487141 (pbk : alk. paper)
Subjects: LCSH: Capitalism—Political aspects. | Power (Social sciences) | Money. |
    Accounting. | Right of property.
Classification: LCC HB501 (ebook) | LCC HB501 .D4625 2018 (print) |
    DDC 330.12/2—dc23
LC record available at https://lccn.loc.gov/2017041092

Printed in the United States of America

For Amanda, Michaela, Vince, Ryann, and Mitch.
May your minds be wide open and your hearts lead you on.

Contents

Foreword

No book is easy. The present work was largely inspired by my last study on the rise of a global petro-market civilization and what I called "carbon capitalism." Therein I explored the transition to fossil fuels as an historical exception, tracing it through Britain, the United States, and capitalist world order more broadly. Given the nonrenewable nature of fossil fuels and the elite penchant for building more energy-soaked built environments, I argued that we are headed toward a general crisis of social reproduction where energy-intensive lifestyles will no longer be reproducible. I concluded the book with the following phrase: "After all it would be the ultimate tragedy of human development 'if the history of the human race proved to be nothing more noble than the story of an ape playing with a box of matches on a petrol dump'" (Di Muzio 2015b: 171). The phrase "tragedy of human development" seemed to flow naturally from my analysis, and I barely gave it a second thought until the book arrived in hard copy months after those words were written. Upon rereading the book, the phrase jumped out at me in bolder reliefs: what would it mean to conceive of human development—indeed our history as a species— as a tragedy? It seemed an open and interesting question, particularly given other renderings of human history as progress or catastrophe. The philosopher Walter Benjamin (1892–1940) had already declared human history one giant catastrophe, a radical statement if there ever was one and a somber philosophy of human affairs given our many achievements. The other extreme is the liberal, progressive view of history as a stadial exercise in human betterment finally realized in a commercial society. Our liberal friends do not always deny the atrocities of the stadial history they recount, but they are heavily discounted. It always seemed to me that this reading of history was far too optimistic and far too injudicious. Too optimistic in the sense that there is a liberal tendency to believe that capitalism and the price mechanism of the market will come to our rescue at every turn, if only in the long run for some. Too injudicious in the sense that our liberal friends are happy to somewhat acknowledge the horrible events of our history but like good capitalists are happy to "write off" or "write down" these events because it stops them from looking forward. Between these two extremes—catastrophe and progress—I believe we find tragedy. I will explain what I mean in greater detail later but for now allow me a few words about the subtitle of this book: a genealogy of capital as power. What I want to demonstrate in this book—if only in outline—is the emergence of a historical contradiction between the logic of differential accumulation, which aims for the greater inequality of power, income, and wealth and the logic of livelihood that is mostly concerned with acquiring those things most closely associated with a decent life. While they overlap, I will argue that these logics are fundamentally at odds and the crux of the tragedy of human development. In a word, the tragedy results because the logic of differential accumulation operates in the interests of the very few and supersedes the logic of livelihood. The weapons of differential accumulation are monetization, commodification, ownership and exclusion, and, ultimately, capitalization and war. We are so used to these weapons that few of us stop to question their historical emergence. They are taken as "self-evident," a part of the "natural" world, as though things have always been this way. But things have not always been this way. In this light, the task I have set for myself in this study is to then, if not fully trace their emergence in all their geographical and historical complexity, at least provide somewhat of a guideline for future study. The task has not been easy given the scale of human history covered in this book and the still mounting array of literature scattered across disciplines. As the reader will be able to tell from the references, this book has been built on the shoulders of giants but it has also no less been constructed on the back of those whose work is lesser known but without which, we would know far, far less about ourselves and our world. I owe a great deal of intellectual debt to their work. But while this book has engaged literature across disciplines, at base it is wholly a work of critical political economy, that master social science that refuses to believe that politics and power can be separated from capitalist accumulation, the price mechanism of the market, and the increasing concentration of wealth and power so prevalent today. This book will have silences, gaps, and disappointments, but I hope these are at least matched by new discoveries, novel arguments, and new questions in need of answers. Ultimately, and whatever the shortcomings of this book, I think we must ask ourselves if it is possible for the logic of livelihood to triumph over the logic of differential accumulation. I will take up this question toward the end of this work when I discuss the biopolitics of global capitalism. But for now it is time to end this foreword and get to the task at hand. For after all, the hurricane of our history cannot roar in opening words alone.

Tim Di Muzio
Sydney, Toronto, Brussels, Paris

Acknowledgments

While the act of researching and writing can be a solitary effort, it is seldom done entirely alone. A debt of gratitude is owed to many people—living, dead and those whom I have not met but whose work I engage. It is impossible to name everyone but I do want to acknowledge the following people. My greatest debt is to Matt Dow who is an exemplary researcher. Without his help this book would not have been possible. I also thank Hanna Kivistö for her patience and thoughtful discussions throughout the period I was engaged with this project. My best friends Tony Guindon and Art Piatek were exemplary hosts in both Toronto and Brussels and they contributed to this book more than they are likely aware. Stephen Gill and Isabella Bakker are a constant source of inspiration and I thank them for their hospitality and our discussions up at the Pines when I returned to Canada on study leave. I owe a debt of gratitude to Tim Onslow for countless discussions, Sydney nights filled with music and for sorting the index. My family both immediate and extended were also a constant source of support and encouragement. Last I want to thank my colleagues and students at the University of Wollongong who have helped make life on campus pleasant and intellectually engaging.

Prologue

THE PLANET OF THE APES HYPOTHESIS

This is a political economy of the present as history. It is about the emergence and development of the capitalist mode of power and the possibility for a general crisis of social reproduction. Our story begins in the municipality of Arecibo, Puerto Rico, where we find one of humanity's most iconic achievements. Built over three years from 1960 to 1963, Arecibo is home to the world's largest radio telescope.[1] It is 305 meters in diameter and has a listening surface of 73,000 square meters. Originally, the giant dish was constructed to help the United States detect incoming intercontinental ballistic missiles during the Cold War. Today, the purpose of the giant radio telescope is rather different and includes "radio astronomy, planetary radar and terrestrial aeronomy."[2] But perhaps one of its more interesting tasks is helping the Search for Extraterrestrial Intelligence (SETI) attempt to find intelligent life in the universe. We human beings have long pondered whether we are the only high intelligence animals in the universe and it is only in the past fifty to sixty years that we have had the capacity to operate large radio telescopes that should be able to detect distant signals from intelligent life-forms light-years away. The notion that there may be intelligent life-forms, not to mention various biological life-forms in general, on distant planets from our own may seem odd to those of us outside the fields of astrobiology and astrophysics. However, using data from the Kepler mission, astronomers have recently estimated that there may be billions of habitable planets in our galaxy alone. If their calculations are accurate, extrapolating the data to account for the 100 billion galaxies observed by the Hubble Space Telescope means the potential for an almost unimaginable number of planets capable of supporting life (Bovaird et al. 2015). To some, what this suggests is that the chances

1

of life on planet Earth being the only life in the universe can be considered statistically slim. But what astronomers and other space enthusiasts care more about is the following question: "Once there is life of any kind, what is the probability that it will evolve into a human-like intelligence that can build and operate radio telescopes?" (Lineweaver in Seckbach and Walsh 2008: 355). Why is the construction of a radio telescope so important? The answer is twofold. First, radio waves are used to communicate across long distances, including interstellar communication. Thus, if there were an intelligent species and they would want to communicate with us, it would likely be by radio waves. Second, a radio telescope is needed to pick up radio waves from outer space. But what is the likelihood of another species developing such a technology? One way this question has been addressed is by the famous Drake Equation named after the astronomer Frank Drake, the founder of SETI. The goal of the Drake Equation is to find out the number (N) of civilizations in our galaxy whose electromagnetic emissions might be detectable. Drake proposed that the number (N) could be calculated using the following formula:

$$N = R^* f_p\, n_e f_l f_i f_c\, L.$$

The components of the equation are as follows:

R^* = The rate of formation of stars suitable for the development of intelligent life
f_p = The fraction of those stars with planetary systems
n_e = The number of planets, per solar system, with an environment suitable for life
f_l = The fraction of suitable planets on which life actually appears
f_i = The fraction of life-bearing planets on which intelligent life emerges
f_c = The fraction of civilizations that develop a technology that releases detectable signs of their existence into space
L = The length of time such civilizations release detectable signals into space[3]

According to scientists at SETI, the first three components are relatively well known and, to a considerable degree, calculable. The difficulty, however, lies in knowing the other four components. As such, the Drake Equation is only a very rough guide for discovering the number of planets with intelligent life capable of communicating with radio telescopes. At a meeting of astronomers in Green Bank, West Virginia, in 1961, Drake estimated N to be about 10,000 whereas the famed astronomer Carl Sagan estimated N to be far higher: in the millions! Others believe, however, that $N = 1$, which translates into the fact that we have been the only species in the universe capable of developing radio telescopes and launching our technology into space. Those who believe that $N = 1$ or that N is an incredibly small number, believe not only that high intelligence of the human kind is exceptional but also that intelligence—again of the human kind—may not be selected out for survival. Those who argue that N is likely a large number typically subscribe to what the astrophysicist Charles H. Lineweaver calls the Planet of the Apes Hypothesis. Lineweaver borrows the terminology for his hypothesis from the popular film *Planet of the Apes* (1968). The film depicts a world where most humans have been annihilated by nuclear war and chimps, gorillas, and orangutans eventually develop "human-like intelligence" and effectively rule the world (Lineweaver in Seckbach and Walsh 2008: 355). In other words, the apes filled an "intelligence niche" and, over time, developed greater intelligence. Thus, the Planet of the Apes Hypothesis argues for the "stupid things get smarter" theory of evolution. This debate was perhaps most famously had by Carl Sagan (mentioned previously) and the eminent evolutionary biologist Ernst Mayr. The question put to Mayr, who started the debate, was whether SETI had any chance of success finding intelligent life on another planet. Mayr's reasoning was relatively straightforward and based on probability. He argued that it was probable that life—in some form—exists on other planets given that there are billions of them in the known universe. But as an evolutionary biologist he argued that all the factors that contributed to making human beings intelligent were likely never to be repeated. Mayr notes how, to the best of our fossil evidence, life on the earth began about 3.8 billion years ago in a very simple form. And yet, of all the life-forms created in the world throughout this time, only one phyletic lineage produced the intelligence to build a radio telescope. The controversy is spelled out by Mayr:

> How many species have existed since the origin of life? This figure is as much a matter of speculation as the number of planets in our galaxy. But if there are 30 million living species, and if the average life expectancy of a species is about 100,000 years, then one can postulate that there have been billions, perhaps as many as 50 billion species since the origin of life. Only one of these achieved the kind of intelligence needed to establish a civilization.[4]

Since one in fifty billion is very rare, Mayr asks himself why this is the case. First, he argues that human intelligence must not be favored by natural selection and notes that there are millions of species getting on fine without the ability to build radio telescopes. A second possible reason for the rarity of high intelligence may be due to the specific factors that allow for a higher Encephalization Quotient (EQ) in human beings. At its simplest, EQ is a measure of the ratio of the brain's mass to body weight. The assumption here is that the larger the brain is relative to the body, the greater the likelihood that the brain can perform more difficult cognitive tasks. Still, even if we can agree that EQ is a good indicator of intelligence, as Lineweaver points out, there is a big difference between "intelligence" as measured by EQ and the capacity for a technological civilization:

> Today there are about a million species of protostomes and about 600,000 species of deuterostomes (of which we are one). We consider ourselves to be the smartest deuterostome. The most intelligent protostome is probably the octopus. After 600 million years of independent evolution and despite their big brains, octopi do not seem to be on the verge of building radio telescopes. The dolphinoidea evolved a large E.Q. between ~60 million years ago and ~20 million years ago. . . . Thus, dolphins have had ~20 million years to build a radio telescope and have not done so. This strongly suggests that high E.Q. may be a necessary, but is not a sufficient condition for the construction of radio telescopes (in Seckbach and Walsh 2008: 363).

Ever the optimist, Sagan's retort to this line of reasoning begins by recognizing the sheer number of habitable planets that can support biological life-forms. From there, he moves to suggest that there may be unimagined evolutionary pathways toward intelligence and that we should not think of necessarily finding humanoids on other planets but any being that develops the technical capacity to make a radio telescope. Sagan adds that some planets orbit a sun that is ten billion years old, which means that any communication is likely to come from a more advanced civilization (our sun is estimated to be about 4.6 billion years old). He rests his case for technological development on the fact that any intelligent civilization will eventually have to stumble upon the physics of radio waves since planets and their populations are under constant (though perhaps not frequent) threat of comets and asteroids. Thus, Sagan suggests that the technology used in the SETI program is likely to be reproduced by intelligent extraterrestrials for their own safety. This is because objects in space emit radio waves and this is one way to tell whether an object is on a collision course with life. In the end, Sagan argues that we ought not judge prior to having sense experience and that to be good scientists we have to experiment and observe rather than rule out hypotheses based on our own narrow experience of life on the earth. In his view, SETI is a worthwhile project and should be supported.

The debate is a difficult one to resolve and given our limited knowledge of many factors, it is unlikely that a clear answer to whether there is intelligent life on other planets will be solved any time soon. There is also the relevant but ignored question of what energy source intelligent beings may have access to and whether this energy source is abundant enough for a complex civilization. On Earth, radio telescopes would not have developed without the scientific and industrial revolutions powered largely by nonrenewable fossil fuels (Di Muzio 2015b). Are we to assume that coal, petroleum, and natural gas will be found in plentiful amounts on other planets? And even if they were, would intelligent life-forms use these resources? Fossil fuels have been around long before humankind, but it is only in the past three centuries or so that we have used them in any considerable amount, far less than 1 percent of time since the dawn of *Homo sapiens* about 200,000 years ago (Harari 2011: ix). Thus, there are a number of factors to consider when we think about the potential for intelligent life on other planets that can build a radio telescope. But the debate does raise a very important proposition to consider about the history of humankind: whether it is better to be smart or stupid, intelligent, or ignorant.

As Chomsky (2004) suggests, we may be entering a period of history where this empirical question may be answered once and for all. We already know that we are the only species on the earth to have developed the capacity to annihilate most life on this planet and that during the so-called Cold War, the United States and Soviet Union came dangerously close to triggering a nuclear war during the Cuban Missile Crisis. It appears that but for a Russian Navy Officer named Vasili Alexandrovich Arkhipov, who refused his captain's permission to launch a nuclear torpedo at a US flotilla, World War III may very well have begun with the Soviet Union and the United States setting off scores of nuclear warheads directed at military bases and major cities (Savranskaya 2005). The Federation of American Scientists, an organization working to reduce the spread and number of nuclear weapons, reports that there are 15,800 nuclear warheads held by nine states: the United States, Israel, Russia, China, Pakistan, India, the United Kingdom, France, and North Korea.[5] All it may take for a nuclear exchange to occur is a simple error let alone political miscalculation, misunderstanding, or a sheer act of self-indulgent bravado by one of the world's leaders. The Doomsday Clock, maintained as a symbol for potential global catastrophe by the Bulletin of Atomic Scientists at the University of Chicago, is also a sad reminder of our potential for self-destruction. Since its inception in 1947, the clock has been adjusted twenty-two times with midnight symbolic of global catastrophe. In early 2017, the clock was adjusted to just two and a half minutes to midnight, the second closest the clock has ever been to midnight. The justification for moving the clock's hand is the rise in xenophobic nationalism, renewed talk about ramping up nuclear weapons, continued nonaction on climate change, and the election of Donald Trump to the US presidency.[6] But even if we do not manage to blow ourselves up, we appear to be doing a stellar job destroying our environment in multiple dimensions. The most obvious threat is global climate change propelled by our use of fossil fuels and killing sentient beings for food in mass-scale factory farms. The Intergovernmental Panel on Climate Change (IPCC) reports that:

> anthropogenic greenhouse gas emissions have increased since the pre-industrial era, driven largely by economic and population growth, and are now higher than ever. This has led to atmospheric concentrations of carbon dioxide, methane and nitrous oxide that are unprecedented in at least the last 800,000 years. Their effects, together with those of other anthropogenic drivers, have been detected throughout the climate system and are *extremely likely* to have been the dominant cause of the observed warming since the mid-20th century (2014: 4).

Scientists anticipate that climate change will impact regions differently, but with varying degrees of certainty, humanity as a whole is likely to witness melting polar ice caps; extreme strains on fresh water; more intense storms; a greater propensity for floods, droughts, and wildfires; the loss of habitable land and species; the acidification of the oceans; and a rise in sea levels, just to name some of the major calamities already experienced in certain regions of the world (IPCC 2014). Such prospects have the likelihood of creating greater refugee crises, heightened tensions between nations, and more armed conflict. As Klein (2014) spelled out in her popular book on climate change: "This changes everything." Many politicians worldwide are of course aware of the potential danger and the economic catastrophes runaway climate change will likely entail. To address the international and interconnected nature of the problem, state representatives met in Paris in December of 2015. Though there was considerable self-congratulations and fanfare when the delegates announced a historically unprecedented accord, scientists who have considered the accord have argued that the proposed measures will only cut emissions by half of what they should be reduced to in order to avoid dangerous climate change.[7] Moreover, it is unclear whether the states that are party to the agreement will necessarily follow through on their commitments.

While most people will be aware that the combustion of oil, coal, and natural gas is a major contributor to climate change, it is only now, thanks to the work of Kip Andersen and Keegan Kuhn in popularizing the facts in their documentary film *Cowspiracy* (2014), that a broader population is becoming conscious of the fact that animal agriculture is potentially the single largest contributor to climate change (FAO 2006; Goodland and Anhang 2009). Indeed, as I have detailed in the previous work, we live in an era of carbon capitalism and our civilizational orders can largely be conceived of as hierarchical petro-market civilizations reliant, though in highly uneven dimensions, on the consumption of nonrenewable carbon energy for economic growth, a good swathe of our food systems, and what Brand and Wissen have called the "imperial mode of living" (2013). This "imperial mode of living" involves high-energy patterns of social reproduction that currently provide a relatively small portion of humanity with material comforts and a reasonable, and in many cases excessive and environmentally ruinous, standard of living (Bakker and Gill 2003; Di Muzio 2015a, 2015b; Gill 1995). In earlier work I have defined what I mean by social reproduction, but it is worthwhile restating the definition in this work. By the concept of social reproduction I mean the ways in which any given historical society produces, consumes, and reproduces its lifestyle; how it understands or interprets this lifestyle; and how it justifies and defends this particular pattern of living against potential challenges and threats. Appreciating the quality, quantity, and type of energy available to society is crucial for understanding any pattern of social reproduction, and this means that we must be keenly aware of the energy source that supports forms of social reproduction in any given epoch (Debeir et al. 1991; Di Muzio 2015b; Hall and Klitgaard 2012; Podobnik 2006; Smil 1994).

Currently, our global energy conundrum is of serious concern (Di Muzio 2015b; Di Muzio and Ovadia 2016; Heinberg 2003, 2007; Hirsch 2005; Klare 2009; Rubin 2009, 2012). According to the International Energy Agency, as of 2013 the world's total energy supply comes from fossil fuels at 81.4 percent, only slightly down from when statistics started to be recorded in 1973 when it was 86.7 percent. Moreover, global energy consumption is fossil fuel–laden. World total final consumption in 2013 was 65.5 percent, down from 75.9 percent in 1973 when statistics first started to be gathered by the International Energy Agency. But since consumption, like production, is highly uneven, if we consider the Organization for Economic Co-operation and Development (OECD), a club of the most "advanced" states, total final consumption is just over 70 percent in 2013, down from 83.8 percent in 1973. What these figures suggest is that we are nowhere near a global renewable energy economy despite popular incantations in the media and some meagre attempts worldwide to invest in renewable energy and low carbon growth. Of all the fossil fuels, oil is the most important for transport and economic growth and many countries have built their economies and environments to support a future vision where oil will be used as a fuel source in perpetuity. The bad news is twofold. First, the combustion of petroleum is a key contributor to climate change and burning what remains will almost certainly cause irreversible damage to a more habitable biosphere. Indeed, the former head of NASA's Goddard Institute for Space Studies, James Hansen, and colleagues established that "burning all fossil fuels would threaten the biological health and survival of humanity, making policies that rely substantially on adaptation inadequate" (Hansen et al. 2013: 25). Second, we are tragically continuing to construct built environments that are oil-dependent when we appear to know that petroleum is a nonrenewable source of energy. According to the most authoritative statistics kept by BP, as of 2015 there were only 50.7 years of oil remaining at current rates of production.[8] To be sure, conservation, economic downturns, and new finds may slow the decline in oil production over time, but the gross failure of our political leaders to collectively address the issue of oil's non-renewability borders on extreme negligence and a myopic politics of the future. Moreover, while estimates vary, coal and natural gas are also in danger of being depleted this century (Energy Watch Group 2011). As I have previously argued, neoliberal solutions that "leave it up to the market" to solve our energy problems are highly likely to fail given that the oil and gas sector remains highly profitable relative to the renewable energy sector (Di Muzio in Gill 2011 and Di Muzio 2012). To be fair, it is a Herculean task but the faster a transition is planned, organized, coordinated, and put into action, the better for future generations if we want to avoid a general crisis of social reproduction (Abramsky 2010; Di Muzio 2015b).

Another worrisome trend, despite our intelligence, is growing inequality within and between nations. Capgemini and RBC note that there are 14.6 million humans on the planet with at least US$1 million in investible assets (2015: 7). This represents a tiny fraction of the planet's population at 0.2 percent. Of these high-net-worth individuals, Credit Suisse reported that there are 120,000 ultra-high-net-worth individuals with at least US$50 million or over in wealth. That number represents a miniscule 0.002 percent of the global population of roughly seven billion. The report also notes that "the top percentile now own half of all household assets in the world" (2015: 19). If we consider the top decile, the top 10 percent of wealth holders own 87.7 percent of all outstanding global wealth. In other words, the wealth of the world is highly unequal with a strong majority of humanity owning nothing but their capacity to labor for others. Figure 0.1 provides a graphic demonstration of the global wealth pyramid drawing on data from Credit Suisse.

It should also be understood that poverty and inequality has a strong gendered and racialized component. The majority of people in the world without assets are nonwhite and women, while the majority of what I have previously called "dominant owners" or the 1 percent are white men from Europe and North America.[9] For example, of the 100 richest billionaires only 11 are women, according to the Bloomberg Billionaire Index.[10] Furthermore, in the developing world a World Bank (2012) report noted that women make up 40 percent of the labor force but hold only 1 percent of all wealth. Thus, if there were intelligent beings somewhere in our galaxy and they had the potential to observe human society they would find an extreme division of life chances based on the radically unequal division of income and wealth, particularly for women and specifically for women of poorer nations by GDP per capita (Di Muzio 2015a). Excluding and

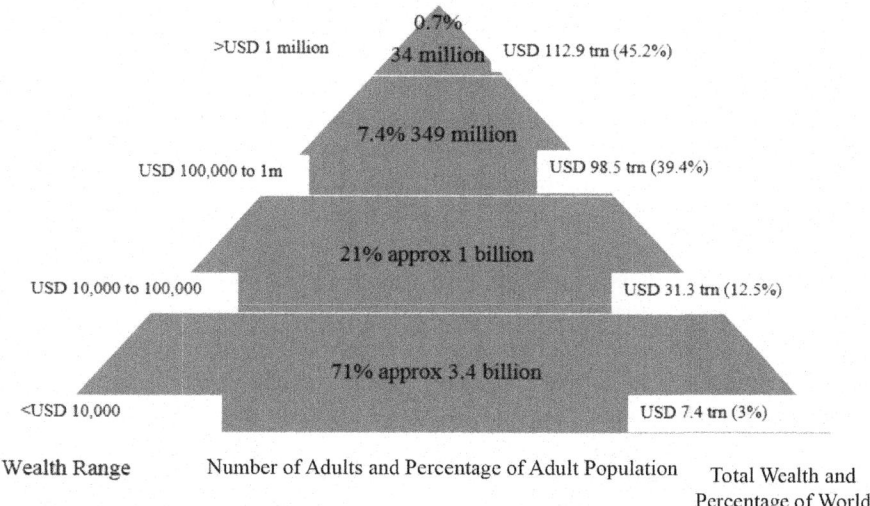

Figure 0.1 World Wealth Pyramid

disadvantaging women and girls, not to mention their targeted murder in various epochs, has a long history, but so too do their struggles against male oppression.

The radical divisions in life chances experienced by many are not a natural point of arrival—some iron law of history working itself out—but the result of past colonial practices, the unequal power and privilege of a few (mostly white) men, political decisions, and the way in which money is generated in capitalist world order. I will discuss the European colonial legacy in greater length and depth in Act II and we will encounter many political choices throughout this work that contributed to inequality, but it is worth briefly discussing money here (for a more in-depth treatment see Di Muzio and Robbins 2016, 2017). As the reader is likely aware, there is considerable confusion over what money is and how it is created in an economy. Economists typically define money by considering its main functions: a unit of account, a medium of exchange, and a store of value. However, ask most professional economists how the money supply expands and you are highly likely, at best, to get the answer that it expands through a fractional reserve system of banking when people make deposits. This is not only incorrect but also logically flawed (Di Muzio and Noble 2017). Werner's seminal research (2014a, 2014b) uncovered that there were three explanations for the expansion of the money supply in the finance and economic literature: (1) the theory that individual banks create money when they make loans; (2) the theory of fractional reserve banking whereby the banking system as a whole expands the money supply because of a reserve ratio; and (3) the theory that banks are not special institutions but simply act as intermediaries between those who save money and those who want to borrow it. Werner argues that the last theory is by far the most dominant theory but that it is incorrect and also as logically flawed as the fractional reserve theory since it too relies on people making deposits. To test the theories beyond logic, Werner conducted an empirical study of a German bank to observe its balance sheet when making a loan—in this case to Werner himself. What was discovered is that new money is created when a bank makes loans to customers (see also McLeay et al. 2014). While certainly not all powerful, what this means is that banks have a tremendous power to allocate new money. Since banks have the power to create new money, governments are *structurally forced* to go into debt if they want to spend more money than they accrue in revenue (e.g., from taxes, fines, fees, and the privatization of public assets). Another way of putting it is to say, following Veblen (1904, 1923), that the money supply of most modern economies has been sabotaged for private profit since publicly listed banks are privately owned institutions. And given the highly uneven pattern of wealth ownership both within and between societies, we can be sure that only a tiny minority benefit from this ownership and act of sabotage. Last, as Rowbotham (1998) noted sometime ago, when banks create money as loans to customers, they do not create the interest charged on the loan. This means that there is *always* more debt in the system than there is the ability to repay. Thus far, it is likely fair to say that most of society has taken the current banking system as self-evident—that it has been this way and always will be and that there is only one way to organize our money system—but this is not the case as a number of academics and civil society organizations such as Positive Money and Monetative argue (Di Muzio and Robbins 2017; Huber 2017; Pettifor 2017). The current system is crisis-prone and a flawed human creation, albeit beneficial to the few who own it. Indeed, at the time of this writing, the Swiss Sovereign Money movement known as the Vollgeld garnered enough signatures to hold a referendum on a proposal that would disallow banks to create new money and put that power into the hands of their democratically elected government through the Swiss Central Bank.[11] In other words, if the referendum is successful, the citizens and their representatives would decide how to allocate new money in Switzerland and citizens would not have to be indebted to private social forces who capitalize their state's ability to generate a revenue stream, largely through taxation.[12] This would also mean that the state is not forced into debt if it desires to spend more money than the revenue it collects. Thus, a key challenge to overcome is the prevailing monetary system that largely benefits a small handful of individuals and families who own the banks.

So, at this conjuncture, humanity faces enormous challenges, and we may, in the decades, if not century to follow, find out whether our intelligence combined with the ways in which we have come to order our societies has ended up getting the better of us. After all, it is one thing to have the technological capacity to be able to build radio telescopes, it is quite another to still be around to operate them. Indeed, the theoretical physicist Stephen Hawking, among others, has advanced the peculiar argument that the survival of the species is contingent on the colonization of other planets.[13] This argument would not seem so strange if it was rooted in our natural curiosity about the potential for life on other planets and greater knowledge about our place in the universe. Instead, Hawking and others in favor of colonizing earth-like exoplanets premise their arguments on the aggressive nature of our species and the observable notion that humanity is depleting its nonrenewable resources and, in the process, ruining the biosphere for future generations. Is it true, as Zizek (2011: 315) claims, that we can now only dream of an "apocalypse at the gates"? And worse, as Barry (2012: 1) suggests, might we be the first species to actively record our own demise? Indeed, how might an objective observer conceive of what humankind has accomplished as a species since our birthday in Africa some 200,000 years ago? The Marx-inspired philosopher Walter Benjamin appears to suggest that human development, if we were to look back upon the magnitude of all the past actions of our species, can be interpreted as one giant catastrophe:

> There is a painting by Klee called Angelus Novus. An angel is depicted there who looks as though he were about to distance himself from something which he is staring at. His eyes are opened wide, his mouth stands open and his wings are outstretched. The Angel of History must look just so. His face is turned towards the past. Where *we* see the appearance of a chain of events, *he* sees one single catastrophe, which unceasingly piles rubble on top of rubble and hurls it before his feet. He would like to pause for a moment so fair [*verweilen*: a reference to Goethe's Faust], to awaken the dead and to piece together what has been smashed. But a storm is blowing from Paradise, it has caught itself up in his wings and is so strong that the Angel can no longer close them. The storm drives him irresistibly into the future, to which his back is turned, while the rubble-heap before him grows sky-high. That which we call progress, is *this* storm.[14]

Organized wars over resources and which supernatural deity should be revered, the torture and sacrifice of bodies, the mass extinction of other species, the deforestation of the earth, the nuclear bomb, the environmental devastation wrought by the extraction of resources, and more are all evidence for Benjamin's thesis concerning human "progress." History as one giant catastrophe—that is certainly one plausible hypothesis for the entirety of the human endeavor. But is this thesis too extreme, bordering on the misanthropic? Doesn't Benjamin's thesis exclude the successes and better nature of our species? Could we not make the claim that while present and past generations have visited horrors upon one another and despoiled many of our environments and possibly our biosphere that things have always been getting better as the arrow of time moves forward and we conquer our biological and political imperfections? Human history as human betterment and progress; this is certainly another plausible hypothesis (e.g., Fukuyama 1989; Ikenberry 2011; Pinker 2011 but the tradition stretches back to at least Godwin and Condorcet; for a critique of this view see Di Muzio 2011 and Jahn 2013). But is this also too extreme—to discount the atrocities of the past and present for the hope that one day when the accounts are finally settled the assets will far exceed the liabilities? Between these two polar extremes, is there not another plausible hypothesis? I want to suggest there is an alternative between these two opposed narratives. The thesis explored in this book is that human development can be understood as a tragedy from the perspective of capital as power. I follow Brecht's idea of "epic theatre" in framing my understanding of tragedy because, as I hope to make clear, many of the historical sufferings we will encounter in this work were not inevitable but the result of the pursuit of power. The relevant passage from Brecht that helps frame this book is as follows:

> The dramatic theatre's spectator says: Yes, I have felt like that too—Just like me—It's only natural—It'll never change—The sufferings of that man appall me, because they are inescapable—That's great art; it all seems the most obvious thing in the world—I weep when they weep, I laugh when they laugh. The epic theatre's spectator says: I'd never have thought it—That's not the way—That's extraordinary, hardly believable—It's got to stop—The sufferings of this man appall me because they are unnecessary—That's great art: nothing obvious in it—I laugh when they weep, and I weep when they laugh (Brecht 1986: 71).[15]

Thus, if human development can be read as a tragedy in the Brechtian sense of "epic theatre," with many sufferings unnecessary or avoidable, we must consider the reasons why these sufferings were (and are) inflicted and enabled when they appear—from a certain angle of possibility—to be unnecessary. And so we must explore the idea that if the destruction of the biosphere along with a multitude of historical sufferings were preventable, that they must have been performed in the interest of definite social forces and not others. The exercise of power was involved at every turn and as the esteemed anthropologist Michel-Rolph Trouillot reminds us, most "history is a story about power, a story about those who won" (1995: 5). Yet "the ultimate mark of power may be its invisibility; the ultimate challenge, the exposition of its roots" (1995:

xix). This is what it means to be radical: to go to the root of the matter of our major challenges. Could it be that the potential for civilizational ruin is all but inevitable because it benefits a tiny powerful minority chasing greater money and power at the expense of everyone else? I have previously called this the Carr-Diamond hypothesis building on the work of E. H. Carr (1981) and Jared Diamond (2005), and I explore it throughout this work from the perspective of capital as power (Di Muzio 2015b). Thus, the idea of tragedy developed here is the notion that human creativity or alternative potentials have been sabotaged and controlled by the logic of differential power and the differential accumulation of money as an end goal among dominant owners. At present this logic is rooted in ownership and registered in the differential capitalization of income-generating assets. In this logic, accumulation knows no mental or theoretical bounds, but it always comes up against resistance (Gill 2008). For this reason the logic of accumulation is in stark contradiction with the logic of livelihood insofar as the quest for ever greater money can be shown to jeopardize both individuals and communities. The end goal of differential accumulation is not the enhancement and security of life but the generation of greater and greater inequality. This is the bare essence of differential accumulation, and to achieve it many have been sacrificed on the altar of profit. I juxtapose this drive for power with what I call and develop in this work: "the logic of livelihood" or the drive for a good life rather than the pursuit of power for the sake of pursuing power, status, and material acquisitions. The logic of livelihood is primarily concerned with the survival and reproduction of the individual, family, kinship network, or community in which they are embedded. But it involves much more than merely securing subsistence and the sexual reproduction of future generations. It means following particular, though changeable, practices that help sustain and enhance the life of the individual and community over time without sacrificing the life chances of future generations for short-term gains, crass materialism, or wasteful consumption of nonrenewable resources. The strange thing about these two logics, at least from the perspective of reflexive sanity, is that while the majority of humanity actually holds almost innately or organically to the logic of livelihood rather than the logical of differential accumulation, the logic of livelihood remains subordinate to the pursuit of more money and power. It is largely the subject of this work to uncover how we arrived at this historical conjuncture where livelihood is trumped by a logic of power and accumulation, but first we must tend to some theoretical and methodological housekeeping before the curtain is lifted and our tragedy unfolds.

Mise-en-scène

Before we open Act I of our tragedy it is necessary for me to provide a greater mise-en-scène for what is to follow. Typically, in the literature largely known as "global history," there are three major revolutions that have transformed the human race after the discovery and control of fire: (1) the Cognitive Revolution (also called behavioral modernity and dated to 40,000–50,000 years ago), (2) the Neolithic Revolution (also called the agrarian revolution or demographic transition and dated to 10,000–12,000 years ago), and (3) the Industrial-Scientific Revolution from about 1750 in Britain. This schema was most recently used by Harari (2011) in his celebrated account of human history. There is little doubt—whether we call these events "revolutions" or not—that these developments were crucial for reconfiguring forms of social reproduction and power relations between and among peoples. However, if the tragedy of human development is inextricably intertwined with the rise of the capitalist mode of power, we must consider four additional underappreciated and interconnected revolutions in human affairs. The first is what I will call the *monetary revolution*, which contributed to at least two major developments: the greater quantification and commodification of society and nature and a profoundly different way of accumulating and exercising power over humans and the natural world than previously experienced by our precapitalist ancestors. I will discuss the emergence and proliferation of money in Act I and follow its impact on society and nature as it developed as one of the most important social technologies for the powerful in a hierarchically arranged social order. The second revolution from the point of view of tracing the tragedy of human development and the genealogy of capital as power is what I will call the *accounting revolution*, which I most closely associate with the gradual adoption of Indo-Arabic numerals and subsequent developments. This revolution runs from what we might call the "primitive accounting" of ancient civilizations all the way up to the gradual popularization of double-entry bookkeeping from the fourteenth century on, to the invention and adoption of gross domestic product (GDP) as the dominant measure of human success or failure after World War II and the capitalized earnings model. As will become clear how we "account" for things is incredibly important for understanding the past, present, and future of social order (Gleeson-White 2011). The third revolution, though still debated and largely understudied, is the gradual, yet somewhat traceable, origins of private property—the *ownership revolution*. Thus far, there is no scholarly consensus on the precise origins of the social institution of ownership, but its traceable history runs from the suppression of women, slavery, the agrarian revolution, and the practice of exclusion and dispossession of some by (typically a minority of) others due to violence, colonialism, or unpayable debt right up to the rise of the capitalized modern corporation. The final revolution is what we might call the *violence revolution*, running from primitive weaponry and tribal warfare to mercenaries, the first national standing armies and the greater application of technology to the art of killing in mass numbers. Though we separate these revolutions out for analytical purposes here, as will become clear, they overlap historically. I will discuss these revolutions as our tragedy unfolds, but it is now time to explore the main arguments of this work before moving on to discussing the rationale for this work, its method, theoretical approach, and the organization of the book.

MAIN ARGUMENTS

To explore what I call the tragedy of human development, this book makes a series of interconnected arguments from the critical political economy perspective of capital as power (Nitzan and Bichler 2009). First, the potential for civilizational ruin is an eventuality that has been preordained by past and present circumstances and is recognized and registered as such in many quarters of the natural and social sciences. It is anticipated and could potentially be avoided but nevertheless may still occur given our current historical trajectory (Amed 2010; Diamond 2005; Hansen et al. 2013; Heinberg 2003, 2007, 2011; Jackson 2009; Klein 2014; Randers 2008; Rockström 2009; Wells 2010).[16] Second, the unsustainable and potentially ruinous civilizational path we are currently traveling down ultimately stems from the fact that it benefits a small minority of what I call "dominant owners" (Di Muzio 2015a). These benefits are recorded as monetary units and expressed in differential ownership (owning claims to more lucrative income streams than rivals) and capitalization (the overall monetary value of capitalized income-generating assets relative to rivals). The magnitude of wealth held by dominant owners is *not* the result of their productive contribution to society, as the production function of neoclassical economic theory would suggest, but their position in the social and international hierarchy as owners and their power to enforce this ownership and inflict damage upon society (Alperovitz and Daly 2008; Di Muzio 2015a; Nitzan and Bichler 2009; Sayer 2015). In many respects, differential capitalization occurs when society and the environment are sabotaged or harmed. For instance, the monetization of all proven oil reserves, not to mention all the remaining fossil fuels, will make the owners of international oil resources incredible sums of money but will almost certainly cause runaway climate change and considerable harm to multiple global communities (Hansen et al. 2013: 25). Third, it is highly likely that the Neolithic Revolution and what I have previously called the fossil fuel revolution were perhaps the two most important human social transformations that allowed for the greater accumulation of power and wealth to pass into the hands of a tiny minority, but the revolutions in money, accounting, ownership, and violence were vital to their quest (Di Muzio 2015a; Manning 2004). Last, overcoming the tragedy requires challenging the logic of illegitimate and harmful differential power, which requires greater education about real-world financial practices and concerted action on inequality, the way we produce money in our economies, climate change, and imagining a post-carbon world order premised on livelihood, community, inclusiveness, gender and racial equality, sustainability, and *informed* democratic decision making. With these arguments noted, I will now turn to the rationale for this book.

RATIONALE FOR THE BOOK

In the history of the world there has probably never been as many books published on all manner of topics. So many books are published yearly that Sartre's autodidact in *La Nausée* would never be able to read them all even if he had multiple lifetimes. So why write another book? What is at stake? I think these are questions that every author should ask, academic or otherwise. Books, of course, are written to be read, but they also have significance for the author. First, in that it is a representation of thought in action, an attempt to synthesize, organize, and present a wealth of research and materials that might not otherwise come together in such an idiosyncratic manner. Second, this book is not solely written to *in*form but also to *trans*form the world; to overcome the tragedy of human development through practical political action. But practical political action requires a proper understanding and diagnosis regarding our current situation. In this sense, my primary purpose for writing this book is to explore the hypothesis that we can conceive of human development as a tragedy from the perspective of capital as power

(Di Muzio 2014; Nitzan and Bichler 2009). As previously stated, the idea of tragedy developed here is the notion that human creativity or alternative potentials have been sabotaged or incapacitated by the logic of differential power and, at a certain point in human history, the differential accumulation of money. At present, the logic of differential accumulation is rooted in the ownership claims to income-generating assets and registered in differential capitalization. It is a logic that threatens greater inequality of life chances both within and between nations, the destruction of the biosphere for future generations of humans and other species, a looming energy crisis of epic proportions, and the potential for greater violent conflict. Taken together, these threats can be conceived of as a general crisis of social reproduction—"a multi-scalar, multi-dimensional and international situation whereby current patterns of energy-intensive production, consumption and reproduction can no longer be sustained" (Di Muzio 2015b: 16). Overcoming the potential for this crisis is what is ultimately at stake and the rationale for this book. But before outlining the organization of this work, it is necessary to discuss its genealogical method and the capital as power approach to critical political economy.

GENEALOGY AND THE SILENCES OF HISTORY

Genealogy is an approach to historical inquiry and writing that seeks to problematize social relations of power that are taken as self-evident truths in the present. Typically, genealogies begin with an assessment and critical question about the present, moving on to problematize the "inevitability," "naturalness," or "self-evidence" of current power relations through a historical investigation that moves back, rather than forward, in time. Genealogies can be considered "effective histories" insofar as they aim to provide a counter-memory to dominant interpretations of history for use in the present. Dominant narratives of human history have a tendency to reinforce rather than critically interrogate present social relations of power. They do so in a number of ways including but not limited to the following: (1) by excluding inconvenient facts from the historical narrative; (2) by silencing the voices of certain social actors and forces; (3) by deliberate manipulation or misrepresentation of facts; (4) by underplaying historical struggle in the constitution of the present; (5) by celebrating and privileging those who have declared victory in a battle, controversy, or conflict; (6) by representing the present as normal, natural, and inevitable; and (7) by relying on a transcendental or transhistorical subject and its immutable necessities.

As a method of historical investigation and writing, genealogies are guided by at least four methodological precautions. The first is a concern for subjectification rather than a transcendental or transhistorical subject. What this means is that genealogies resist interpreting history by relying on a transcendental subject such as God, divine providence, a chosen people, a "spirit of the age," "manifest destiny," or an asocial transhistorical subject such as *homo economicus*. Rather, a genealogical method traces the historical constitution of the subject in "interrelations of power, knowledge and truth" (Hutichings in Lloyd and Thacker 1997: 108). In this sense:

> Genealogy is concerned with the descent rather than the evolution of events in history, a movement backwards rather than forwards in time. One such series of events is the way the self 'fabricates a coherent identity' from 'numberless beginnings'; tracing the forward evolution of such a self would too readily produce an image of progressive unity. If we reverse the focus on historical study, and work backwards, then this fiction of a unified subjectivity is less likely . . . to captivate us (Thacker in Lloyd and Thacker 1997: 34).

Dispensing with a unified or changeless subject of history opens up the possibility of considering how relations of power produce and reproduce subjects practically at the level of the body and consciousness and discursively when they are taken as objects of knowledge and intervention. For example, public health officials in India are currently alarmed with the presence of a new historical subject in India—a subject whose practical and discursive existence did not exist a decade ago: the obese person. With rising incomes for some and the introduction of Western fast-food corporations, marketing, and advertising, diets and perceptions of food are in the process of radically changing. In New Delhi for instance, 29 percent of the population is obese, up from 16 percent only two years ago. Whereas studies have shown that the obese subject in most developed economies is typically poor, in India the obese tend to be rather wealthy by comparison. The constitution of this new subject shows how relations of power—in this case the power to consume and the power of multinational corporations to influence perceptions about food and social status—are inscribed on the body and how they shape the consciousness of India's new middle class. But this new subject is also constituted discursively. For example, along with the rapid increase in obesity an official medico-financial discourse about what to do is in the process of being formed—particularly since there is also a corresponding rise in diabetes linked with overweight individuals and worries about how obesity and its related illnesses will strain public finances.[17]

However, while genealogies express a concern for existence rather than essence, and becoming rather than an immutable being, I offer one caveat to this anti-essentialist stance: what has remained constant throughout human history is the fact that humans are *social beings* who produce and reproduce their livelihoods with the capacity for conscious life activity.[18] So while the forthcoming genealogical account of the capitalist mode of power does not posit a human nature or essence that has to be reconciled at a later point in history—which would lead to a teleological reading of history—it does recognize that human history is always a *social* history and that the survival of humanity and its multiple cultural achievements and failures require a constant metabolism with the natural world. Thus, my own genealogy is informed by a social ontology that takes real human beings in their changing relations as the subjects of history.

A second concern of genealogical approaches to problems in the present is with rupture and discontinuity rather than the evolution and progress of a species, an institution, a people, an individual, or a concept. To operate in an evolutionary and progressive register risks viewing the present as some natural and necessary point of arrival, as though things could not have been otherwise. It also risks viewing the present as a stage in human improvement—ignoring reversals, resistances, and the radically uneven distribution of resources both within and between states. For example, one of the dominant discursive constructions in international relations argues that "failed" political communities must emulate the Western development model since its product—liberal-capitalist societies—is reasoned to be pacific and prosperous (Morton 2005). This creates a sort of optimal civilizational benchmark to be achieved while completely ignoring developmental variation, different understandings of development and human well-being, and how the violence of colonial and post-colonial power relations contributed to a "developed" West (Berger and Weber 2014; Bowden 2009; Rist 2008; Stavrianos 1981; Wallerstein 1974; Wolf 2010). Such reasoning also effaces the gross inequalities and violence that go on within Western states, or, as Allen Ginsberg noted in the case of the United States: the powerful "say nothing about [their] prisons nor the millions of underprivileged who live in [their] flowerpots under the light of five hundred suns."[19] Outside of the poet's register, others have avoided interpreting history as a singular undertaking to improve the well-being of all humanity from Malthus to Benjamin and Neo-Malthusians like Al Bartlett and Paul R. Ehrlich.

The counter-history I provide in this study is also concerned with an alternative view of history—one that is sensitive to historical transformations rooted in collective human struggle, and one that is highly suspicious of teleological narratives of human progress. This is so because what looks like progress to some may very well look like retrogressive social transformations to others as Bodley's (2015) work has amply demonstrated. For example, while Marx appreciated some of the advances associated with capitalist social property relations, he also understood how this radical break transformed the terrain of social reproduction in ways that intensified human insecurity for a majority of people forced into pauperism or forced to work for others. Almost a full century later, and from a different angle, Polanyi would also note that the attempt to instantiate a free market represented a "singular departure" from past forms of human economy that resembled "more the metamorphosis of the caterpillar than any alteration that can be expressed in terms of continuous growth and development" (Polanyi 1957: 42). Thus, the genealogical method applied in this work will be sensitive to rupture and discontinuity rather than tracing the destiny, evolution, improvement, or progress of humanity. This does not mean that "progress" does not happen, that things cannot improve, but we must question—progress for who and what purpose (Wright 2005)?

A third methodological precaution when producing genealogies is the recognition that they cannot provide a precise and exhaustive historical account of a complex emergence. Genealogies admit that "any historical narrative is a particular bundle of silences" (Trouillot 1995: 27). As such, genealogies are never complete, nor do they intend to be the final word on the subject under study. In this sense, they do not lay claim to an ultimate truth or to be able to narrate "what actually happened" as empirical nominalism and some positivist accounts of history attempt to do (Davies 2003). They admit a complex and potentially undecipherable web of causality yet seek to bring out how relations of power have shaped the present through an analysis of struggle. Their ultimate aim is to render a problem intelligible by questioning the self-evidence of taken-for-granted "truths." In this way, genealogists are concerned to bring out what is strategically at stake in the present by problematizing dominant interpretations of who we are and what we can become.

Insofar as genealogical approaches aim to provide counternarratives, they overlap with the concern by some social historians to provide "histories from below." This tradition of historical writing is most closely associated with England's Communist Party Historians Group which featured Christopher Hill, E. P. Thompson, and Eric Hobsbawm, among others.[20] These studies differ from traditional historiography insofar as they seek to recover what has been silenced in official or dominant narratives of the past. Whereas traditional historiography has tended to focus on the powerful, wealthy, and famous, "histories from below" attempt to capture and reveal the practices of the ordinary, exploited, and oppressed people in the making of history.[21] These works have not only demonstrated that alternative accounts of the past are possible, but that dominant interpretations of history have practical consequences for actions in the present.

For this reason, and to paraphrase Robert Cox (1981), the view taken in this study is that "history is always for someone and some purpose."[22] This is not to suggest that that history is "infinitely susceptible to invention" or that it can be manipulated toward any ends the author sees fit (Trouillot 1995: 8). As Chris Lorenz has noted, one check on the infinite malleability of history is that it is an "intersubjective enterprise":

> In contrast to authors of fiction, historians deal with an object and with defini-
> tions of the object that are open to *public* scrutiny and debate. And so is the
> *evidence* they use to back up their *arguments*, because as a consequence of the
> public character of historical narratives cannot just be *presented*, as are their
> fictional counterparts, but they stand in need of constant empirical and logical
> backing (1998: 326, emphasis original).

Thus to say that "history is always for someone and some purpose" is *not* to say that the historicity of human events and the "debatability of the past" is open to complete fictionalization or interpretation. However, what it does suggest is that "the production of historical narratives involves the uneven contribution of competing groups and individuals who have unequal access to the means for such production" (Trouillot 1995: xix). What this suggests is that the writing and interpretation of history cannot be separated from questions of power and the political beliefs and subject positions of those involved in "producing" history. To take two quick examples that illustrate this point, consider the case of new history textbooks in Iraq, and a comprehensive study of high school history books in the United States.

Upon occupying Iraq in 2003, one immediate priority of the United States military was to collect, assess, and ultimately replace Iraqi history textbooks. According to the US-led Ministry of Education in Iraq, history textbooks glorified Saddam Hussein and the Baath Party, vilified the United States and Israel, and misrepresented a number of historical events such as the Iran-Iraq War and the Gulf War. For instance, Iraqi history textbooks claimed that Iraq had won both the Iran-Iraq War and the Gulf War. The point here is that as the ruling government, the Ba'ath Party had history written to serve the repro-duction of its rule. However, with the US occupation of the country, the US Defense Department had the chance to rewrite Iraq's history with the help of a Western-friendly Ministry of Education. Texts were introduced that have removed any reference to Israel, the United States, Kurds, the Baath Party, or controversial events such as the Gulf War and the UN sanctions regime. As one Defense Department official charged with advising the Ministry of Edu-cation claimed, "Entire swaths of 20th-century history have been deleted."[23] In effect, the United States and its handpicked allies in the Ministry of Educa-tion began the process of rewriting Iraq's history to serve the interests of the occupation and the future of what promises to be a very different Iraq.

The power relations involved in the production of history are of course not confined to Iraq alone. In his study of twelve major high school history textbooks in the United States, James Loewen argued that students are presented with a distorted picture of the history of the United States—one that omits significant facts and, by doing so, produces a certain understanding and image of its political community. For example, Loewen notes that while the history textbooks he reviewed mention Woodrow Wilson's presidency, not a single one discusses his administration's intervention to overturn the Russian Revolution and its historical consequences (Loewen 1996: 14). The point here is that omissions shape how students think about the history of US foreign policy.

What these two examples demonstrate is that the production of history is inseparable from power relations so that different interpretations of history become possible while others are marginalized and silenced. Thus, while history is not infinitely malleable, it can be used as a weapon insofar as understandings of the past can inspire, motivate, or mollify action in the present. This is perhaps why the control over the production of history and daily news events in Orwell's dystopia, *1984*, was so important for the totalitarian party that sought to rule Oceania in perpetuity. Indeed, one of the Party's understandings of its rule was encapsulated in the following statement: "Who controls the past controls the future: who controls the present controls past" (Orwell 1990: 260).

Thus, the genealogical method used in this study understands that the production of history cannot be dissociated from relations of power, and that these unequal relations and their competing interpretations bear on the making of the future and its political possibilities. This is one reason that this book seeks to problematize the carefully protected claim that liberal-capitalist societies offer the best opportunities for improving the well-being of the vast majority of the planet's inhabitants. It will be shown that the tragedy of human development is intertwined with capital as a mode of power. But to do so, we must begin in the present and explore what it means to say that capital is power.

CAPITAL AS A MODE OF POWER

To explain historical development, most historical materialists rely on the concepts of class struggle and how struggles between various classes emerge out of the many ways in which human beings have related to each other in the production of their livelihoods.[24] This is what Marx referred to as a "mode of production" and he suggested that in all historical modes of production, contradictions eventually lead to conflicts between classes until a new class emerges victorious and institutes a new mode of production with different social relations. However, from the capital as power perspective, focusing on a "mode of production" is far too narrow for an understanding of the emergence and development of capitalism. Instead, capital is broadly understood as a mode of power rather than a mode of production most closely associated for Marxists with industrial production.[25] What we are concerned with then is "the specific architecture of power and the logic that creates and recreates a given hierarchical, class society where the emphasis is on scrutinizing and historicizing organized institutional power rather than *only* forms of production and labor practices" (Di Muzio 2015b: 37). Braudel had a similar concern in his three-volume history of capitalism and civilization:

> On a world scale, we should avoid the over-simple image often presented of capitalism passing through various stages of growth, from trade to finance to industry—with the mature industrial phase seen as the only true capitalism. In the so-called merchant or commercial capitalism phase, as in the so-called industrial phase, the essential characteristics of capitalism was its capacity to slip at a moment's notice from one form or sector to another, in times of crisis or of pronounced decline in profit rates (1983: 433).

This is not to say that social labor and production are unimportant, but to solely focus on how people produce risks not gaining a knowledge of wider power processes that may be more important for understanding how capitalist power operates and is reproduced. For this reason the capital as power approach to critical political economy focuses on something that Braudel put his finger on but did not identify: the act of capitalization, the chief ritual of capitalists (Nitzan and Bichler 2009: 270). Capitalization has two meanings. First, capitalization is the act of discounting to present value a future flow of income adjusted by some calculation of risk. The reason why capitalists discount anticipated future income when they purchase claims to income-generating assets is the time value theory of money. This financial theory suggests that money is worth more today than it is in the future since money earned today can start generating returns right away. Second, capitalization also means the market value of a firm. For example, the market capitalization of Facebook as of January 5, 2017, is US$342 billion. Thus, when we say that someone capitalizes a corporation or government security, we mean that they are investing money to obtain a claim to a future flow of income. What this means is that "capital" is either money invested in an income-generating asset or money intended to be invested in an income-generating asset (Di Muzio and Dow 2017). But what is money? Money can and has been represented by various mediums from notes and coins to cattle and sea shells, but ultimately money is an imaginary social institution with very real effects (Davies 2002; Ingham 2004). Money can primarily be conceived of as an abstract claim on society and natural resources denominated in a unit of account (e.g., dollars, euros, or pesos) and used for payment (Di Muzio and Robbins 2017). Since money's major role is primarily a *claim* on society and natural resources, the more money one has, the more claims one can make on society and natural resources. In this sense, capitalism is not so much about the production of commodities, as important as this is to accumulation, as about the accumulation of money and therefore the accumulation of greater differential power/claims on society and natural resources. We should note here that high-net-worth individuals or what I have previously called dominant owners do not hold the majority of their wealth as cash but as an array of income-generating assets such as equities and government securities (Di Muzio 2015a). For this reason we can use the term "differential capitalization" to think about both the power and the relative disparity of ownership (Nitzan and Bichler 2009: 310). For example, as of January 2017, Bill Gates had capitalized assets worth US$91.5 billion while Mark Zuckerberg had capitalized assets worth US$51.6 billion. Thus the ratio of differential capitalization here is 1:1.8—a relatively minor disparity. However, as we saw previously, the majority of humanity has wealth of US$10,000 or under, so the ratio of Bill Gates to one of the 3.4 billion people with this threshold level of wealth would be: 1:9,150,000—an enormous disparity in need of explanation and justification. With some of the key terms used in the capital as power approach defined, it is now time to summarize the meaning of capital as power more fully and provide a definition of capitalism.

Whereas Marx argued that an understanding of capitalism required that we first consider the commodity, Nitzan and Bichler (2009) argue that ownership and the corporation should be our starting point. While there are many small and medium-size firms, most of the world's goods and services are provided by publicly listed, but privately owned, corporations. The corporations with the largest market value or market capitalization are referred to as "dominant capital" and their owners can be referred to as "dominant owners" (Di Muzio 2015a; Nitzan and Bichler 2009: 315). When dominant owners and other minor investors capitalize a firm, they are concerned primarily about corporate earnings and whether the corporation is meeting, beating, or falling behind an average benchmark rate of return such as the S&P 500. Generally, corporations that exceed the average rate of return typically see their share prices go up, while corporations that fail to keep up with the average rate of return see their share prices adjusted downward. But earnings are not a simple matter of producing for the market but the result of a broad power process (Nitzan and Bichler 2009: 218). In order to accumulate differential earning and therefore greater capitalization, corporations must exert power over the social process *writ large*. This is because earnings are contingent upon a number of factors from government regulation and advertising to trade deals and government contracts. For example, when the BP-leased Deepwater Horizon experienced an uncontrollable blowout in the Gulf of Mexico, its capitalization was cut by nearly half by investors. Part of the reason investors headed for the door was that it took BP months to seal off the well, causing the larg-est oil spill in US waters and a raft of legal challenges, compensation claims, and federal fines in the billions.[26] We will encounter additional examples of how multiple factors bear on corporate earnings throughout this work, but the main takeaway here is that earnings and differential accumulation rely on corporate power to shape and reshape the terrain of social reproduction for the benefit of corporate owners. However important corporations are in shaping social reproduction, the state is equally, if not more, important. In fact, as Nitzan and Bichler contend, one might make the plausible argument that states were the first capitalized "corporation" through the issuance of financial bonds (2009: 294). Through their national debt, the vast majority of nation states are, in effect, capitalized entities insofar as a portion of state rev-enue is redirected to bondholders. To recall, in the present historically created system, if governments want to spend more than they take in in taxes, fines, and fees, the modern monetary and fiscal system *structurally forces* them to go into debt to private social forces. As Nitzan and Bichler (2002: 13) have argued, capitalizing the state effectively privatizes a portion of its income when bondholders are paid interest on their principal investment. As we will discuss in the last act, mounting national debt is one of the chief reasons for neoliberal austerity policies and the fiscal crisis of the state (Di Muzio and Robbins 2016; O'Connor 1979). But while states are capitalized through their national debt, state policies have an incredible impact on differential accumulation. These policies and regulations are enormous and range from the privatization of public assets and environmental regulations to defense contracts, patent protection, and trade agreements. All of these policies and more bear on differential accumulation and the level of a firm's capitaliza-tion. Thus, rather than seeing the state separate from "the market" or the corporate universe, in the capital as power approach to critical political econ-omy, they are unavoidably intertwined. We will encounter many examples of how state policies intertwine with the process of differential accumulation throughout this work, but now it is time to provide a definition of capitalism before moving on to outline the organization of this work. "Capitalism is a politico-economic system premised on the social property relations between hierarchically arranged owners and non-owners whereby income-generating assets are differentially capitalized based on the institutional power of busi-ness and governments to generate income streams by shaping and reshaping the landscape of social reproduction through the market and price system" (Di Muzio and Dow 2017: 9). Thus, at least three main things are important to capitalism: (1) the act of capitalization; (2) the institution of ownership or private property and the ability to exclude others from owning; and (3) the ability of social institutions—corporations or governments—to generate earnings in the case of firms and revenue in the case of governments.

ORGANIZATION OF THE BOOK

Rather than chapters per se, this work is divided into a series of acts to flesh out how we might conceive of human development as a tragedy by examining differential power over the course of some of the major events in human history. Since each act has an introduction, my outline here will be brief.

The presence of differential power within social relations is perhaps unavoidable in human communities but perhaps what matters most is the degree of that differentiation—the magnitude of the power imbalance, the reasons for this magnitude, and the long-term consequences of unequal power relations for society and the natural world. Boehme (2001) informs us that as hunters and gatherers our species was relatively egalitarian—at least within the community if not in the family. Why, then, did we lose this tendency for egalitarianism? The question is not intended to romanticize the past—to beg for a return to some bygone era—nothing of the sort is intended here. Our concern is with the *why* and *how* of greater differential power. Since it seems, by most accounts, that the decisive break was the transition to agriculture known commonly as the Neolithic Revolution and the invention of money, Act I focuses on these developments. Much is still obscure to us about these early great power civilizations, but there is enough evidence to strongly suggest that the desire of a small minority with the ability to dominate others and the natural environment by force or mysticism was at play (Flannery and Marcus 2012). If these events were decisive moments in the tragedy of human development, the loss of egalitarianism and the formation of rigid social hierarchies where a small minority appropriated greater social wealth and power for themselves, then Act II discusses Western colonization and the transatlantic slave trade that served the powerful by making world order more unequal. Though I separate this out for analytical purposes, Act II overlaps with our Act III: the fossil fuel revolution and the rise of military-industrial complexes, scientific progress, scientific racism, and the industrial slaughter of World War I and World War II. Act IV in the tragedy of human development is the rise of corporate capitalism—the greater concentration and institutionalization of the quest to monetize human labor and the natural world and a way of organizing ownership for greater control over human social production and reproduction. Act V explores the era of "human development" proper sparked by Point Four of Harry S. Truman's infamous Inaugural Address and questions the pursuit of growth, the prevalence of debt, and the biopolitics of global capitalism (Berger and Weber 2014; Rist 2008: 70). The epilogue of the tragedy—Saturn and World Civilization—examines the major contradictions of our present state of affairs and discusses the trajectory of possible transformations in the decades to come.

NOTES

1 The radio telescope was featured in films *Goldeneye* (1995) and *Contact* (1997).

2 About, The Arecibo Observatory. http://www.naic.edu/general/index.php?option=com_content&view=article&id=149&Itemid=631 (12/8/2015).

3 SETI Institute Frequently Asked Questions. http://www.seti.org/faq#seti2 (12/9/2015).

4 The debate is available online http://www.astro.umass.edu/~mhanner/Lecture_Notes/Sagan-Mayr.pdf (12/9/2015). But it originally appeared in the Planetary Society's *Bioastronomy News*, starting with vol. 7, no. 3, 1995.

5 International Campaign to Abolish Nuclear Weapons, The Facts. http://www.icanw.org/the-facts/nuclear-arsenals/ (12/10/2015).

6 Bulletin of the Atomic Scientists: Doomsday Clock. http://thebulletin.org/time line (3/21/2017).

7 Coral Davenport (2015) "Nations Approve Landmark Climate Accord in Paris" *New York Times*, December 12.

8 BP Oil Reserves. http://www.bp.com/en/global/corporate/energy-economics/statistical-review-of-world-energy/oil/oil-reserves.html (1/2/2017).

9 Dominant owners are the tiny but global group of individuals and families who own most of the world's income-generating assets and/or a greater proportion of them.

10 Bloomberg Richest of the Rich. https://www.bloomberg.com/graphics/info graphics/bloomberg-markets-100-top-billionaires.html (3/21/2017).

11 Vollgeld Initiative Home. http://www.vollgeld-initiative.ch/english/ (2/1/2017).

12 Mehreen Khan (2015) "Switzerland to vote on banning banks from creating money," http://www.telegraph.co.uk/finance/economics/11999966/Switzerland-to-vote-on-banning-banks-from-creating-money.html (12/28/2015).

13 Andrew Griffin (2015) "Stephen Hawking: Space Travel Will Save Mankind and We Should Colonize Space," *The Independent*, February 20. http://www.indepen dent.co.uk/news/science/stephen-hawking-space-travel-will-save-mankind-and-we-should-colonise-other-planets-10058811.html (4/17/2016).

14 https://www.marxists.org/reference/archive/benjamin/1940/history.htm (12/14/2015). See also Vogel (1996) on Marx's dialectical understanding of historical development and the twin legacy of the Enlightenment belief in human rights/dignity and progress.

15 It is well known that Brecht distanced himself from a certain form of tragedy he believed to be too conservative. (See Carney 2005.)

16 Of course life on Earth will eventually end once the sun's hydrogen is fully burned out in about five billion years—a scale that ought not to concern us here.

17 On the recent trend in Indian obesity, see Amelia Gentleman (2005) "India's Newly Rich Battle with Obesity" *The Observer*, December 4; Somini Sengupta (2006) "India Prosperity Creates Paradox; Many Children Are Fat, Even More Are Famished" *New York Times*, December 31; and ANI (2016) "Childhood Obesity and Exploding Nightmare" *Times of India*, June 16.

18 It should be noted here that by the concept "becoming" I do not imply a teleo-logical view of subject formation where it is possible to have a knowledge of what the subject will "become" at the end of a process. The concept, as used here, simply implies a dynamic process of subjectification whereby human agency and identity is constituted socially and historically. In other words, it is a formative view of becom-ing rather than a teleological view of becoming that I want to stress here.

19 Allen Ginsberg, "America." Accessed online: http://www.writing.upenn. edu/~afilreis/88/america.html (4/12/2017).

20 For a general survey of how Marxists have approached and understood history, see Matt Perry, *Marxism and History*. (Basingstoke: Palgrave), 2002.

21 For a general overview of this approach to historical writing, see Jim Sharpe, "History from Below," in Peter Burke (ed). *New Perspectives on Historical Writing*. (Cambridge: Polity Press), 1991: pp. 24–41. Classics of this genre include but are not limited to: E. P. Thompson, *The Making of the English Working Class*. (New York: Penguin Books), 1991; Christopher Hill, *The World Turned Upside Down: Radical Ideas during the English Revolution*. (New York: Penguin Books), 1991; Eric Hobsbawm, *Primitive Rebels: Studies in Archaic Forms of Social Movement in the 19th and 20th Centuries*. (New York: W. W. Norton and Company, Inc.), 1972; George Rudé, *The Crowd in the French Revolution*. (Oxford University Press), 1959; Howard Zinn, *A People's History of the United States 1492-Present*. (New York: HarperPerennial), 1995; Ray Raphael, *A People's History of the American Revolu-tion: How Common People Shaped the Fight for Independence*. (New York: Harp-erPerennial), 2002; Peter Linebaugh, *The London Hanged: Crime and Civil Society in the Eighteenth Century*. (London: Verso), 2006; and Peter Linebaugh and Marcus Rediker, *The Many-Headed Hydra: Sailors, Slaves, Commoners, and the Hidden His-tory of the Revolutionary Atlantic*. (Boston: Beacon Press), 2000.

22 Keith Jenkins, *Rethinking History*, 2nd ed. (London: Routledge), 2003, p. 21. Jenkins expresses the same point as Cox by noting that "history is never for itself; it is always for someone."

23 Neil King Jr. (2003) "For One Small Education Company, Iraqi Schools Are a Huge Challenge" *The Wall Street Journal*, April 14; Christina Asquith (2003) "New Textbooks Rewrite History in Iraq through Omission" *The Christian Science Monitor*, Monday, November 10; and Christina Asquith (2003) "A New History of Iraq," *The Guardian*, November 25. On other aspects of rewriting Iraq's present his-tory, see Robert Fisk (2004) "Rewriting Iraq's History" *UK Independent*, May 27.

24 I have previously summarized the capital as power approach in Di Muzio (2014) but because many readers may not be familiar with the approach, I find it necessary to outline it here.

25 The conflation of capitalism with the industrial revolution or industrial produc-tion has been a major setback for Marxist theorizing.

26 BBC "BP Loses Latest US Oil Spill Appeal" December 8, 2014. http://www. bbc.com/news/business-30375089 (accessed 6/1/2017).

Act I

The First Power Civilizations

To understand the emergence of capital as a mode of power and the tragedy of human development, we need to consider earlier modes of power and the rise of complex human hierarchies. It has been suggested by scientists of complexity that any complex system such as human political communities follows certain rules of interaction that results in certain outcomes while at the same time restricting alternative possibilities. What this suggests to us is that within any mode of power there will be fairly particular rules of interaction that tend to reinforce, but yet perhaps at times undermine the social relations of power, privilege, and hierarchy. It is the task of Act I to begin our genealogy of capital as a mode of power by considering the historical and anthropological literature on the emergence of human hierarchies and inequality and to consider some of the rules of interaction that were followed to reproduce power relations that were non-capitalist. By what mechanisms and justifications were these rules of interaction instantiated and how did they buttress early social relations of power between dominant and dominated? To set the scene this act begins with a few basic facts about the emergence of modern *Homo sapiens* and the "Out of Africa" Hypothesis. The hypothesis suggests that modern *H. sapiens* emerged in East Africa about 200,000 years ago and, over time, spread throughout the habitable continents of the world. I will then consider one of the most significant transformations in human history: the transition from hunting and gathering/foraging to agricultural-based societies. This period of human history, though it begins in fits and starts in geographically differentiated spaces, is commonly known as the Neolithic Revolution. Some date this revolution in human affairs from 12,000 to 7,000 years ago and it took place "in the Near East, New Guinea, China, Central and South America, and eastern North America" (Ehrlich and Ehrlich 2008: 105). While we could examine developments in any of these regions, the transition to agriculture and the revolution in human affairs it caused takes or will take us to Mesopotamia and Ancient Egypt, where we have reasonably clear records on the emergence of three main things that are important for explaining the development of capital as power: counting, accounting, and money as a unit of account. Act I then moves to focus on developments in Lydia, Greece, and Rome, where we find a very curious and revolutionary development: money, not simply as a unit of account, store of value or a means by which to measure the relative value of people and things, but money as relatively standardized gold and silver coin. The steadfast belief, primarily among rulers, traders, and mercenaries that gold and silver were the only true money—and how this idea spread throughout the world—not only shaped the modern world and intersocietal relations but also laid the groundwork for the capitalist mode of power. As I will explicate, while qualitative things had become "accounted" for at least since the rise of the first agrarian civilizations, from the sixth century BCE, qualitative things came increasingly to be "accounted" for in gold and silver coin. As we will uncover, the adoption of coin as money had tremendous consequences for political and social developments and the lives of countless peoples.

OUT OF AFRICA

The prevailing hypothesis on the origins of *H. sapiens* is that anatomically and genetically modern humans emerged in eastern Africa at least 150,000, if not 200,000, years ago. The evidence is based on DNA patterning of current members of the human family and skeletal remains (Mellars 2006: 9381). Though heavily debated, new studies have argued that rather than one dispersal from Africa there were two migration waves. The first is believed to have occurred 130,000–115,000 years ago. Some suggest that, for reasons that are not quite clear, this initial population either retreated back to Africa or died out (Armitage 2011). But a recent discovery of teeth in Fuyan Cave in southern China suggests that this might not be the case (Wu et al. 2015). A team of researchers have argued that the forty-seven teeth are unequivocally those of modern humans and date to at least 80,000 years ago. The fossil evidence suggests that modern humans were highly likely in China before the second wave of migration into the Levant and Europe, believed to have taken place from 40,000 to 74,000 years ago (Appenzeller 2012). Since China is east of Africa, this suggests that modern humans may have also been in other Eurasian regions as well. The reason for this migration is largely lost to history but some scholars have suggested technological developments that made new environments easier to adapt to, climate disruptions that threatened preexisting habitats, the search for more appealing environments, and population

growth as all possible answers (Mellars 2006). Both debates on the disper-
sion of modern humans and the reasons for departing Africa will continue as
archeologists and geneticists uncover new evidence, but one thing is certain:
H. sapiens gradually spread throughout the habitable earth and populated
new territories and, in Eurasia, replaced early hominins such as Neanderthals.

As Harari (2011: 16ff) points out, there are two major lines of reasoning
when it comes to explaining what happened to our earlier ancestors. The first
theory holds that as *H. sapiens* migrated out of Africa they lived, survived,
and interbred with the Neanderthals largely found in Europe and *Homo erec-
tus*, largely found in Asia. In this sense, interbreeding would ultimately lead
to a mix of DNA between *H. sapiens* and earlier members of the homo genus.
There is indeed some evidence for sexual relations between the two species
as scientists discovered in 2010. However, as Harari warns us, further tests
must be done before we fully adopt the interbreeding theory to explain the
disappearance of our close cousins. The second theory, the one most commonly adhered to, is called the replacement theory. The idea here is that the
H. sapien diaspora into Eurasia led to the killing off of earlier settled peoples.
Though the debate continues, some scholars argue that *H. sapiens* were better mentally equipped than their counterparts and had better technology and
organizational abilities. This suggests that acts of violence would have been
easier to accomplish against a less technologically and mentally sophisticated
species. This is certainly plausible and, as Harari suggests, the move out of
Africa to the Eurasian landmass may prove to be "the first and most significant ethnic-cleansing campaign in history" (2011: 19). However, there is the
possibility of another culprit: tropical disease. Some scholars have suggested
that the migrating *H. sapiens* may have brought diseases from tropical Africa
that our early cousins had no previous exposure to, and thus, no proper immu-
nity from newly introduced pathogens (Houldcroft and Underdown 2016).
The jury is still out on the precise reasons other members of the genus *Homo*
disappeared altogether from the historical record save for their remains, but
it is highly likely that while there may have been some interbreeding and
mixing of DNA, the replacement by "violence and disease" hypothesis has
considerable archeological weight behind it. In fact, a recent finding in Africa
on the shore of Lake Turkana in Kenya suggests that prehistorical hunter-
gatherers may have been just as prone to violent conflict as are more settled
agrarian societies. At Lake Turkana, archeologists found the following gruesome evidence of an early massacre 10,000 years ago:

> Of 12 relatively complete skeletons, 10 showed unmistakable signs of violent
> death, the scientists said. Partial remains of at least 15 other persons were found
> at the site and are thought to have died in the same attack. The bones at the lake,
> in northern Kenya, tell a tale of ferocity. One man was hit twice in the head by

arrows or small spears and in the knee by a club. A woman, pregnant with a 6- to 9-month-old fetus, was killed by a blow to the head, the fetal skeleton preserved in her abdomen. The position of her hands and feet suggest that she may have been tied up before she was killed.[1]

This not only suggests that hunters and gatherers, like their more settled counterparts, had the propensity for violence, but also that this tendency toward overcoming hardship or adversity through violence was a possibility even among what were previously thought to be more peaceful and communal peoples eking out a living by foraging and hunting live game (Boehm 2001). But while *H. sapiens* may be hard-wired for aggression and violence, we must remember that environmental conditions also influence intergroup interactions. The stress of survival could be very real just as much as the potential for a lack or exhaustion of local resources. However, given the magnitude of the African and Eurasian landmass, the diversity of species edible by human omnivores, and the fact that the population of the time would have been extremely low, it is difficult to fathom that there would necessarily be "resource wars" encouraged by "resource shortages." This does not mean that there could not be conflict over local resources from time to time or that two unrelated groups, prompted by some grievance, could not war or fight with one another. I merely suggest here that it seems a bit far-fetched to hold to the view that our ancestors were hyper-competitive for a shortage of resources given the territory open to them and the overall size of the incipient human population. Despite our lack of concrete evidence that would allow for a general theory of *H. sapiens* interacting with and perhaps more likely massacring non-sapiens, we end this section of Act I with an undeniable fact: modern *H. sapiens* colonized, in fits and starts and over tens of thousands of years, the habitable regions of the earth. What some groups would do with their surrounding environment would have profound consequences for the tragedy of human development and the eventual emergence of capital as a mode of power.

THE NEOLITHIC REVOLUTION

When most scholars consider the Neolithic Revolution or what is sometimes called the Agrarian Revolution they focus on what appears to be a troublesome riddle: why did hunters and foragers abandon their seemingly easily reproducible lifestyles with what is generally assumed to be nutritious (or at least diverse) diets for a more difficult life of working the soil? After all, archeological evidence suggests that sedentary agriculturalists were relatively malnourished compared to hunters and gatherers and had far less time for leisure. Before we can consider this riddle we can dispense with the idea that this transition to social reproduction based on agriculture production happened suddenly, as most evidence suggests the two practices—settled agriculture and hunting and gathering—were synchronous. Again, hypothesizing about the distant human past leads to little absolute certainty but are there some more convincing explanations for the transition, despite the fact that there is scant academic consensus on the issue and our gaps in knowledge remain fairly vast, particularly given regional differences among early farmers? Though most scholars believe that hunters and gatherers did not become farmers overnight and that there was likely a considerable amount of oscillation or comingling between the two practices, one leading explanation has it that a warmer climate and the natural tendency of early humans to intervene in their environment contributed most to a gradual transition (Barker 2009). Another view is that early farmers or their progeny eventually dispersed to new regions where little was known of farming, bringing skills and knowledge to new parts of the world (Bellwood 2005). A final hypothesis does not necessarily discount climate change or past practices of human intervention into their environments in order to acquire sustenance, but focuses more on the social relations of power in more hierarchically arranged human groups. In this vein, hunters and foragers became farmers over time because of a power struggle between a minority in a position of strength and a majority who submitted to paying tribute in forms such as grain and animals to their would-be rulers who likely claimed some special privilege such as knowledge about the spirit world or afterlife (Bell and Henry 2001; Henry in Wray 1994: 79–98). In hierarchical prescientific civilizations rulers invented, inherited, or adopted religious or mystical ideas about the natural and cosmological order and what happened after death. The adoption of a superhuman world served to justify certain actions while at the same time prohibiting others. The evidence that the transition to agriculture was primarily about consolidating the power of privileged elites is of course scant, but for some, such as Richard Manning, the built environment of some early agrarian civilizations is highly suggestive:

> Farming did not improve most lives. The evidence that best points to the answer, I think, lies in the difference between early agricultural villages and their pre-agricultural counterparts—the presence not just of grain but of granaries and, more tellingly, of just a few houses significantly larger and more ornate than all the others attached to those granaries. Agriculture was not so much about food as it was about the accumulation of wealth. It benefited some humans, and those people have been in charge ever since (2004: 38, see also Wells 2010).[2]

Whether the shift to agriculture was the result of a gradual power process or the result of happenstance and experimentation, one thing is certain: the gradual shift toward agriculture provided the enabling conditions for the accumulation of greater power in the hands of a minority in all early "agrarian command economies" (Ingham 2004: 91). But what does seem beyond dispute is that with the rise of agrarian civilizations we witness the first forms of complex hierarchy where the majority is clearly subordinated to a ruler or a ruling priestly caste. To be sure, the transition to agriculture will continue to generate interest among scholars and we may never have a precise answer to such a direct and seemingly simple question given how far the transition lingers in our distant past. But while credible explanations for the transition loom large, an equally important question can be asked once humans start to domesticate plants, animals, and, in many ways, themselves.[3] This question is not so much a probe into why hunters and gatherers become farmers, but more about the cosmology, organization, and unique developments that happened to early agrarian societies. There appears to be a general agreement that the cosmology held by hunters and gatherers and early farmers differed. However, due to a lack of historical evidence, it is difficult to say with any precision how different groups of hunters and gatherers understood the universe and their place within it and how these understandings may have diverged from those of the first farmers organized into a social hierarchy. While the debate on the transition to agriculture is important, it is in the first agrarian empires where we start to witness the first kernels of capital as power.

MESOPOTAMIA

By about 3200 to 3600 BCE, one of the first major agrarian civilizations had emerged in Mesopotamia (more or less modern-day Iraq). For a time, those residing in Mesopotamia had the good fortune of relying on the flooding of the Euphrates and Tigris rivers that provided the surrounding soil with rich nutrients suitable for growing grains. The region and its cities showed virtually all the trappings of a civilization: a division of labor, a farming sector capable of generating a surplus, a priestly caste, monumental architecture, money and record keeping, and a hierarchy of power and privilege (Copeland 1974; Ezzamel 2002, 2009; Hudson 2000; Hudson in Wray 2004: 99–127; Keister 1963; Powell 1996). But, while there are many interesting things to discuss about the broader cultural aspects of Mesopotamia, our focus is on the financial developments happening in the region. Goetzmann (2016) makes the argument that any complex civilization such as the city-states of Mesopotamia would develop financial techniques as a way of coordinating communal order and the social reproduction of its hierarchical community. He, like other scholars, sees some of the early trappings of capitalism in Mesopotamia if we hold to the straightforward view that capitalism is largely about investing money to make more money. This is not to suggest that ancient Mesopotamia was a full-blown capitalist economy with market dependence and a developed price system gradually becoming a crucial aspect of everyday life—far from it (Ingham 2004: 93). But it should not be overlooked that there are indeed some elements of capitalism to be discovered in ancient Mesopotamia. These elements may surprise students and scholars who conflate capitalism with the industrial revolution and the systematic production of commodities in Europe of the nineteenth century, but the facts are difficult to deny. First, from our available records, there were certainly some forms of enforceable private property rights rooted in ownership, thus signaling the exclusionary power of some over others. Though we can find evidence for property rights earlier, the Code of Hammurabi in the second century BCE makes it clear that property rights are to be respected and protected by law. Second, there is undoubtedly a culture of lending at interest going on with creditors being in the minority and debtors mostly borrowing money in the short term at high interest rates (Goetzmann 2016: 64; see also Graeber 2011: 39). There is no conclusive evidence, but most scholars of money think that the idea of charging interest stems from the ability of livestock to generate new generations of livestock (Graeber 2011: 215). Unlike metallic money, animals are reproductive and can breed more offspring useful for farming or for sustenance. The practice of lending at high interest rates was often contested, and debts periodically forgiven in order to ensure some modicum of social harmony when debt crises intensified and threatened the breakdown of social order. But considerable evidence suggests that debt was used as a technology of power to expropriate land or encourage labor services from debtors, a legacy that continues today in various forms (Di Muzio and Robbins 2016; Graeber 2011: 180). Third, ancient Mesopotamia had a virtual form of money represented by a system of record keeping and an early form of accounting for credits and debts measured in grain, silver, and, sometimes, labor time. The accounting and record keeping appears to be primarily connected to the temple and palace authorities and there is evidence that the population was taxed, though there is little indication by precisely how much and exactly what was owed by the entire community and why some people may have paid more than others. Fourth, there is evidence that a small spectrum of society—including temple and palace authorities—with financial means capitalized entrepreneurial ventures in the expectation of a return. One venture was the maritime expeditions to Dilmun to trade for copper. Wealthier Mesopotamians would purchase a stake in the venture and, if it was successful, hope to get some form of return on their investment just as modern investors expect a return on the money they invest. Another equity capital–like venture was the silver trade with

Anatolia funded with the similar hope of a return on investment (Goetzmann 2016: 64). A third form of capitalization for which we have evidence is the capitalization of war making. As Goetzmann relates:

> Ochus, son of the Babylonian concubine Costmartidus and satrap of lower Mesopotamia, was living in a spacious rented residence in Babylon when his half- brother ascended the throne. One of Sogdianus's first imperial acts was to summon his powerful halfbrother to the imperial city of Susa—perhaps to put him under the sword and consolidate his own power. When the summons came in the form of an official cuneiform tablet delivered by royal messenger, Ochus had to work fast. His supporters urged him to fight, but they could not immediately provide the means for him to do so—they were land rich but cash poor, and the mercenaries and supplies to fight Sogdianus could only be obtained with silver. With Sogdianus pressing for a reply, they turned to the Murašu family for help. Ochus's backers mortgaged their vast property holdings in the Euphrates valley to the Murašu and used the proceeds to hire an army. Deserters from the disaffected Persian regulars soon joined them, and when Ochus rode into the city of Susa, it was not as Sogdianus's prisoner but as his successor. The usurper was usurped. Ochus took the royal title of Darius II. The overthrow of Sogdianus may be the *first war we know of to have been fought on borrowed money,* but it certainly was not the last (2016: 67, emphasis added).

What this passage reveals is that war-making capacity was financed in the hope that Ochus would be victorious in battle. Once in a position to rule after the violence quelled down, the supporters of Ochus expected him to use his newfound power to support all those who had backed him politically and financially. As Goetzmann points out, many of the land-rich, but cash-poor, farmers remained mired in debt after the victory, with some ultimately losing their land to their creditor, the Murašu family. In this sense, capitalizing violence may not have been profitable for the supporters of Ochus but for the Murašu family, the expropriation of more tracts of arable land likely would have extended them greater wealth and power.

Last, while many people think of money as notes and coins, the first form of money was a virtual money of account (Ingham 2004: 93–95). To the best of our knowledge, in Mesopotamia the most common form of money—essentially an accounting device—was based on silver as a unit of weight and tied to a certain amount of grain (Powell 1996: 226). Debts to the temple or palace, while registered in silver, were more often than not repaid in grain or other material goods rather than in silver (Goetzmann 2016: 59). Why silver was used as a unit of account remains a bit of a mystery since the metal is not native to Mesopotamia. The most credible answer, Goetzmann suggests, using the work of Van De Mieroop, is that it helped to overcome the fragmentation of early city-states by giving them and other distant trading communities a recognizable unit of value and medium of exchange for large and foreign transactions. This was particularly important for the region to acquire copper from abroad to make bronze with. And as Goetzmann has observed of this era: "Without bronze there are no weapons. Without weapons there is no empire" (2016: 59).

In sum, we can trace at least five elements of the capitalist mode of power back to Mesopotamia, even though the region was in no way fully capitalist. First, we have the institution of differential ownership (e.g., unequal ownership across the social hierarchy), which creates the fertile soil for differential accumulation and exclusion. Second, we find relationships between debtors and creditors and ways of mobilizing debt to dispossess others of their property, a family member, or their labor, primarily through very high interest rates. In other words, we have the act of lending at usurious rates. Third, we find the presence of an accounting system that keeps records in a monetary unit of account, facilitating the quantification of qualitative things including humans and their labor (Keister 1963). Rendering quality into quantity is essential for capitalism, though far from its only feature. Fourth, during this era there are some instances where a potential future income stream is capitalized by willing investors in both the copper and silver trade. And, last, we have an intersocietal money of account measured in silver that facilitated trade between communities of the region. On this foundation, the world's first militarized empire—the Neo-Assyrian Empire (c. 934–c. 605 BCE)—was erected. The Kingdom of Assyria ruled over Mesopotamia for centuries, extracting tribute from those it subjugated and penalizing subjects with severe violence if they disobeyed the imperial center. Another goal of war during the reign of the Neo-Assyrian empire was the capture of slaves, a practice that would be repeated elsewhere over the course of history (Chaliand 2014: 48–51; see also Bedford in Morris and Scheidel 2009: 30–65).

ANCIENT EGYPT

Egyptian civilization would likely have been impossible without the Nile and its periodic flooding. As food surpluses became more prevalent, the division of labor extended until a very particular hierarchical order started to emerge around the Pharaohs—the monarchs of Egypt—and a supportive priestly caste. Henry (in Wray 2004: 79–98) argues that the pharaohs likely originated from a class of hydraulic engineers with specialist knowledge invaluable for the survival of the population and its agrarian way of life. Over time, Henry argues that this class of engineers elevated themselves above the population and invented a religion to justify their rule and appropriation of resources and labor services. As a complement to their religious ordering of the mortal and supernatural worlds, the rulers of Egypt invented their own standard units of account to measure the relative value of things and to impose taxes across the population. These units were called the *khar* and the *deben*. As Ezzamel and Hoskin remark:

> In ancient Egypt, items begin to be valued through the use of monies of account by being named and counted as worth so many "khar" of grain, or "deben" of copper, silver or gold—i.e. the measuring is done in terms of a standard, recognised measure, already in use, as a commodity account which now, in signifying the worth of other entities in a precisely denominated way, appears to have a value in itself. These monies of account then become employed in a whole range of economic contexts: in stewardship accounts, in exchange transactions, in recompense contracts, and in legal disputes. Thus it is arguable that, beyond writing and counting, another kind of new sign, enacting a new and distinct kind of signifier-signified relation, is hewn out of accounting. As a signifier, the money sign follows on, like writing and counting, from the accounting token, in being a visible sign and an outside yardstick, which denotes and denominates (2002: 336).

As in Mesopotamia, we thus find a few crucial components of capitalism in ancient Egypt: the presence of money and a system of recording pecuniary transactions. We also find some semblance of private property—at least the recognition of usufruct rights—despite the fact that the land "technically" belonged to the gods and their earthly representatives: the pharaohs. Thus, from a juridical standpoint, there was no conception of absolute or exclusive private property, only various forms of tenure associated with rent and tax obligations. What seems to be absent in Egypt, unlike in Mesopotamia, is the capitalization of expected future profit from entrepreneurial adventures. Instead, we find a society largely geared toward the production and redistribution of local produce, the construction of temples, and a preoccupation with death, burial, and the afterlife rather than the accumulation of money as an end goal (Ezzamel 2009).

THE MONETARY REVOLUTION IN LYDIA-ATHENS-ROME

There have been metallic representations of money before Lydian Kings happened upon electrum—a gold and silver alloy panned in the Pactolus River. But it was arguably the transformations made to metallic money in Lydia (modern western Turkey) that would have a long-lasting legacy on Western monetary and fiscal affairs for over 2,000 years. The fetishization of silver and gold metal coins as the only "true" money would also have profound consequences for the non-European peoples of the world, who largely viewed these metals (where they could be found) as decorative objects rather than a medium of exchange. We will explore these consequences in more detail in Act II of our tragedy but here we ask: what happened in Lydia around 640–30 BCE that so shaped the tragedy of human development and the emergence of capital as power? To recall, earlier systems of money in the agrarian command economies of the Near East were based on a unit of account represented by silver or some amount of grain (typically convertible into units of silver). Money, then, was primarily a unit of account and a way of settling debts and credits owed to both secular and temple authorities, with rulers typically claiming to mediate between the supernatural and the material world. In Lydia, money was to gain a more material and standardized footing than it previously had in any other civilization. The electrum panned from the Pactolus River was struck or hammered into relatively uniform coins, typically with the emblem of a lion (Davies 2002: 63; Weatherford 1997: 31). This uniformity eased transactions because weight and purity were guaranteed by the governing authorities and the coins only represented a few days labor or a small portion of a farmer's produce—meaning they could circulate more broadly rather than represent a simple store of wealth. Once metallurgy developed further, it was also possible to separate the gold and silver from the amalgamated alloy and to strike separate gold and silver coins. By accounts of the time—particularly those of Herodotus—the Lydians became a nation of shopkeepers as coins circulated in the community and called forth the greater marketization and monetization of social life (Weatherford 1997: 32). For his part, King Croesus spent lavishly on building construction and for mercenaries. His paid soldiers, however, were no match for the Persian king, Cyrus the Great, who conquered Lydia in 546 BCE. But despite the defeat of Croesus's kingdom, the Lydian invention of stamped gold and silver coinage spread like wildfire eastward through the Persian Empire and westward through the Aegean islands to Greece and later Italy (Davies 2002: 66). Davies notes the world historical consequences of this new technology: "Money has always meant more than simply coins; but it was coins that thereafter in the main constituted money and also provided a simple and therefore universally understood and accepted base and reference point for all other financial accounting devices and exchanging media" (2002: 65). Pandora had been let out of her box: though it would take some time to spread throughout the rest of Eurasia, a new belief would gradually take hold among most rulers, merchants, and even some commoners: "real" money was gold and silver coins; everything else was derivative, representative, or worthless. International or high-powered money was no longer just a metaphor that could correspond to any number of physical objects from cattle to cowrie shells (though this remained true in many quarters of the globe for centuries until these "primitive" currencies were demonetized during the course of European colonialism). The dominant money of command—the money that could attract wanted goods, slaves, and mercenaries—now corresponded with only two physical objects: gold and silver coins (Hollander 2007: note 3; Ingham 2004: 97; Schaps 2007: 106). The political communities of Greece and Rome would help spread this new technology to Western Europe and, by extension, the wider world (Davies 2002: 66–112).

Though Greece is often celebrated as the cradle of democracy, it is in its monetary dimension where the importance of Greece for capitalist order is perhaps most acute. The historical turning point for the greater monetization and commercialization of a civilizational order appears to have happened in Greece. At the time when its neighbor—Lydia—was producing coinage of electrum, gold, and silver, Greece was a fragmentary political and cultural community of city-states run by aristocratic oligarchies. Scholars are not certain why Athens and other Greek city-states adopted coinage, but it appears that Greece's lack of generous farmland may have forced the hands of rulers to exploit its plentiful silver in exchange for foreign grain. This is highly plausible, as the Greeks generally only had to bring silver with them when abroad and, with it, could avail themselves to virtually every commodity they may have desired (Goetzmann 2016: 90). Whatever the reason for the turn to a system of money based on silver coinage, that this was a decisive turn away from Homeric Greece can hardly be in doubt (Peacock 2006: 642; Weatherford 1997: 43). As Peacock notes, there is no money-thing in Homeric Greece and where the search for profit rather than glory in battle is mentioned at all, the pursuit of wealth is denigrated as unworthy of a hero. But with the introduction of coinage by separate city-states, the Grecian world was turned upside down. Greek coins were stamped and had a fiduciary (nominal) rather than intrinsic value. Above a swathe of city-state issued coins stood the Attic silver standard—the *drachma*, followed by coins of lesser denomination (Davies 2002: 75). After the mining and minting process, Greek coins were spent into the economy to pay for soldiers, jurors, and additional goods and services demanded by state officials such as infrastructure and sacrifices. But why did ordinary and aristocratic Greek people accept coins in payment for actual goods and services when this practice represented a radical break from previous forms of non-market and non-monetary social reproduction? Peacock (2006), among others, suggests that the coins were made valuable by government decree and the prevalence of monetary taxation. First, the coins had to be accepted as payment for goods and services within the local community, and this was backed up by the force of governing authorities. Second, once taxes were commuted into coins, the taxpaying population required coins in order to pay their obligations to the state. Monetary taxation not only created a demand for coins among the community, but it also helped to gear agricultural production toward the market and emerging price system—a trend that would continue as the monetization of taxation proceeded in additional political communities. Aristocratic farmers with little money but productive land would have to convert part of their produce into cash in order to settle their obligations to the state. Once again, we do not have a full-blown capitalist economy with the introduction of coined money in Greece, but we do see the emergence of a completely new way of organizing society: around money as coin, with the push and pull of state spending and taxation. We should note here that this relationship between the state as the money issuer and user of coin and the population as a whole is an interesting one and historically novel and part of what I have called the monetary revolution. Since the state cannot recall its entire coinage system through the mechanism of taxation, private social forces are able to accumulate wealth in the form of coins by providing goods and services to the state or to their fellow citizens. What this suggests, as Harrington's political theory would later confirm in England, is that private citizens can come to amass more wealth and power than political rulers, making it possible for an overthrow of authority by a wealthy class who can afford to pay an army easier than a royal authority with less finance (Pipes 1999: 32).[4] Regent after regent in Europe had to practically beg financiers for loans in order to finance their aristocratic and religious wars, eventually weakening their powers and, in some cases, leading to political upheaval and revolution. In any case, this potential to amass private wealth in the form of coins appears to happen in Greece for the first time and is noticed by Aristotle, who makes a distinction between money for household use and well-being and trade for the endless accumulation of money:

> Wealth acquired in household management is naturally limited by the needs of the family or state. Exchange is legitimate if it is limited to the acquisition of necessities. Aristotle contrasts this mode of acquisition with another, unnatural, one—"retail trade"—which has its origin in money. The goal of retail trade is not the provision of useful objects but the acquisition of money which, in principle, has no limit. The "most hated" acquisition of money is through usury, because it not only serves the end of monetary enrichment but does so in its most direct form, without the intermediary of an object of exchange. The unlimited acquisition of coin could lead to large inequalities in wealth, something which put the justice of "exchange" in the polis into question (Peacock 2006: 646).

What this passage suggests is that with the introduction of coinage, a new societal motive was introduced as a world historical fact: the desire to accumulate greater and greater amounts of coin as evidence of wealth and power rather than to merely manage one's household for a decent livelihood or make a short-term gain in a venture or transaction. Schaps encapsulates the revolution:

> If coins had been merely a convenience, a more effective way of transferring items from one to another, their effect on Greece would probably have been limited to increasing market trade, making trade and exchange a larger part of the society's experience. This effect they surely had; but their influence went much deeper. The conceptual revolution that identified coins with wealth turned money into an item of which one could never have too much, or, indeed, enough. Not all the Greeks subscribed to this judgment; but some did, and as their ideas became more influential, they had effects more profound than mere increase of trade (2007: 175).

To be sure, the entire monetization of the emergent Greek market society depended upon the labor of slaves working the Laureion and other mines in horrible conditions. It is estimated that the Laureion mines alone may have had up to 30,000 slaves working to excavate the new coinage of the realm (Davies 2002: 70). If Fritz Lang was looking for inspiration for his film *Metropolis*, he could hardly have gotten better inspiration than the silver mines of Greece. We should also note that even at this early stage of money's introduction, Aristotle remarked on the potential for greater inequality within the *polis*. Given what we know today about the radically unequal distribution of income and particularly wealth in the global economy, it appears that Aristotle's concern was more than prescient. But if Greek civilization underwent a fundamental transformation by adopting coinage as its monetary medium, it would be Alexander the Great's military advances that would press the dimensions of coinage beyond new territorial and cultural barriers.

While coinage in Greece was emitted by fragmented city-states, mines in the Macedonian Kingdom were the exclusive property of the king and thus there was a highly centralized form of ownership over coinage and its allocation. Macedon was rich in gold, silver, iron, and copper, all of which by custom belonged to Alexander when he assumed the throne in 336 BCE (Davies 2002: 82). This centralization of ownership facilitated the financing of Alexander's empire and likely its vast scale. Davies recounts how Alexander's soldiers were well supplied with both coin and provisions, with adequate extra-military support for long campaigns of conquest far from home. Soldiers were apparently banned from looting treasure from their conquered peoples and were instead encouraged to spend their salary to obtain local produce and services. Alexander would also tax his new subjects in his own coinage, thereby ensuring a demand among locals for Alexander's money. According to Davies, Macedonian hegemony and the financial consequences of Alexander's imperial ambitions came to an end in 197 BCE when the Roman general "Quinctius Flaminius defeated Philip V at the battle of

Cynocephalae" (2002: 87). Though Rome was undergoing socio-economic transformations before this date, thereafter, it would take center stage in the tragedy of human development and the rise of capital as power.

The cash nexus that developed in the Greek city-states took on new dimensions with the rise of Rome and its eventual control over the regions and peoples of the Mediterranean basin and further far afield. Once again, we have to be careful not to fall into the trap of conflating capitalism with industrialization. Just because there was little to no industrial production in Rome, this does not mean that there was an absence of capitalist practice. As Runciman argued, "The ownership of private property was both absolute and exclusive" and Rome's rulers—the patrician and equestrian class—were "no less intent on the pursuit of profit" than capitalists in later centuries (1983: 158). The major point of difference between Romans chasing money and capitalists of later centuries chasing the same may be how the pursuit of profit was carried out.

Rome was founded on the Tiber River in 753 BCE and developed into a hierarchical social order under kingly rule until Roman senators put an end to the institution of monarchy and established a republic based on their rule. Before the turn toward republicanism, the second Roman King, Numa (716–672), introduced a bronze coinage. It is not known whether this was a strategic move, a move out of geographical necessity (there were few, if any, silver and gold mines in Italy) or just a fortuitous circumstance. While the precise reason for the adoption of bronze coin is uncertain, Zarlenga (2002: 50) holds that this was ultimately a wise decision since the largest deposits of gold and silver were in the east and a considerable amount of it stowed away in temples as offerings to priests and gods. Moreover, the bronze coins had a fiduciary value in law, not an intrinsic one measured by the weight of metallic content. In other words, the bronze coins had value because Roman rulers said they had value. To be sure, Rome's rulers did command its moneyers to strike silver and gold coin, but this was mainly for use in trade abroad, not for the domestic market, where bronze coinage appeared to be ideal for the payment of the army and the circulation of domestic goods and services. Another benefit was that bronze, unlike gold and silver, could be found in greater quantities, thus helping to ease one of the crucial problems of the era: the shortage of coin for purchase transactions.[5] However, during its militant expansion, Roman soldiers came across different political communities, many of whom traded in silver coin rather than bronze. It is likely that these inter societal interactions forced Rome to adopt a silver coin, the denarius, in order to pay for goods outside of the republican and, later, imperial center. By 269 BCE, Roman rulers were regularly striking silver coins in the Temple of Juno Moneta, the Roman goddess of warning and from where the English derive the words "money" and "mint" (Davies 2002: 89; Weatherford 1997: 48).[6] The new silver coin was called the denarius and its smaller silver cousin, the sesterce, represented one-fourth of a denarius. However, while adding silver coins to the official stock of Roman money may have been expedient given that many eastern political communities wanted silver, rather than bronze, coin, this move would serve to force the republic's hand, right down to the final days of the Roman Empire in 476 CE. The reason for this monetary straightjacket can be largely explained by Roman geology. Rome and the wider communities of modern-day Italy had no significant deposits of silver on its territory, making the acquisition of silver coin/bullion or silver mines a key explanation for the expansion of the Roman Empire. It is true, as we will discuss subsequently, that Roman rulers financed war in order to gain more territory, but it is equally true that without military conquest and expansion, there would be no silver to pay the army and precious little silver leftover to pay for luxury goods from the east—particularly from Anatolia, India, the Baltic, and China (Weatherford 1997: 51, 56).[7] In fact, the draining of silver (and later gold) coin eastward was a constant threat to the Roman money supply and one of the key reasons for periodic deflation and renewed military conquests to find and takeover more silver mines. For instance, Rome's conquest of Spain in 206 BCE allowed Roman rulers to take over her gold and silver mines and extract a steady stream of tribute over a ten-year period (Davies 2002: 94). These newly acquired mines belonged to the Roman state and later became the direct personal property of the Emperor. But the conquest of new territories and mines also meant capturing other people and enslaving them on plantations or in the mines themselves. Thus, building on Ingham's original formulation of a "military-coinage complex," Graeber has called Rome's regime a "military-coinage-slavery complex" (2011: 229). The interactive rules of the complex can be summarized as follows: Roman rulers use an initial outlay of coin to finance (or dare we say capitalize) an army to gain useful land, mines, and slaves from outside its original jurisdiction. Captured slaves are used to mine for gold, silver, and copper so that these metals can be converted into a new flood of coins to finance a larger army to expand the initial search for more mines, territory, and slaves. The search for slaves continues because of the rapid death rate in the mines, and the search for mines continues because rulers are always short of coin to finance the military and its luxury spending abroad. The process repeats itself until there are diminishing returns or some other calamity such as the debasement of the currency or a mass slave or provincial revolt calls the entire operation into question. To what extent can we call this "complex" capitalist? The answer may become clear once we ask an additional question: what was the primary aim of Roman rulers and how did they reproduce themselves as a class? There are at least two ways to answer this question—the first is at the level of the state the rulers directed and controlled—be it through the senate during the

Republic or later through the office of the emperor with some senatorial input. The second is at the level of the individual patrician or equestrian—what were their individual strategies of accumulation? Let us consider the state first.

The Roman Republic and later the emperor not only owned and controlled the production of coins but were the main issuer of new runs of bronze, silver, and, later, gold currency. We know that the overwhelming expense of the Roman state and later the empire was the military. According to Davies, "to support just one legion cost Rome around 1,500,000 denarii a year, so that the main reason for the regular annual issue of silver denarii was simply to pay the army" (2002: 89). The main task of Rome's legions was to conquer new territory, capture slaves, and enforce tribute and taxation to the center, not to mention pacify local populations newly absorbed into the centripetal force of the Roman 1 percent's avarice. Since Rome never accumulated a national debt, it is impossible to say that the Roman state was capitalized by private lenders who sought a return from government taxation. Instead—and this will get reversed later in our story—rather than the Roman state being capitalized, the Roman state itself capitalized the military in the hope of a return on their investment. The return was directly tied to successful territorial conquests, the capture of mines and slaves and increasing coinage which would have expanded state spending for the army, and additional projects such as infrastructure, monumental architecture, and additional public spectacles and works. But though the state was in constant need of coin to finance its ongoing reproduction, the Roman state never became a debtor to private social forces with money to lend. So while conquest could increase state coffers and therefore state spending, the capitalization of the army served primarily to renew the hierarchical social structure of Roman civilization.

But if we move from the state to the individual patrician or equestrian, we go from state/imperial reproduction and accumulation to private accumulation. As mentioned previously, what were the individual interests of these privileged individuals? Undoubtedly, it was to maintain their power or aggrandize it, and this meant gaining and maintaining wealth. First, in order to even consider becoming a member of the senate, a patrician had to have at least 250,000 denarii while an equestrian had to have wealth worth 100,000 denarii (Goetzmann 2016: 105). And even this accumulation of wealth did not guarantee one a seat in the senate. But how was one to accumulate private wealth? Patricians only had a few options open to them. In essence, patricians were supposed to garner their wealth from the sale of their agricultural produce generated on their estates (Goetzmann 2016: 106). However, by most accounts this activity was not enough to earn, let alone maintain, a substantial fortune (Goetzmann 2016: 108). For this reason, most if not all senators were moneylenders and engaged in commerce at a distance through intermediaries and go-betweens. Since senators were not legally permitted to engage in commercial activity, investing at a distance in entrepreneurial activities afforded them with plausible deniability while at the same time providing them with an opportunity to make profit and maintain their status within Rome's hierarchy of class privilege. The equestrian class (Roman Knights) was not so restricted and could engage in commerce without any subterfuge. What were some of the opportunities available to them? As it turns out, most of the opportunities to make a fortune were associated with state contracts, particularly after the Second Punic War (218–201 BCE). As Goetzmann asserts:

> Rome expanded relatively rapidly throughout the Mediterranean world. This expansion created challenges for the Republic. It had to supply a large standing army; build and maintain a vast urban infrastructure; and tax remote, newly conquered provinces. Rather than build a governmental bureaucracy to do all these things, Rome auctioned off government contracts to private consortiums called *societas publicanorum*—publican societies. The publican societies bid for government contracts at public auctions—particularly for contracts to collect provincial taxes, but also for other services ranging from construction and maintenance of public monuments to supplying and provisioning the armies. Roman legal historians are convinced that these firms were not only large- scale business enterprises, but that they also had ownership shares that were liquid and tradable (2016: 122, emphasis original).

The Amsterdam Stock Exchange, opened in 1602, is typically credited as the world's first stock exchange (Petram 2014). However, as Goetzmann points out, the trading of shares in publican societies at the Roman Forum may represent the world's first true stock market. Investors could buy and sell claims to the anticipated income streams generated from government-financed contracts. Under the empire, these contracts started to dry up, as the imperial machinery increasingly took on the task of providing public works (Goetzmann 2016: 127).

Yet another way to accumulate great wealth was to confiscate the property and wealth of others. This not only happened as the empire expanded, but was internal to Roman politics, and later religion, as well. The proscriptions of 82 and 43 BCE set the stage for such great dispossessions. The first proscription was declared by Lucius Cornelius Sulla, a statesman and military general who captured power in Rome by force. Once in power, Sulla had the senate draw up a list of names of those who were deemed enemies of the regime. The names were posted on the Roman Forum and rewards were offered for their capture and murder. Proscribed men were typically decapitated with their heads displayed in the Forum or throughout the city as a warning to other potential traitors. Those citizens who killed proscribed men could confiscate part of their property, with the remainder going to the state to auction off for money. Sulla's treasury would be filled with the riches of his opponents. The second proscription was issued after the assassination of Julius Caesar in an effort to avenge his murder. As in the first proscription, a list of names was drawn up and rewards were offered for decapitated heads. The property of the condemned could also be confiscated, thus providing a powerful incentive for Rome's citizens to track down and ultimately murder proscribed men. What is more, the sons and grandsons of condemned men could never take up public office and the widows and daughters of the proscribed forbidden to remarry or wed. It is estimated that 300 senators and 2,000 members of the equestrian class were killed during this purge.[8] A third and final "great dispossession," also motivated, in part, by money, was the adoption of Christianity as the official state religion by Constantine in 313 BCE. For centuries, Rome had persecuted Christians but in 313 BCE, the Roman Emperor Constantine and his eastern counterpart, Licinius, issued the Edict of Milan, effectively decriminalizing Christian worship. The exact motives for this move are unclear but scholars have suggested that elevating Christianity to the official state religion allowed a financially weak Constantine to confiscate the loot of pagan temples:

> Unable to finance his administration from taxation and unable to loot new lands, Constantine began confiscating the riches in the temples of his own empire. He conducted a systematic looting of these temples, and with the gold and silver, he minted gold coins to finance the construction of his new capital, Constantinople. The building of the new capital cut off the money supply to Rome and further depressed the economic condition of the Roman lands (Weatherford 1997: 60, see also Davies 2002: 107).

Thus, while not totally conclusive, it appears that there is a case to be made that Christianity was elevated as a state religion in order for Constantine to loot the far wealthier non-Christian temples. The spoils could then be added to imperial coffers for Constantine's new capital in the East. Whatever Constantine's ultimate motivation, the adoption of Christianity as the Roman Empire's official religion had profound historical consequences for the peoples of the world. From a tiny sect in the Levant, in the hands of imperial Rome, Christianity became a world historical fact (there are believed to be about 2.2 billion practicing Christians) and one of the world's three major Middle Eastern–born monotheistic religions sandwiched historically between Judaism and Islam.[9] Many of the tragedies inflicted upon humanity over the coming centuries would be justified in the name of one or more of these gods. Such has been the power of human belief that these religions remain with us today, despite overwhelming evidence that all religion is a human construction.

END OF ACT I

The opening act of this work watched how *H. sapiens* spread throughout the habitable continents of the earth where they displaced, by violence, disease, or interbreeding, other hominins. To the best of our knowledge, in six regions of the world former hunters and gatherers were gradually experimenting with settled agriculture and the domestication of certain animals. This experimentation gave way to what Ingham (2004: 91) called the first "agrarian command economies," where we find a growing division of labor, a more developed class structure between rulers and ruled, a belief in supernatural gods, and the storage of agricultural surpluses. To be sure, Mesopotamia and ancient Egypt were not capitalist societies with a developed price system, market dependence, and the overwhelming desire of its ruling class to accumulate money as the primary goal of social life. However, as I argued, in these early political communities we can find some of the key trappings of the capitalist mode of power: private property, simple accounting, and money as a unit of account used to assess the value of people, animals, and products of the natural world. The qualitative social and natural world was being gradually quantified within a system of organized power that chiefly benefited powerful rulers backed by force and interested in accumulating tribute and slaves. We then considered how the first standardized coins of gold and silver led to a revolutionary transformation in monetary affairs. Beginning in Lydia, the belief that "real" money was gold and silver coin spread throughout Eurasia through trade and the violence of imperial rulers and their armies. To leverage the power of violent force meant having enough coin to pay for soldiers, mercenaries, and weapons. Thus, it could be said that the desire to accumulate money and the slaves who would work the mines became, perhaps for the first time, *a primary goal* of ruling classes. This goal was intimately intertwined with ruling class power and their ability to maintain and socially reproduce their rule. As we will see in Act II, this "monetary revolution" is integral for explaining so much of the trajectory of the tragedy of human development. In fact, it could be said that without the development of money as coin and its ability to be accumulated by both rulers and ruled, much of human development, economic growth, and the emergence of the capitalist mode of power could not be explained. Weatherford captured the importance of this new social technology:

Prior to the invention of money in the form of coins, the chapters of history overflow with stories of many civilizations on different continents speaking different languages and worshiping different gods, but we see in virtually all of them a common pattern. Whether we consider the ancient Egyptians or the Aztecs, the Hittites or the Babylonians, the Cretans or the mysterious people of Mohenjo-Daro, we see that they all appear to have risen only to a similar level of civilization. It is almost as though each of them encountered the same invisible wall, which they were unable to penetrate (1997: 42).

Money and the greater monetization of social relations and nature, it seems, was about to change everything.

NOTES

1 James Gorman (2016) "Pre-Historic Massacre Hints at Warfare among Hunter-Gatherers" *New York Times*, January 20.

2 See also Manning (2005: 37–41).

3 Manning (2005: 41) suggests a co-evolutionary pattern: the domestication of wheat also meant the domestication of agricultural societies.

4 James Harrington (1611–1677) was an English political theorist. His most famous work is *The Commonwealth of Oceana* (1656). In it, Harrington tried to account for the downfall of the monarchy, arguing that political power ultimately rested on wealth since, political rule ultimately depends on force and an army must be paid.

5 As should become clear by the end of this book the problem of money in capitalist society is not that there is too much of it chasing too few goods and services, but that there are too many goods and services chasing too little money. This is a structural feature of capitalism as will be explained later on.

6 According to Weatherford: "The coins seem to have flowed out of the mint in a constant stream, and it is from the Latin word *currere,* meaning 'to run' or 'to flow,' that the modern word *currency* is derived, along with other, related words such as *current* and *courier*" (1997: 48).

7 As we will see, this draining of gold and silver coin to the east was not unique to Rome but would end up being a constant problem throughout the age of money as coin in Western Europe.

8 'Proscripto' in Murray, John (1875) *A Dictionary of Greek and Roman Antiquities.* (London: np). http://penelope.uchicago.edu/Thayer/e/roman/texts/secondary/smigra*/proscriptio.html (14/4/2017).

9 'World's Muslim Population Will Surpass Christians This Century, Pew Says' April 2, 2015. http://www.npr.org/sections/thetwo-way/2015/04/02/397042004/muslim-population-will-surpass-christians-this-century-pew-says (5/24/2017).

Act II

Colonialism and the Transatlantic Slave Trade

If money was starting to change power dynamics and social relations in the Greco-Roman world of the Mediterranean, the fall of the Western Roman Empire in 476 BCE was, in many senses, a reversal of these visible but ultimately unsustainable transformations. In most of Europe, there was a turn from the urban and the cash nexus of the market to new forms of social reproduction less reliant on cash transactions we typically call "feudalism" (Weatherford 1997: 62). Why this sudden reversal? The historiography on the decline of the western empire is still a matter of dispute and, given the evidence that remains from the fourth and fifth centuries, it is unlikely that any one theory will prevail (Goldsworthy 2010). However, Zarlenga (2002: 110) has proposed that the ultimate decline of the Western Roman Empire may be sought in three main factual events. First, money was being heavily concentrated in the possession of the powerful, particularly in the Eastern Roman Empire, leaving less coinage for the people to use in their daily transactions. Second, money was constantly being transferred to the east for luxury goods and because the exchange rate of silver into gold was higher in India than it was throughout Europe, more coin was drained to the east than otherwise would have been the case. Third, old mines started to dry up and there was a general absence of new mining, and therefore new metal by which to make coins for the realm. In other words, it is entirely possible that the empire was relatively demonetized over time, throwing the price system and market relations that supported urban forms of social reproduction into chronic decay. Unlike the sack of Rome or cultural decadence thesis, Zarlenga's argument has the merit of demonstrating how one of the first most heavily monetized societies could gradually undergo a civilizational decline due to a lack of money to circulate goods and services (see also Burnett 1987; Duncan-Jones 1998). As we will uncover, the lack or dearth of money for the majority of humanity is not an exception of history, but a general rule embedded in the way money was produced as coin and how it is currently created by commercial banks. Though there are additional things to consider about our current fiat monetary system, in regard to coined money Bernstein points out the obvious: "A society that uses metal for money will always be constrained by the supply of that metal" (2000: 52). But before we get too far ahead of ourselves, it is now time to outline Act II of the tragedy of human development and our genealogy of capital as power.

In this act, we move from the money-making vectors of the Mediterranean to the development of what Thomas (1993) has called the "Atlantic economy" throughout the centuries' long history of Western colonialism and the transatlantic slave trade. Once again we find that those doing the most significant harm to workers, slaves, and the environment are the ruling 1 percent of society for the private benefit of greater money, power, and to a considerable extent, religion, and prestige. We begin with the investments made into a series of Christian crusades, largely, though not always exclusively, to regain the "Holy Land" of the Levant from those practicing the newest monotheistic religion of the Middle East: Islam. The crusades had a number of financial consequences that would, to some extent, revitalize the quest for gold and silver coins that could finance greater trade with the East and fund new Christian crusades. The act then moves to consider European colonial encounters and the motives for exploration and, eventually, the colonization of much of the non-European world. I will then demonstrate how the desire for differential accumulation in money (primarily gold and silver) motivated and sustained the violence of the transatlantic slave trade over centuries. As I will discuss, the biopolitical violence of the slave trade was ultimately capitalized through the creation of a permanent national debt and the expansion of the credit system by the newly formed Bank of England (1694). This development, I will argue, is a watershed moment in the emergence of the capitalist mode of power and helped set England (later Britain in 1707) on a radically divergent developmental trajectory. The act closes by discussing how scientific racism emerged and informed colonial and imperial practice in the midst of a geopolitical and increasingly militarized battle for Western supremacy that would introduce the horrors of World Wars I and II to a global population yet uninitiated to the terror of industrial warfare.

CHRIST, CRUSADES, AND GOLD

According to Weatherford (1997: 58–63) and historians of feudalism, after the fall of the Western Roman Empire in 476 BCE, the classical monetary economy of the Mediterranean fell into abeyance. Money as coinage and urbanism did not disappear altogether, but urban centers and coin seemed to have played far less a role in social life across Europe than it had in classical Rome for about a thousand years (Bloch 1962: 65–69; Cipolla 1993: 92). Weatherford captures the essence of the structural shift:

> The medieval era, which might also be called the manorial era because of the importance of manors, represented a major departure from classical Mediterranean culture; whereas classical culture focused on the city, medieval culture focused on the country manor. Whereas classical culture emphasized commerce, medieval culture emphasized self-sufficiency; and whereas classical economy focused on money, medieval economy focused on hereditary services and payment in kind. Medieval culture, then, departed radically from that of the classical era, especially in that the medieval world virtually gave up the use of money. Rather than collect taxes in coins, landowners required payment in crops and service from the peasants. Rather than manufacture trade goods, each manor sought to be as self-sufficient as possible by producing its own food and clothing and even by making its own tools. No longer able to sell their services, people became serfs who were bound to the land (1997: 62).

Once again, we do not know with complete certainty why this transformation came about, but Zarlenga's stress on the lack of money appears to be convincing if only for the fact that had the region remained heavily monetized, it would seem highly unlikely that a new feudal mode of power based on "hereditary services and payment in kind" would have developed. What changed this relationship has been heavily debated, but Weatherford argues that key to understanding the re-monetization of social order in Europe were a series of Christian crusades to liberate the "Holy Land" from Muslim rule. He writes: "After centuries of slumber, the system gradually returned to life during the era of the Crusades, when western Europeans invaded the Muslim lands of the East. Money acquired a newly important role in financing the extensive new trade routes opened between East and West and in financing the large military expeditions that were launched over great distances for long periods of time" (1997: 63).

Raised in Mecca from 570 CE, the Prophet Mohammed and his army of 120,000 supporters moved swiftly to spread their new religion of Islam both east as far as India and west as far as Spain by 711 (Zarlenga 2002: 105). By 1095, upon the request of the emperor of Byzantium (Constantinople) Alexius I Comnenus, Pope Urban II issued a call for Western European Christians to recapture the "Holy Land" from Muslim authority (Tyerman 2004). Though historians debate the exact number of Crusades, 1096 marked the first in a series of intermittent Crusades that are generally said to have come to an end in the mid-fifteenth century (Davies 2002: 153). For the Arabs, the Crusades represented an attempt by Europeans to colonize the Middle East, whereas the European Christians thought they were expropriating Islam from Christian lands that had been unjustly seized (Ferro 1997: 3). Roughly two centuries of battle and bloodshed were fought to prove once and for all that one religion and one god were the correct ones and that all other belief systems were heretical. In return, soldiers and mercenaries of various religious sects were promised a world beyond the physical world they had come to know. Roughly a century later, the fear of hell, the promise of an "afterlife," and an unwavering Manichean worldview continue to motivate religious faith in "needed" atrocities. But the initial Crusades to recapture the "Holy Land" did not come cheap. In order to facilitate the movement of millions of soldiers and pilgrims to the "Holy Land," an entire financial apparatus was erected around the Knights Templar. The organization was founded in 1118 in order to safeguard the right of pilgrims to enter the "Holy Land," transfer funds from one geographical space to the next, and assist in whatever way possible with reclaiming the "Holy Land" for Christendom. Members of the Knights Templar took an oath not to accumulate any private fortune from their activities and those who were found accumulating money were said to have fallen outside the grace of God, given an unceremonious burial, and "condemned to eternal damnation" (Weatherford 1997: 67). But what was true for the individual was not true of the organization as a whole. Supporting princes and kings and the younger sons of noblemen on their quest to liberate the "Holy Land" was a lucrative enterprise. As Davies notes, "Payment for supplies, equipment, allies, ransoms and so on, from time to time required vast resources of cash and the means of safely and quickly transferring such money" (Davies 2002: 153). But the Templars, as an organization, not only grew rich from innovations in banking and their role as financial intermediaries and creditors. The Templars were also viewed as a prominent charitable organization, obtaining gifts of money, land, and buildings from the wealthy elites of Europe who supported the cause to retake the "Holy Land" from infidels. Once again, both activities would have the effect of creating a dearth of currency in parts of Europe. First, in the fact that money flowed eastward and second in that it was hoarded by the Templars. In fact, Spufford called the Crusades "a new means of draining Europe of coin" (1988: 98). One significant center of accumulation was just outside Paris, where the Templars would effectively become the victims of their own success.

King Phillip IV had debased the silver currency of France and was in considerable debt to Jewish moneylenders and the Knights Templar. By July 1306, Phillip expelled his Jewish creditors from France and less than a year later plotted to raid the wealth of the Knights Templar by denouncing the order as a group of heretics. On Friday, October 13, 1307, members of the organization were rounded up and forced to confess to abominable crimes against the Christian faith and European morality. Under severe torture, "the elderly officers of the order signed confessions that provided lurid details about their activities as idol worshipers, profaners of sacred objects, conspirators with the devil, and perpetrators of sexual deviance upon one another. . . . The charges included accusations of Templars having sex with the corpses of noblewomen, worshiping a cat, eating the bodies of dead knights, and making bonds of blood brotherhood with Muslims" (Weatherford 1997: 69; see also Tyerman 2007). The accusations were all fabricated, but the falsities of the king's claims were covered up by the vigor of French prosecutors, whose charges condemned the Templars to death by fire or a life in prison. Cowering to the king of France, Pope Clement V abolished the order in 1312, effectively complementing by religious decree what had already been accomplished by courtly and royal force. The largest, richest, and most extensive financial network in Europe had been destroyed, and its riches usurped by an indebted regent.

However another event during the era of the Crusades is likely to have also increased the money supply of Europe. Zarlenga, citing the work of William Jacobs on precious metals, argues that the Sack of Constantinople (1204) by Venetians (among other Crusaders) may have been a watershed moment for re-monetizing Western Europe with coin. According to Jacobs, the Sack of Constantinople likely "transferred more metallic wealth to western Europe than all the commerce of the centuries that preceded it" (cited in Zarlenga 2002: 155). This may be true, but we must take the statement with a grain of salt. It appears that hoarding, the purchase of eastern luxuries by elites, wear and tear of the coinage and gifts to churches and shrines continued to plague most of Western Europe with a dearth of coinage even in the opening of the fifteenth century (Spufford 1988: 348, 356). The problem of the dearth of coinage, rooted in the false, yet nevertheless powerful belief, that only gold and silver were "real" money, continued to plague most of Europe, particularly as it sought luxury goods from the east and had very little to offer Indian and Chinese merchants in return but precious metals.

The problems created by the shortage of coin across Europe were compounded by the takeover of Byzantium (Constantinople and later Istanbul) by Ottoman Turks in 1453 (Ferro 1997: 4). The Turks did not fully block trade with Western powers but their regulation of trade and their ability to impose taxes and fees on merchants made the eastern route to India and Chinese riches far less desirable—particularly for Spain on the Western edge of Europe (Anievas and Nişancioğlu 2015: 115–16; West 1992: 259). The Turkish obstruction of trade prompted discussion on the possibility of finding a western route to the eastern trade, one that would also be motivated by Christianity and, what appears most important, the search for gold and silver.

One Italian seaman and adventurer's accidental discovery became the spark that set off a spectral fire in the minds of fifteenth-century adventurers and merchants that would last centuries.

Cristoforo Colombo (1451–1506), better known by his Anglicized name, Christopher Columbus, was a citizen of the city-state of Genoa. In his youth and young manhood, Columbus garnered considerable experience making maps and navigating the Mediterranean (West 1992). Using the instruments available to him at the time and digesting the geographical and cosmological theories of the age, Columbus became convinced that there must be a western sea route to India and the grand Khan of China. In 1484, Columbus pled with King John of Portugal to finance his expedition west into the Atlantic but the king's counselors advised against financing the venture (Ferro 1997: 23). Columbus would have to wait until 1492 for King Ferdinand and Queen Isabella of Spain to sponsor his transatlantic mission to find gold, spices, and a new route to the east that would avoid better known but dangerous paths by land and sea. While certainly concerned to uncover a new trade route to eastern riches, we must also recall that Columbus's undertaking was a capitalized expedition. In other words, Columbus had financial investors in his scheme to find gold and other riches and they expected a return on their initial capital lent—in this case 114,000 maravedis (Spanish copper coin and a monetary unit) or 14–15 kg of gold. A potentially lucrative new trade route was viewed as a key avenue by which greater differential wealth could be obtained. In short, the exact trade route was secondary to the goal of finding gold or goods that could be turned into gold on the budding world market. There can be little doubt that Columbus had spiritual or religious motivations in searching for gold. Indeed, he did not only aim to enrich himself and his family but to find gold so that he and the Spanish regents could finance a new crusade against Muslims in the Near East (Bernstein 2000: 118; Vilar 1984: 64). According to Vilar, Columbus's diary "mentions gold at least 65 times" and "he even took the trouble to convince" the Taino natives of Hispaniola that "gold was the only thing he was interested in" (1984: 63–64; see also Williams 1984: 23–29). But while Columbus had investors in his enterprise, he also had his own terms spelled out with his investors:

> Columbus had to wait patiently for the funding of his first transatlantic voyage, and then he had to promise the future unknown profits to his benefactors. His contract with the Spanish crown was extraordinarily complex: he received not only political favors but also 10% of future revenues from transatlantic trade. He also negotiated an option to invest up to 1/8 share of any commercial enterprise organized to exploit his discoveries. Without this intertemporal contracting, he might never have set sail (Goetzmann 2016: 10).

What this passage suggests is not only that Columbus's "enterprise of the Indies" was a capitalized venture—money was invested to make more money at some point in the future—but that Columbus himself was rewarded on the basis of future expectations. As one historian of gold and money points out, though Columbus did not find a western sea route to India or China, he did discover gold in Hispaniola (or Santo Domingo) and other Caribbean islands (Vilar 1984: 65). In Hispaniola, Columbus found that what little gold the native Taino had was used for ornamentation rather than for commercial exchange and the accumulation of capital. According to Vilar, in the beginning it was easy for Columbus and his men to exchange what trinkets they had for the Taino's gold (1984: 64). On his return to Spain, the gold Columbus "discovered," while small in amount, was enough to convince the Spanish Crown and other adventurers and investors to embark upon the first capitalized "gold-rush in the history of the modern world" (Williams 1984: 23). Indeed, the gold and silver mined in the New World were used to finance further expeditions and conquests in the region while fueling war in continental Europe.

By all accounts, the Spanish gold rush in the Caribbean and what later came to be known as South and Central America was a most brutal affair. Almost twenty years after Columbus's discovery of the New World, a Dominican preacher is said to have given the following sermon in Santo Domingo:

> Tell me by what right of justice do you hold these Indians in such a cruel and horrible servitude? On what authority have you waged such detestable wars against these people who dealt quietly and peacefully on their own lands? Wars in which you have destroyed such an infinite number of them by homicides and slaughters never heard of before. Why do you keep them so oppressed and exhausted, without giving them enough to eat or curing them of the sicknesses they incur from the excessive labor you give them, and they die, or rather you kill them, in order to extract and acquire gold every day (Fray Antonio de Montesinos in de las Casas 1993: 66–67).

A former slave owner and a participant in the violent conflicts against the Taino peoples, who himself eventually became a Dominican friar, Bartolomé de las Casas, confirmed the observation made by the Dominican friar in 1511:

> Now the ultimate end and scope that incited the Spaniards to endeavor the Extirpation and Desolation of this People, was Gold only; that thereby growing opulent in a short time, they might arrive at once at such Degrees and Dignities, as were no wayes consistent with their Persons. Finally, in one word, their Ambition and Avarice, than which the heart of Man never entertained greater, and the vast Wealth of those Regions; the Humility and Patience of the Inhabitants (which made their approach to these Lands more facil and easie) did much

promote the business: Whom they so despicably contemned, that they treated them (I speak of things which I was an Eye Witness of, without the least fallacy) not as Beasts, which I cordially wished they would, but as the most abject dung and filth of the Earth; and so sollicitous they were of their Life and Soul, that the above-mentioned number of People died without understanding the true Faith or Sacraments (2007, published originally in Seville, Spain in 1552).

As the Spaniards searched for gold in and around the islands, the native population of the Caribbean was virtually liquidated, dying from European diseases, forced labor, or at the hands of superior weaponry. The forced labor of the native populations that remained flooded Spain with gold and silver. With a royal monopoly on all mines found in the New World until 1584, the Crown appropriated half of the gold and silver siphoned from the territories conquered by the Spanish (Williams 1984: 24). It is not known with precision how much gold and silver was stripped from the mines of the New World, but that it was substantial can hardly be in doubt (Vilar 1984: 147).

ACCUMULATION, COLONIZATION, AND DOUBLE-ENTRY BOOKKEEPING

Two years after Columbus set sail across the Atlantic, a book was published in his native Italy that would profoundly shape the modern world and our understanding of how qualitative things get quantified. Lucca Pacioli (1447–1517), an Italian mathematician and Franciscan friar, published the first systematic treatise of double-entry bookkeeping and to this day he is known to us as the "father of accounting" (Chatfield and Vangermeersch 1996; Gleeson-White 2013). It would take considerable time for double-entry bookkeeping to become the standard for maintaining and comparing merchant and financial accounts, but the practice of double-entry bookkeeping, a simple, yet at times sophisticated recording technique, would eventually be adopted the world over by emerging joint-stock companies, the modern corporation, and, ultimately, the state with its national accounts. The basic principle of double-entry bookkeeping is that there are always two entries for every transaction: a debit entry and a credit entry. Though seemingly neutral and innocuous, double-entry bookkeeping has profound consequences for the way we think about our world and how humans organize their personal and business affairs:

> The genius of double-entry bookkeeping is that it was a means to reduce errors in documentation. But it also has a subtle effect. Once you begin to use it, you start to think of the world in terms of accounts. A household is not only a family, it is a sequence of expenses and periodic income. Even a soul can be envisioned as an account, with sins and penance needing to be totaled before passing on.

The ledger becomes the quantitative essence of the organization—the numerical measure of its life (Goetzmann 2016: 247).

While Pacioli popularized and helped promote double-entry bookkeeping in the fifteenth century, the practice was already common among Venetian merchants and may stretch back to the Western Roman Empire. For example, Kats (1929) argued that double-entry bookkeeping can be traced back to the dynamic between master and slave in ancient Rome and the need for the master's claims to be matched with a borrower's obligations in the books kept by his slave. Though Kats's argument is not definitive, there is considerable evidence that some of the educated slaves of Roman patricians—patricians being unable to engage in commercial transactions directly—did keep accounts for their masters. Regardless of the precise origins of double-entry bookkeeping, we know that this method of keeping accounts proliferated and was a key organizing factor in the colonization of the world by European powers and their chartered companies. Human beings and the natural world would be subject to their ledgers of profit, loss, and, ultimately, the accumulation of money—the differential abstract power of command over society and natural resources.

As we have seen with Columbus and the conquistadors that followed in his wake to the new world, at the heart of colonial adventures was the search for wealth—particularly gold and silver, but also exotic goods that could be sold on the emerging world market to accumulate money. For instance, the Portuguese cared little for settling land in new found territories than they did in enforcing a lucrative monopoly on trade routes. As Ferro notes:

> It was not land that the Portuguese wanted, but control of the sea trade. Dazzled by the wealth of India they intended to secure its traffic for themselves. Refusing to grant to others the right to sail in that part of the ocean, they henceforth confiscated the cargo of anyone who did not have their authorization. Any ship caught sailing without their permission, the cartas, was treated as a pirate and seized. Consequently the Portuguese flooded Europe, via Lisbon, with the calico of Calicut, with pepper and other spices (1997: 25).

Once again, we find the dynamic of exclusion—more often than not enforced by violent means—at the heart of accumulating money for a minority of private social forces. One of the key signals of such exclusion was the construction of settled fortifications in trading ports, an advance made most famously by the Dutch on the less organized Portuguese but copied by other imperial firms on the hunt for exotic goods to monetize in Europe and elsewhere (Ferro 1997: 43). But settlers defending trading posts differed from the enterprise of settling new land and commercializing it. Colonial violence would reach genocidal proportions when late colonial powers not only wanted to secure trade routes and exploitable resources, but when they wanted to settle native land and subject it to the imperative of profit making. So while the search for metallic treasure or goods that could be converted into metallic coin was at the forefront of colonial minds, there were additional opportunities for profit in converting native land into commercial agriculture and private property.

In the "New World" ownership and private property in land was anathema to native tribes whose cosmology, however different from each other and from Europeans, could not comprehend the alienation of land by sale let alone its commodification (Friedenberg 1992: 29). This lack of commodity logic can be gleaned from the great Shawnee leader Tecumseh's statement that: "No tribe has a right to sell, even to each other, much less to strangers, who demand all, and will take no less. . . . Sell a country! Why not sell the air, the clouds and the great sea, as well as the earth?" (Friedenberg 1992: 308). Nor was there a discourse that made improving the land a condition of absolute private property, something that early settlers and their posterity used as a justification to confiscate or otherwise expropriate the land of first peoples (Roediger 1999: 21). This is not to suggest that there were no territorial con-flagrations among local populations before the arrival of European colonists. To be sure, territorial disputes and violent conflict were, if not commonplace, at least present from time to time, particularly when scarce resources became an issue of survival and social reproduction or when one tribe encroached upon another's hunting grounds. But whatever conflicts existed, they were extremely limited compared to the imperial taking of land by Europeans. While various forms of land tenure existed across Europe during the period of colonial adventures, there was an understanding—particularly among the English—that land could not only be privately owned but *should be* improved to yield an appropriate income stream commensurate with the technology of the time and the quality of the land (Weaver 2003; Wood 2002). The tell-tale sign of this development was the growing role of land surveyors scouring the countryside assessing the monetary value of tracts of land, typically owned by a small coterie of aristocrats that could trace their ancestry back to the vio-lence of the Norman Conquest of England in 1066. In fact, the monetization of the land and its products can be taken as the starting point of political econ-omy as a field of knowledge. The question of the time was not so much what the land could yield in produce but how much surplus produced on the land could be monetized to ensure that the monetary yield outpaced the monetary expenditure on wages and implements. But the problem of land in the colo-nies was the precise opposite of the problem of money in Europe. Whereas there was a constant complaint of the dearth of money to circulate goods and services, in Europe, the problem of land in the colonies was that there was way too much of it. At least theoretically, if not in practice, the problem was most enthusiastically broached by Edward Gibbons Wakefield, a British politician and strategic thinker on the issue of colonialism. Wakefield's "problem" turned on a very simple issue connected with the social reproduction of capitalist hierarchy: how is it possible to create a situation where there are enough laborers to work the land of a landowner when land is in abundance and settlers are likely to work a plot of land for themselves and their family's social reproduction? In short, Wakefield was asking how the many (laborers) could work for the few (owners). Wakefield's answer was that land had to be priced out of the reach of most settlers arriving to the New World (Di Muzio 2012; Piterberg and Veracini 2015). In this way, Wakefield reasoned that those entrants without sufficient money would be forced to work for wages on land owned by those who could afford to purchase tracts of workable land. An assigned price, then, was a mechanism of power and exclusion that would compel new settlers to work for others in order to socially reproduce. Development and improvement for minority profit required that the majority be excluded from producing for themselves and their families—at least until they earned enough money working for property owners to purchase their own plot of land or earned rights as improving squatters (Weaver 2003: 5). But this new property regime also meant the active destruction of previous forms of native social reproduction that were not premised on alienable private property, the commercialization of land, and the accumulation of money as an end goal. As Wolfe (2006) has spelled out, if not the logic of genocide, then the logic of elimination was at work in settler colonial societies. For Wolfe the logic of elimination is conceptually broader than genocide since while it requires the elimination of alternative modes of indigenous life, it does not necessarily have to involve the wholesale murder of a people. For example, Wolfe argues that assimilation may be a better strategy for settler colonists (2006: 401–2). But while assimilation may be part of the logic of elimination, it is highly questionable how broadly it was applied in the colonies. An example from revolutionary America highlights the potential limitations of Wolfe's argument.

In order to prevent future wars with Indians in what was to become the continental United States, the British Empire forbade further settlement west of the Appalachians (Royal Proclamation 1763). The British had just fought a costly war with the French and various Indian nations and did not want to provoke further costly wars by antagonizing the native population west of the Appalachians. British merchants also had an interest in maintaining native hunting grounds since they traded with various tribes and did not want to lose the trade to colonial settlers. Though the reasons for the American Revolution are multiple (the Declaration of Independence is essentially a list of grievances against royal authority), there is little doubt that the proclamation line forbidding further settlement west gained the ire of investors whose companies desired to capitalize the sale of western land. Not surprisingly, one of the first acts of the revolutionary government was to abolish the royal decree.

By the time of the revolutionary period, American Indians had a strong interest in supporting the proclamation line because it provided them with a refuge from further colonial advances. Fearing a loss of their independence if the proclamation should be lifted, and premised on more than a century of experience confronting colonial settlers and their violent militias, many Indian nations sided with the British during the war.[1]

However, once the thirteen colonies declared victory in the War of Independence, one of the major governmental challenges became how to dispossess Indians of their land (Horsman 1961: 35). This problem was connected to the massive debt the colonies had accumulated during their war against Britain. Rather than tax themselves at a sufficient level to pay for the war, one of the ways the ruling elite financed the war was by issuing securities to wealthy investors. Once the Treaty of Paris had been signed, the Confederation reasoned that one of the only ways to repay the confederation's creditors and thereby increase the institution's creditworthiness was by the sale of Indian land (Horsman 1961: 36). Without a strong national army, however, expropriating Indian land would be a near impossibility.

Since many Indian nations fought on the side of Britain during the war, colonists argued that by virtue of conquest, the Indians had forfeited their land in defeat. However, while colonists held fast to this principle of victory, they also understood that the Indians would not give up the land they occupied without protracted struggle (Jennings in Young 1976: 319–48). Doing so would have meant abandoning their mode of social reproduction and governance. The strategy favored by early American Indian policy, however, was precisely that Indians should abandon their way of life by adopting the sinews of commercial civilization. For instance, Secretary of War Henry Knox contended that "the United States are highly desirous of imparting to all the Indian tribes the blessings of civilization, as the *only means* of perpetuating them on the earth" (Horsman 1961: 45, emphasis added). In other words, first peoples had a choice between reconstituting their communities or dispersal and annihilation. As Horsman argued, the failure of Indians to adopt a colonial or gentlemanly way of life was derided by colonial Americans and used as an excuse to exterminate them:

> In general the Indians by the latter years of the seventeenth century were despised because they had tried to remain Indian and had shown little desire to become gentlemen. The Indians could therefore be thrown off the land, mistreated, or slaughtered, because in rejecting the opportunities offered to them

they had shown that they were sunk deep in irredeemable savagery (Horsman 1981: 103–4).

After the revolution, native Indians became the target of a protracted war that would systematically dispossess them of their direct access to the means of survival and therefore the reproduction of their way of life (Gilje 1996: 177). Against the extermination of their livelihood, Indian nations fought many battles to secure their own liberty and independence against colonial encroachment. However, with the desire for land and profit, a belief in manifest destiny, and with firm notions of racial superiority that would later be buttressed by new "sciences" such as phrenology, white colonists continued their conquest of Indian territory. What Jefferson would later call an "empire of liberty" would be built on the foundations of a war to exterminate a people and a mode of social reproduction premised upon livelihood and community rather than the accumulation of money as a form of social power. The point here is not to stress that a better way of living was increasingly encroached upon and destroyed by American armies, settlers, and powerful land companies. Rather, it is enough to point out that the liberty of Native American communities threatened the security of white colonial civilization and the differential accumulation to be had by commodifying and commercializing land.

The most comprehensive study on colonial land settlement in the New World has been carried out by Weaver (2003), who distinguishes British colonial practice from those of Portugal, Spain, Germany, Russia, and the Netherlands. Weaver argues that the key distinction was an English (later British) obsession with land as a private asset to be improved for profit and to be used for collateral for credit (2003: 43). It was this belief that propelled a series of atrocities as the doctrine of improvement for profit collided with the social structures of first peoples. According to Weaver:

> In history the clash between the doctrine of improvement and the status quo, between newcomers and first peoples, was profound. This means not that indigenous peoples were inactive and peaceful prior to contact with Europeans but that the newcomers—particularly the English—carried an ideology that insisted on making the land bountiful, even if that required the confiscation of land, which is what the English government practiced on several occasions in Ireland before and after the 1641 uprising. The idea of material improvement motivated and informed the legal and political processes that colonizers used to evaluate the colonized. In the colonies, the dispossession of a number of first peoples . . . advanced under the most revered regimental pennant of colonizers, "Improvement" (2003: 82).

But while the hierarchy of white settlement was primarily a matter of elite white privilege and price used as a weapon to exclude many poor whites and new immigrants from obtaining land without servitude or mortgaging their labor to a property company, a more nefarious form of servitude would be indispensable to elite capitalist development: the trade in human flesh and muscle power.

THE BIOPOLITICAL VIOLENCE OF THE TRANSATLANTIC SLAVE TRADE

As we have previously encountered, slavery has deep roots in the human past—its ubiquity linked up with the rise of hierarchical civilizations based on an extensive division of labor, war, and the desire of the powerful to increase their wealth or display their power in monumental architecture or in sacrifices to supernatural deities. However, while slavery as a form of labor servitude can be traced to the first civilizations, the forms and reasons for enslaving people have differed over time (Davis 2006: 32, 37; Dresche and Engerman 1998; Heuman and Burnard; Nikiforuk 2012). There is, according to Davis, however, one commonality throughout the ages:

> It is also important to remember that in most societies, even the most privileged slave—the wealthy farm agent in Babylon, the Greek poet or teacher in Rome, the black driver, musician, blacksmith, or boat captain in Mississippi—could be quickly sold, or stripped and whipped, or raped, or sometimes even killed at the whim of an owner. All slave systems shared this radical uncertainty and unpredictability . . . Whatever privileges she or he may have gained could be taken away in a flash—leaving the slave as naked as an animal at an auction. This absence of a past and a future, of a place in history and society from which to grow in small increments, made each slave totally vulnerable. This may be the very essence of dehumanization (2006: 37).

Davis is likely correct that the unity among different historical forms of slavery may be the "uncertainty" and "unpredictability" that comes with being subject to the will of another human. But there were historical differences in the constitution of human slavery as well. If Greece was the first political community to be dependent on slaves for the social reproduction of its hierarchical order (unlike other societies that merely possessed slaves), it would only be a forerunner to the territories of domination, subordination, and capital accumulation that would be created with the discovery of the New World and the transatlantic slave trade (Davis 2006: 41). At most, ancient Greece may have had 80,000 slaves. Compare this with the millions of Africans that were captured, shackled, imprisoned, and then transported to the New World through the Middle Passage. Estimates vary on the precise amount of human cargo transported across the Atlantic to the Americas and

Caribbean, but a reasonable estimate is that "the total number of people leaving Africa in the Atlantic slave trade between 1501 and 1866 was 12,521,336. Of this number, 10,702,656 are known to have disembarked from the ships they were carried on" (Burnard in Heuman and Burnard 2011: 118). The remainder died, committed suicide, or were killed along the Middle Passage. Originally, Portuguese merchants were interested in African gold and ivory in modern-day Ghana, but as the demand for plantation labor to produce cash crops in the New World intensified, they became interested in purchasing slaves from African rulers and middlemen. It is true that slavery existed in Africa before the Europeans arrived, but the scale and scope of enslavement was nothing like what would transpire during the centuries of the transatlantic slave trade. The commercial value of the African slave trade soon attracted additional European interlopers—particularly when prices for slaves escalated by 1,013 percent from 1680 to 1830 (Davis 2006: 89). As is well known in the literature, a triangular trade developed between Europe, West Africa, and the New World, with Western Europeans and African slavers fighting among themselves to corner the majority of the trade.

What appears to be less well known—or at minimum, underplayed in the history of capitalism and slavery—is the Asian connection and its link to the capitalization of European firms involved in the slave trade. The majority of slaves on the African West coast were purchased for some combination of cowrie shells that originated (until other sources of supply were found) in the Maldives and other goods. The Dutch East India Company was the major supplier of the West African currency, acquiring the shells from Asia. Back in Europe, the Company would proceed to sell the cowries to European merchants, who would then use the shells as currency to purchase African slaves (Hogendorn and Johnson 1986). What this suggests is that the Dutch East India Company's capitalization, in part, depended on acquiring the currency necessary to purchase slaves. To be sure, Europeans also traded an entire coterie of goods with West Africa to obtain slaves and other cherished goods like gold and ivory. According to Alpern, who scoured "thousands of surviving bills of lading, cargo manifests, port records, logbooks, invoices, quittances, trading-post inventories, account books, shipping recommendations, and orders from African traders," hundreds of goods were coveted by African rulers and traders (1995: 5). These included cloth from India and Europe, clothing, semi-processed metal, metal containers and tools, firearms in the tens of thousands, jewelry, alcohol, tobacco, glassware, ceramics and paper, seasonings, drugs, and exotic food, just to name some major categories of goods exported to West Africa in return for slaves. A considerable portion of these products came not just from Europe and Asia but from the very plantations in the New World where newly captured Africans would be sent to work in the biopolitical apparatus of slavery and differential accumulation.

As suggested by the Dutch East India Company and its trade in cowrie shells with the Maldives, Europe, and Africa, we need to take a closer look at how the transatlantic slave trade was capitalized and financed and eventually linked up with the power of the British state and Bank of England once the asiento was wrested from the Spanish kingdom after the War of the Spanish Succession (1702–1715). We have to recall that the trade in African human beings lasted centuries rather than decades and that this trade was financed and capitalized for profit in at least two ways. First, the companies and their ships that transported the slaves to the New World were investment opportunities for rich capitalists looking for a return on their money. What this means is that capitalization and profit depended upon a ready supply of Africans who had to be forcefully removed from their families and communities, degraded, and made to work for European/white elites in the New World (Blackburn 2010; Zook 1919). The Portuguese, Spanish, and Dutch were the most prominent slave traders until English slavers overtook them all by capturing the right to provide Spanish America with slaves in 1713 (Wood in Heuman and Burnard 2011: 97). Originally, as with other charters granted to merchants seeking a private fortune from overseas trade, the Royal Africa Company (1672) was given a monopoly on the trade with West Africa. But in 1713, the asiento was given to the South Sea Company in the hope that a profitable trade in slaves with Spanish colonies would take place. The British government desired to reduce and consolidate its mounting "national" debt due to continued warfare on the continent. Toward this end, the South Sea Company was chartered to engraft a portion of the government's debt into the new company. Holders of government bonds were given the opportunity to swap their government securities for tradeable shares in the South Sea Company (Carswell 1960). In this sense, both holders of the "national" debt and shareholders in the South Sea Company capitalized the company's ability to earn a profit stream from buying and selling West Africans who would be enslaved in Spanish America and the Caribbean. As Wennerlind has recounted, "debate surrounding the South Sea Company therefore came to focus on the extent to which the investing public believed that the company's slave trade would be profitable enough to generate an adequate rate of return" (2011: 198).

But the capture, purchase, transport, and sale of African humans was only one part of the slavery-capitalization-profit equation. Money could also be made by lending to New World planters or by absentee investing in a plantation venture. For example, many southern planters in colonial America were indebted to British creditors who were capitalizing the income stream derived from slave productivity on plantations that had been stripped from native Americans in one form or another (Banner 2005; Di

Muzio and Robbins 2016: 66–68). In 1766, a British Parliamentary commit-tee discovered that nine-tenths of the £4.5 million in debt owed to British creditors and merchants was incurred by Southern planters (Friedenberg 1992: 149; Holton 1999: 35–36; Sosin 1964: 175 nt. 4). This relationship of debt and absentee capitalization continued well after the creation of the United States. One indication of this trend can be found in Draper's (2010) research on the compensation received by British absentee slave-owners for the loss of their "property" when the Slavery Abolition Act of 1833 passed Parliament. In fact, Draper argues that without the promise of £20 million set aside to compensate British slave-owners, it was unlikely that the Slav-ery Abolition Act would have passed Parliament. This is hardly a surprise when Draper's research demonstrates that between 1820 and 1835, one hundred Members of Parliament were found in the official compensation records. Two-thirds of Members of Parliament were found to be slave-owners, while the remaining one-third proved to be trustees or executors of estates of slave-owners (Draper 2007: 90). Since Britain had an extremely regressive tax system and the compensation that slave-owners received was financed by British government debt, the working classes of Britain effec-tively financed the vast majority of the compensation (Ferguson 2006: 194; Michie 2001: 72).

But it was not just slave productivity on the land that could be capital-ized by creditors extending loans to planters, slaves themselves were often pledged as collateral for mortgages, contributing to the system of credit in the Antebellum south. For whatever reason—a fall in commodity prices or a bad harvest, for instance—if slave-owning planters could not finance their mortgages, creditors could seize the slaves pledged as collateral by their debtors. Seized slaves would then be used to work off the debt, or they could be sold on the regional slave market for ready cash. In sum, slaves were often the underlying "asset" that secured the mortgages of their masters (Kilbourne 1995).

What can we learn from the human tragedy of the transatlantic slave trade? From the point of view of capital as power that does not make the mistake of conflating the industrial revolution with capitalism, slavery didn't "contribute" or "lead" to capitalism, it was capitalism. The brutality and inhumanity of the transatlantic slave trade was a fully capitalized enterprise and, as Wennerlind pointed out in the quote earlier, investors in slave com-panies expected a particular rate of return. In other words, the violence of the transatlantic slave trade was carried on for the profit of the few. As Black-burn argued in his unrivaled study of New World slavery "the link between modernity and slavery gives us good reason to be attentive to the dark side of progress" (2010: 5).

THE DISCOURSE OF "SCIENTIFIC" RACISM

As the transatlantic slave trade was gradually abolished in the nineteenth century, a nefarious discourse on the physical variation of human beings started to emerge to explain and justify the oppression and subjugation of slaves, the poor and colonial subjects. But this new "scientific" discourse, like previous forms of racial discrimination, was also inseparable from a belief in progress, improvement, and development. Its widespread acceptance among imperial elites, capitalists, and politicians in Europe and the colonies paved the way for the elimination of millions, just as the logic of accumulation and racism born of colonialism and the transatlantic slave trade encouraged the atrocities against native and enslaved populations. This new discourse of "scientific" racism would build on the racism congenital of colonialism and the transatlantic slave trade, but it would take on new dimensions inspired by Darwin and Wallace's scientific observations about the natural world. Separately, what both men put forward was the notion that species evolved through a process of natural selection within a competitive environment for limited resources. Eventually, Darwin would come to call this the "struggle for existence" and the full title to his monumental work, often shortened to the *Origin of Species* bears this out: *Origin of Species by Means of Natural Selection, or the Preservation of Favoured Races in the Struggle for Life.* But while Darwin and Wallace's provocative works contributed to (and one could argue gave credence to) the emerging discourse of "scientific" racism in the nineteenth century, the tenets of which we will identify momentarily, the roots of their thought stretches back much further to the social problems and transformations in the English countryside. While it is well recognized in the literature that Darwin and Wallace were heavily influenced by Thomas Malthus's *Essay on the Principle of Population* (1798), we should begin, as Polanyi suggests, with the earlier figure of Joseph Townsend (1739–1816) (Polanyi 1957: 112–3; Young 1969).

Townsend was a vicar from the county of Wiltshire in England and is most famous for writing *A Dissertation on the Poor Laws* in 1786. In his work that prefigured Malthus's principal contribution to political economy, Townsend's overall aim was to argue that the Elizabethan poor laws served only to "increase the number of the poor, and greatly to extend the bounds of human misery."[2] Townsend argued that the poor began to appear with the dissolution of the monasteries ordained by Henry the VIII (1536–1541) and that their numbers were increasing due to parish relief. As long as the poor had access to food, Townsend reasoned, they would not only avoid waged work but would multiply. To demonstrate this, Townsend contrived a parable of an island in the "South Seas" where a certain John Fernando imported a male and female goat. Finding ample pasture, the goats bred and multiplied. Over time, English pirates raiding Spanish galleons for treasure came to use the island as a source of food. Townsend relays what happened when the Spanish discovered this fact:

> When the Spaniards found that the English privateers resorted to this island for provisions, they resolved on the total extirpation of the goats, and for this purpose they put on shore a greyhound dog and bitch. These in their turn increased and multiplied, in proportion to the quantity of food they met with; but in consequence, as the Spaniards had foreseen, the breed of goats diminished. Had they been totally destroyed, the dogs likewise must have perished. But as many of the goats retired to the craggy rocks, where the dogs could never follow them, descending only for short intervals to feed with fear and circumspection in the rallies, few of these, besides the careless and the rash, became a prey; and none but the most watchful, strong, and active of the dogs could get a sufficiency of food. Thus a new kind of balance was established. *The weakest of both species were among the first to pay the debt of nature; the most active and vigorous preserved their lives.* It is the quantity of food which regulates the numbers of the human species (emphasis added).[3]

If we pay close attention, what this passage suggests, and what Townsend is at pains to emphasize throughout his dissertation, are two major lessons. First, population numbers are regulated by the amount of food available. A lack of food must ultimately result in a drop in population just as additional food resources would allow for an increase in population. But while this might seem like a historical truism or immutable law of nature, Townsend does little to discuss the origins of inequality and depravation in his native country. His constant trope is to make a steadfast division between two types of people: those who are diligent and acquire property and those who are idle, lazy, and prodigal. In Townsend's formulation, there are no power processes or relations that contribute to inequality and the pauperism. For instance, there is no discussion of the waves of expropriations of land in the English countryside that ejected direct subsistence producers from their historical tenures. Thus one of the primary causes of increasing pauperism was at best overlooked by Townsend and, at worst, blatantly ignored. As Polanyi argued:

> Enclosures have appropriately been called a revolution of the rich against the poor. The lords and nobles were upsetting the social order, breaking down ancient law and custom, sometimes by means of violence, often by pressure and intimidation. They were literally robbing the poor of their share in the common, tearing down the houses which, by the hitherto unbreakable force of custom, the poor had long regarded as theirs and their heirs. The fabric of society was being disrupted (1957: 35).

The waves of enclosures in England, Scotland, and Wales dispossessed peasant farmers and their families of any land to cultivate for subsistence. Consolidated landownership for the powerful and wealthy was largely used for sheep pasturage, reducing the amount of arable land (Clay 1984: 67; Palgrave 1894: 406–7; Thomas 1993: 67; Wood 2002: 108). The three social causes that encouraged the process of enclosure was the Black Death that served to depopulate rural districts, thereby reducing the labor force available for arable farming. Second, even where labor could be found, Palgrave (1894: 407) notes that there was often a dearth of money to pay for labor services. And third, the wool provided by sheep walks was a new source of profitability and wealth for the landed class. Thus, a massive transformation in social property relations in the English countryside was afoot by at least the fourteenth century. For Polanyi (1957), the centuries long mix of violent and juridical expropriations that consolidated landownership in the hands of a minority was the true source of a "surplus" population of paupers (see also Marx 1887: Section 8). But this fact did not stop men like Townsend from arguing that the poor of England resulted from their being of a race of idlers. Townsend's staunch belief in the division between the diligent and industrious and the idle and prodigal comes home more forcefully when he considers what a more just and fair division of property in Great Britain might lead to:

> If a new and equal division of property were made in England, we cannot doubt that the same inequality which we now observe would soon take place again: the improvident, the lazy, and the vicious, would dissipate their substance; the prudent, the active, and the virtuous, would again increase their wealth.[4]

In other words, there is a historical law at work between two very different races of people, with Townsend clearly favoring the race of wealthy and prudent men. No tinkering with unequal property ownership, the maldistribution of resources, the concentration of economic and political power, or allowing the poor access to land so they could cultivate their subsistence will ever overcome this iron law of nature for Townsend.

The second thing to note in the parable of the dog and goats is Townsend's comparison of human beings with the animal world. For Polanyi, this was a radical turn in political economy away from Adam Smith's humanism:

> Hobbes had argued the need for a despot because men were like beasts; Townsend insisted that they were actually beasts and that, precisely for that reason, only a minimum of government was required. From this point of view, a free society could be regarded as consisting of two races: property owners and laborers. The number of the latter was limited by the amount of food; and as long as property was safe, hunger would drive them to work . . . hunger was a better disciplinarian than the magistrate (1957: 114).

Polanyi believed that this turn to "naturalism" (or comparing humans to animals) was the result of Townsend and other emerging political economists' inability to convincingly explain the misery and suffering of the lower classes (1957: 123). If men were indeed beasts for Townsend, the only way to spur them to work for others was to ensure that there was no danger of relief from hunger. The unstated claim here is that should the poor not be able to find paid work, they should starve and die out because they, like the goats unable to flee the dogs on the South Sea island, were of a weaker stock than their more cunning and therefore better fed counterparts. But Townsend's dubious and cruel understanding of social order—a division of the strong and the weak where the weak must perish—was not the first formulation of what Wolfe (2016) has called "the logic of elimination." Though Townsend is more specific that the poor should simply starve rather than be relieved—a logic of elimination by starvation—in the European settler colonies of the New World, this logic involved a number of strategies including protracted violence in the pursuit of developing the land for commercial profit. But if this kind of logic was already in operation in the colonies, it was about to take on a new "scientific" and biological twist. Polanyi captured the new discourse of political economy rooted in Townsend's thought: "The biological nature of man appeared as the given foundation of a society that was not of a political order" (1957: 115). Malthus's essay on population, intellectually indebted to Townsend, inspired both Darwin and Wallace to see in society what they discovered in the natural world: a struggle for survival.

Thomas Robert Malthus (1766–1834) was an English cleric and political economist. His major contribution, still debated today, was *An Essay on the Principle of Population* (1798). Malthus argued that an increase in food production inevitably meant an increase in population. However, Malthus argued that population growth would eventually outstrip the ability to produce and procure food, leading to greater poverty and misery, particularly, if not exclusively, among the lower classes without access to money or land. Similar to Townsend's formulation, the tendency for the population to outstrip the food supply was an immutable law of history, unchangeable by political recalibration of the existing distribution of wealth. In the second edition to his essay, Malthus colorfully illustrated Townsend's argument:

A man who is born into a world already possessed, if he cannot get subsistence from his parents on whom he has a just demand, and if the society do not want his labor, has *no claim of right to the smallest portion of food*, and, in fact, has no business to be where he is. At nature's mighty feast there is no vacant cover for him. She tells him to be gone, and will quickly execute her own orders, if he does not work upon the compassion of some of her guests. If these guests get up and make room for him, other intruders immediately appear demanding the same favor. The report of a provision for all that come, fills the hall with numerous claimants. The order and harmony of the feast is disturbed, the plenty that before reigned is changed into scarcity; and the happiness of the guests is destroyed by the spectacle of misery and dependence in every part of the hall, and by the clamorous importunity of those, who are justly enraged at not finding the provision which they had been taught to expect. The guests learn too late their error, in counter-acting those strict orders to all intruders, issued by the great mistress of the feast, who, wishing that all guests should have plenty, and knowing she could not provide for unlimited numbers, humanely refused to admit fresh comers when her table was already full (Malthus 1992: 249, emphasis added).[5]

What this passage suggests is that any compassion toward those struggling to find sustenance can only result in ruin for everyone. To avoid the potential for a catastrophe, the hungry should be subject to nature's cruelty and presumably starve to death (see also Di Muzio 2015a: 108–10). In this formulation, human compassion leads to chaos while leaving the weak, poor, and hungry to die is merely following nature's intention. Malthus's vision of a struggle for survival going on within the social order would profoundly influence Darwin and Wallace and elevate a current of thought already percolating within nineteenth-century Europe to a new level: that some were naturally superior contributors to social development while others were inferior social burdens and therefore unworthy of charity at best, and worthy of elimination at worse.

This new discourse later became known as Social Darwinism and according to Hawkins (1997) it entailed five propositions, three of which, Claeys (2000: 234) argues, were already in circulation before the *Origin of Species* (1959) was published. The first assumption was that all of organic nature—humans included—were governed by biological laws. Second, the struggle for existence resulted from population growth and limited resources. Third, some with special physical or mental abilities have an advantage in the struggle for reproduction and can transmit these advantages to future generations through breeding. Fourth, this process of selection through breeding culminates, over time, with the development of new species and the elimination of weaker species who have failed to appropriately adapt to their environment. The fifth proposition of Social Darwinism holds that the biological laws governing nature "extends to not just the physical properties of humans but also to their social existence and to those psychological attributes that play a fundamental role in social life, e.g. reason, religion and morality" (Hawkins 1997: 31). To be sure, notions of superiority and inferiority between political communities had been noticed and discussed before, even before the discovery of the New World (Borstelmann 2001: 7; Claeys 2000: 238; Foucault 2003). But whereas what we might call the "old" racism explained the differences in physical appearance and the different cultural practices of diverse human groups as largely rooted in environmental conditions, the new, "scientific" racism was premised on the Malthusian/Darwinian notion of a struggle for existence and the claim that some races were more favored for existence than others. As Claeys suggests, Darwin's work did not cause a complete revolution in social thought, but his metaphor of the struggle for existence and notions of fitness tied to biology and reproduction remapped "a preexisting structure of ideas" that largely derived from Townsend and Malthus and their interlocutors in industrializing Britain (2000: 228; see also Gale 1972).

However, in conceptualizing humanity from the biological side, the naturalists encountered a problem. Fitness was originally defined as fertility or fecundity—the ability to pass on inherited traits. In this way, success in the struggle for existence was evidenced by the number of offspring—the more offspring, the more fit. But since the poor and working classes tended to have more children than the rich and well born, it was thought that if biological reproduction be the main criteria for identifying "fitness," then the "degraded classes would most likely dictate the future of man" (Claeys 2000: 238). Out of this recognition, Darwin and his many interlocutors changed fitness to intelligence rather than fecundity and identified "intelligence" with the "white" races (Claeys 2000: 240). Thus, out of a country with radically unequal property relations and undergoing massive social change due to capitalist industrialization emerged a new "scientific" discourse to not only explain and justify the "hierarchy" of races internationally but also why some groups of people had perished or were in the process of being eliminated. The irony of Darwin's application of what he witnessed in the natural world onto the social order was not lost on his contemporary, Karl Marx:

> Darwin, whom I have looked up again, amuses me when he says he is applying the "Malthusian" theory also to plants and animals, as if with Mr. Malthus the whole point were not that he does not apply the theory to plants and animals but only to human beings—and with geometrical progression—as opposed to plants and animals. It is remarkable how Darwin recognizes among beasts and plants his English society with its division of labour, competition, opening up of new markets, "inventions", and the Malthusian "struggle for existence". It is Hobbes's *bellum omnium contra omnes*, and one is reminded of Hegel's Phenomenology, where civil society is described as a "spiritual animal kingdom" while in Darwin the animal kingdom figures as civil society (cited in Gerratana 1973: 73–74).

But while Marx recognized that Darwin was likely projecting his own competitive, industrializing, capitalist Victorian society onto the natural world and then reflecting this vision of the natural order back on to society, the claim that there was indeed a struggle for survival among civil society and the international seemed true enough to him. At home, the problem of pauperism had largely dwarfed into the problem of an unruly and better organized wage-laboring class clamoring for social and economic change. On the international level, the entire world appeared to be a battlefield for European access to resources and the accumulation of money. The problem, for Marx, was not struggle per se but the locus of this struggle and what could be done to overcome it. In Marx's view, social evolution and development did not result from a biopolitical struggle for existence among distinct races but a struggle between classes that capitalism had simplified by creating a minority owning class and a majority working class dependent upon wages for social reproduction and survival. Before we discuss how Marx's interpretation of human development was counteracted by the discourse of race struggle as it became connected to nationalism and imperialism, we need to consider how threatening Marx's interpretation of history was for the powerful owners of capital and a liberal political economy that celebrated private property and improvement for profit. As we will see, Marx's entire problematic of the class struggle and his support for international communism rested on an analysis of capitalist private property and the origin of surplus money in the exploitation of the working class.

CLASS STRUGGLE AND THE VEILED CIVIL WAR OF KARL MARX

In 1843–1844, after having begun his intellectual journey of critique by engaging Hegelian idealism, Marx encountered the ideas of liberal political economists. In his first manuscripts to engage liberal political economy, Marx set up his intellectual problematic by subjecting the liberal concept of private property to historical scrutiny:

> Political economy proceeds from the fact of private property, but it does not explain it to us. It expresses in general, abstract formulae the material process through which private property actually passes, and these formulae it then takes for laws. It does not comprehend these laws, it does not demonstrate how they arise from the very nature of private property. . . . It assumes as fact, in historical form, what has to be explained (Marx cited in Morgan 1992: 1159–60).

What had to be explained, for Marx, was the origin of capitalist private property since:

> Political economy confuses on principle, two different kinds of private property, one of which rests on the labour of the producer himself, and the other on the exploitation of the labour of others. It forgets that the latter is not only the

direct antithesis of the former, but grows on the former's tomb and nowhere else (Marx 1990: 931).

But liberal political economists were not just guilty of conflating two very different kinds of property. In so doing Marx chided them for normalizing the existing property regime by refusing to consider how capitalist private property was not a timeless and natural social relation but a historical product:

> The selfish misconception that induces you to transform into eternal laws of nature and of reason, the social forms springing from your present mode of production and form of property—historical relations that rise and disappear in the progress of production—this misconception you share with every ruling class that has preceded you. What you see clearly in the case of ancient property, what you admit in the case of feudal property, you are of course forbidden to admit in the case of your own bourgeois form of property (Marx and Engels cited in Morgan 1992: 1204).

In order not to admit the contingency of their own form of property, Marx argued that liberal political economists relied on an idyllic narrative that explained how the unequal distribution of property ownership was the historical product of a minority of diligent, intelligent, and frugal individuals who accumulated wealth while their counterparts without property originated from prodigal and idle ancestors who failed to accumulate wealth. Contrary to this reading of history that can at least be traced to Townsend we have already discussed and Adam Smith's *Wealth of Nations*, Marx reminded his audience that "in actual history, it is a notorious fact that conquest, enslavement, robbery, murder, in short, force," played the greatest part in producing the unequal division of property (1990: 874). For Marx, Adam Smith's account of the division between property owners and wage workers was nothing other than the ensemble of practices that divorced "the worker from the ownership of the conditions of his labor; it is a process which operates two transformations, whereby the social means of subsistence and production are turned into capital, and the immediate producers are turned into wage-laborers" (1990: 874).

Working with this understanding of what Marx called "primitive accumulation," in section eight of *Capital Volume 1*, Marx offered a counter-narrative of the liberal political economy's version of "original" or primitive accumulation as a way of reminding the ruling class of property owners that their political rule and property ownership did not originate from their personal frugality, intelligence, or industry, but from a real war of ruthless terrorism and fraud that expropriated the majority of independent producers from direct access to the means of work and subsistence:

> The spoliation of the Church's property, the fraudulent alienation of the state domains, the theft of common lands, the usurpation of feudal and clan property

and its transformation into modern private property under circumstances of ruthless terrorism, all these things were just so many idyllic methods of primitive accumulation. They conquered the field for capitalist agriculture, incorporated the soil into capital, and created for the urban industries the necessary supplies of free and rightless proletarians (1990: 895).

In Marx's account of primitive accumulation as war, part of this "ruthless terrorism" included "bloody legislation" that effectively criminalized the poor and sanctioned torture and, at times, execution for members of the newly created class of "free and rightless proletarians" who would not, or could not, find employment. In addition to the laws that sanctioned corporeal punishment, Marx also considered how capitalists employed the power of the state to violate the liberal law of supply and demand by forcibly suppressing wages to guarantee private capitalists their profits. However, the English government did more than simply suppress wages to secure capital.

Rather than use the celebratory rhetoric of liberal political economists who admired the Glorious Revolution (1688) for making the Crown subservient to Parliament, Marx noted how Parliamentarians used the power of the state to expropriate public property by redistributing it to themselves and their peers:

The "glorious Revolution" brought into power, along with William of Orange, the landed and capitalist profit-grubbers. They inaugurated the new era by practicing on a colossal scale the thefts of state lands which had hitherto been managed more modestly. These estates were given away, sold at ridiculous prices, or even annexed to private estates by direct seizure. All this happened without the slightest observance of legal etiquette. The Crown lands thus fraudulently appropriated, together with the stolen Church estates . . . form the basis of the present princely domains of the English oligarchy (1990: 884).

Here, Marx's historico-political discourse on the Glorious Revolution differs significantly from the liberal narrative that the revolution secured an ancient constitution of liberty from its monarchical usurpation. It also significantly differs from the liberal historiography that capitalist private property emerged through "the private frugality and good conduct of individuals" where the state does not facilitate, but impinges upon, the wealth-generating activities of industrious individuals (Smith [1776] 2005: 283). For Marx, state power was an indispensable mechanism of primitive accumulation—a power that early capitalists could not do without.

While other states were implicated in processes of expropriation and dispossession on an international scale, Marx argued that four major institutions connected to state power in England were "systematically combined" and integral as domestic and foreign expropriating agents:

> The different moments of primitive accumulation can be assigned in particular to Spain, Portugal, Holland, France and England, in more or less chronological order. These different moments are systematically combined together at the end of the 17th century in England; the combination embraces the colonies, the national debt, the modern tax system, and the system of protection. These methods depend in part on brute force, for instance the colonial system. But they all employ the power of the state, the concentrated and organized force of society, to hasten, as in a hothouse, the process of transformation of the feudal mode of production into the capitalist mode, and to shorten the transition. Force is the midwife of every old society which is pregnant with a new one. It is itself an economic power (1990: 916).

For its part, the colonial system, primarily organized and operated by joint-stock monopolies, served to concentrate surplus wealth in the hands of its owners, while at the same time dispossessing indigenous communities of their resources and wealth. The slave trade and the violent destruction of indigenous political communities were testament to these expropriations. Profit earned from these expropriations could then be reinvested in domestic manufacture, government securities, or other trades. According to Marx, the national debt, funded by a system of taxation, also served to concentrate wealth in the hands of government bondholders while at the same time leading to the extension of credit instruments and the expropriation of direct producers through over-taxation. The national debt and heavy taxation also had the added benefit of making workers "submissive, frugal, industrious, and overburdened with labour" (Marx 1990: 916).

The system of high tariff protection also served to facilitate the accumulation of money for the few. High tariffs protected domestic manufacturers from foreign competition while simultaneously supplying the state with revenue to repay security owners and finance colonial trade and war. This system also served to destroy domestic industry in the colonies through unequal competition. While England sheltered its manufacturers through high import tariffs, in the colonies it used the threat of violence to maintain an importation regime free of tariffs. As a consequence, many domestic independent manufacturers could not compete with the cheap goods thrown into circulation by the imperial power and thus lost their independent livelihoods. So while for liberal political economists such as Adam Smith, the state is more likely to encumber the wealth of nations than to promote it, in Marx's historico-political discourse, state power was a central mechanism by which the wealth of private individuals was formed. Thus, in Marx's historico-political discourse of primitive accumulation as war, he emphasized how violence and state power were indispensable moments in the making of a majority of non-owners compelled to work for wages in order to survive.

But Marx's project was not simply to recall the point of departure for this new relationship of domination. What Marx wanted to show was that this series of battles and dislocations was not as important as how it recoded itself in the everyday social relations of capitalism (Perelman 2000: 29–32). One of Marx's central messages, then, was that the war between classes does not come to an end once violence recedes into the background of everyday social relations—it is made permanent because over generations, it is encoded as the natural order of things:

> The advance of capitalist production develops a working-class, which by edu-cation, tradition, habit, looks upon the conditions of that mode of production as self-evident laws of Nature. The organization of the capitalist process of pro-duction, once fully developed, breaks down all resistance. The constant gen-eration of a relative surplus-population keeps the law of supply and demand of labour, and therefore keeps wages, in a rut that corresponds with the wants of capital. The dull compulsion of economic relations completes the subjection of the labourer to the capitalist. Direct force, outside economic conditions, is of course still used, but only exceptionally. In the ordinary run of things, the labourer can be left to the "natural laws of production," *i.e.*, to his dependence on capital, a dependence springing from, and guaranteed in perpetuity by, the conditions of production themselves. It is otherwise during the historic genesis of capitalist production. The bourgeoisie, at its rise, wants and uses the power of the state to . . . keep the labourer himself in the normal degree of dependence (1990: 899).

What this passage reveals is Marx's assumption that once the initial war of expropriation is complete, the minority of owners can largely rely on their structural power within society to continue their exploitation of the working class. Indeed, Marx notes that through "education, tradition, and habit," work-ers are conditioned to accept their social position as natural and inevitable; this is the real advance of capital according to Marx: it masks exploitation and the origin of profit. This is why in each nation where the capital relation was already deeply embedded and property highly concentrated, Marx argued that a "veiled civil war" raged within society. However, while the terrain of battle was primarily conceptualized on the level of the individual nation states of Western Europe, Marx put forth the universal historical narrative that the sub-ordinate social forces of all nations would eventually have to revolt against the appropriators of their surplus wealth. Here, Marx largely assumed, as do some scholars today, that capitalist social property relations significantly pervaded every national space of the globe and that the introduction of these relations would have rather uniform consequences for revolutionary activity.[6] With this universalizing trajectory in mind, Marx rearticulated and repositioned the war going on within society as an international class struggle for *human* emancipation and democratic social development.[7]

Yet for Marx, revolutionary struggle was a political project with at least two dimensions. First, it was a political project to lift the veil that masked the civil war going on within capitalist society. This required an active and ongoing struggle to organize and raise the consciousness of workers concerning both their exploitation and possibilities for social and political change. Second, it entailed developing strategies and tactics for revolutionizing the social order—that is, the practical initiatives that would have to be implemented in order for workers to reappropriate, and then direct, the social resources that had been historically plundered from them or their ancestors.

Here, however, Marx seemed to have assumed that outside of considerable and decisive revolutionary activity, the structural power of capital over the laborer was sufficient to reproduce the liberal-capitalist order. This made the militant tactics and direct violence of primitive accumulation somewhat exceptional in Marx's more theoretical accounts of the class struggle. In this way, primitive accumulation was largely relegated to the past by Marx, if only because of two major assumptions. First, Marx generally assumed that capitalist social property relations were already firmly entrenched in Western Europe. Second, he assumed that all other nations would eventually resemble advanced capitalist political economies. Yet when Marx argued that the war between labor and capital was recoded as a permanent war operating through "the silent compulsions of the market" and the structural power of capital over the laborer, his writing appears sensitive to the fact that where there is significant potential for revolutionary activity, the violent force of state power will be called on to crush it. A hint in this direction is offered by Marx's interpretation of the Paris Commune of 1871. Marx interpreted this autonomous movement by workers to constitute their own political community as a powerful sign of the advance made by the working class in their struggles against their rulers. In writing about the violent attack on the Commune by governmental forces (the Versaillese), Marx offered the following:

> The civilization and justice of bourgeois order comes out in its lurid light whenever the slaves and drudges of that order rise against their masters. Then this civilization and justice stand forth as undisguised savagery and lawless revenge. Each new crisis in the class struggle between the appropriator and the producer brings out this fact more glaringly. . . . The self-sacrificing heroism with which the population of Paris—men, women, and children—fought for eight days after the entrance of the Versaillese, reflects as much the grandeur of their cause, as the infernal deeds of the soldiery reflect the innate spirit of that

civilization, of which they are the mercenary vindicators. A glorious civilization, indeed, the great problem of which is how to get rid of the heaps of corpses
it made after the battle was over! (Marx cited in Tucker 1978: 646).

What this passage suggests is that the veil masking the civil war is often
lifted once an alternative politics of human development constitutes itself as
a threat to the unequal liberties and property of a minority. While Marx was
not the only tactician promoting these kinds of revolutionary struggles against
the exploitation of industrial capitalism, his historico-political discourse on
exploitation and permanent war was arguably the most influential for exciting
twentieth-century national and international movements to challenge capitalist ownership and development.

While his ideas were surely not adopted overnight, Marx succeeded in providing a new narrative of human development, one premised on class struggle
and the necessity of revolution. Revolution and the fear of revolutionary
challenges confronted the capitalists of Europe, governors, and imperialists
(often one and the same) with new practical and theoretical problems. The
key challenge was how to counter the praxis of a revolutionary discourse of
class struggle. As we shall see in the following section, to counter the notion
that the state and the dominant institutions of civil society were little more
than organized forces waging a permanent war on the workers of the world,
the belief in a biopolitical struggle for existence became stronger.

IMPERIALISM AND RACE

Whereas Polanyi places the official birth of the English working class in
1832 with the reform of the poor laws, Thompson has argued that in the
five decades preceding this date, a distinct working-class identity began to
emerge. As common experience gave way to a shared identity and common
concerns forged alternative political projects that threatened the prevailing
distribution of ownership and liberty, those protected by the constitutional
order became more attuned to their own interests as a class (Thompson 1991:
11). Undoubtedly, the political actions of the working class throughout the
nineteenth century ebbed and flowed and were characterized by a diversity
of political opinion and projects. However, whether and to what degree this
movement gained in coherence and actually won political victories is perhaps
not as important as the fear working-class politics instilled in their social
superiors because of its *potential* for social transformation. Thus, while some
histories of this period certainly discount or ignore working-class agency,
what is undeniable is that ruling class forces took working-class challenges
to the liberal order as serious threats throughout the nineteenth century. One

indication of this fear of *potential* revolutionary agency emerged as early as 1792 in the midst of the French Revolution and Thomas Paine's political treaties on the rights of man. The quasi governmental organization—The Association for Preserving Liberty and Property (APLP)—and the related associations it inspired throughout industrializing Britain not only aimed to coerce those seeking political reform but also sought to encourage an uncompromising loyalty to the government through propaganda and intimidation. In the view of the APLP, Parliament was no engine of oppression and social enslavement but the institution that secured the existing distribution of property and freedom (Smith 2005).

Despite these efforts, challenges from below continued and even intensified throughout the nineteenth century—as did the often-violent responses to them. What made these challenges even more complicated for those who wanted to maintain the existing order of ownership in Britain was the threat posed by newly industrializing economies such as the United States and Germany. Whereas Britain in no way industrialized under a regime of free trade, by mid-nineteenth century, the doctrine of free trade—however strategically nuanced in practice—was upheld by the vast majority of public officials. It was also recognized that the reproduction of Britain's hierarchical social order largely depended upon its access to foreign land, raw materials, and markets. For example, in 1888 as parts of Africa were being incorporated into the British Empire, Joseph Chamberlain noted the importance of foreign trade to the social reproduction of Britain's domestic economy:

> We have suffered much in this country from depression of trade. We know how many of our fellow-subjects are at this moment unemployed. Is there any man in his senses who believes that the crowded population of these islands could exist for a single day if we were to cut adrift from the great dependencies which now look to us for protection and which are the natural markets for our trade? . . . If tomorrow it were possible, as some people apparently desire, to reduce by a stroke of the pen the British Empire to the dimensions of the United Kingdom, half at least of our population would be starved (cited in Porter 1975: 80).

As this excerpt suggests, the maintenance of the British Empire was not interpreted as an extravagance but an unquestionable necessity—a fundamental question of life, death, and the preservation of internal order. This concern was echoed by others who noted that colonies were invaluable to the social reproduction of the liberal order at home because they provided work opportunities for the superfluous poor and over time, it was reasoned, this new employment abroad would create additional markets for British manufacturers, further stimulating trade and employment (Hobsbawm 2001: 69–70; Porter 1975: 81). Thus, there is significant reason to suggest that imperial policies were inextricably intertwined with relieving national class tensions. The most acute recognition of this fact, but by no means the only, came from the mouth of one of the nineteenth century's most renowned imperialists, Cecil Rhodes:

> In order to save the 40,000,000 inhabitants of the United Kingdom from bloody civil war, we colonial statesmen must acquire new lands to settle the surplus population, to provide new markets for the goods produced by them in the factories and mines. The Empire, as I have always said, is a bread and butter question. If you want to avoid civil war, you must become imperialists (Porter 1975: 132).[8]

This statement is not only important for what it says but for what it fails to consider. What it says is that imperialism is the only means by which domestic class antagonisms can be resolved without a "bloody civil war." What it refuses to countenance is any alternative political project that would encourage domestic reform, a redistribution of income or property, or a new plan of government. In Rhodes's view, then, the only way in which the nineteenth-century domestic property relations of Britain could be secured was through a strategy of imperialism. In this formulation, as with others during this period, the capture of foreign territory and resources was intimately connected to the avoidance of social revolution at home. What this largely entailed was the development of an imperial governmentality centered on the question of primitive accumulation in newly established colonies and rationalized, in the last quarter of the nineteenth century, by a belief in Anglo-Saxon racial superiority and, to a considerable extent, historical inevitability.[9]

Perhaps the most detailed analysis of this linkage during the age of empire was offered by the left-leaning British liberal political economist J. A. Hobson (1858–1940). Writing at the dawn of the twentieth century, Hobson discussed imperialism with specific regard to the "lower races" in his *Imperialism: A Study*. Hobson's overall purpose in writing this section was threefold: (1) to argue that engagement with the "lower races" was inevitable because the material prosperity of white European races depended upon the ongoing cultivation of and access to world resources, (2) to suggest that however inevitable, the governance of "lower races" by European powers was, at present, disorganized, openly exploitative, and thus likely to cause revolt of the "slave races," and (3) this being the case, to suggest that imperial practices be sanctioned by some form of official trust that would advise newly encountered or conquered peoples on the virtues of becoming civilized and industrious in developing their own resources for the benefit of international trade (Hobson 1972: 223ff).

What is perhaps most interesting in Hobson's analysis from our point of view is the fact that he criticizes the view that "the biological struggle for existence" is "the sole or chief instrument of progress" and chastises European imperialists for their naked and brutal exploitation of indigenous labor and the expropriation of their land (Hobson 1972: 234). Hobson believed that if given proper tutelage, force, though necessary in some cases, would not have to play the greatest role in effecting a transition to capitalist sociality in the colonies. Since Hobson argued that "the arts of progress" could potentially be communicable to some of the colonial natives, it would be difficult to label him a committed biological determinist, as were many of his peers during this period. What is also interesting about Hobson's observations on imperialism and the "lower races" is his remark that when Britain and other imperial countries speak of the "national interest" it "commonly signifies the direct material self-interest of some small class of traders, mine-owners, farmers, or investors who wish to dispose of the land and labor of the lower peoples for their private gain" (Hobson 1972: 226).

However, despite these seemingly critical observations, Hobson is still operating with the notion that Anglo-Saxon civilization—and white European civilization more broadly—is superior to the civilizational practices of the newly conquered natives. The problem for Hobson is that the natives of the colonies have too much liberty. They have too much liberty because they can secure the social reproduction of their communities with relative ease and have few wants or desires that would raise them above a subsistence lifestyle. But there is a second problem with native liberty for Hobson. Not only are the natives too free, but they have failed to use this freedom to progress, develop, and cultivate the territories on which they lived—which, according to Hobson, is the true mark of civilization. This, for Hobson, is a major problem because the development of foreign resources was understood to be of "vital importance to the maintenance and progress of Western civilization." In other words, without destroying this form of liberty and promoting what might be called the "will to improvement" among the natives, the social reproduction of the liberal order of Britain would be jeopardized (Edgell and Jules Townshend 1992: 406–8).

What is perhaps most fascinating about Hobson's line of argumentation is his reasoning that a *peaceful* transition to capitalist sociality in the colonies was possible. Though he did realize that on occasion force would have to be used, in the main he believed that this historical process could be accomplished through instruction and learning. What he did not comprehend, contra Marx, was that force plays the greatest role in the transition to capitalist sociality since peoples do not generally expropriate themselves for the benefit of investors or the "progress of Western civilization."[10] Slightly over a decade later, a more critical and less naïve voice would reinforce Marx's original point:

> Since the primitive associations of the natives are the strongest protection for their social organizations and for their material bases of existence, capital must begin by planning for the systematic destruction and annihilation of all the non-capitalist social units which obstruct its development. . . . Each new colonial expansion is accompanied, as a matter of course, by a relentless battle of capital against the social and economic ties of the natives, who are also forcibly robbed of their means of production and labor power. Any hope to restrict the accumulation of capital exclusively to "peaceful competition", i.e. to regular commodity exchange such as takes place between capitalist producer-countries, rests on the pious belief that capital can accumulate without mediation of the productive forces and without the demand of more primitive organisations, and that it can rely upon the slow internal process of a disintegrating natural economy. Accumulation, with its spasmodic expansion, can no more wait for, and be content with, a natural internal disintegration of non-capitalist formations and their transition to commodity economy. . . . Force is the only solution open to capital; the accumulation of capital, seen as an historical process, employs force as a permanent weapon, not only at its genesis, but further on down to the present day. From the point of view of the primitive societies involved, it is a matter of life or death; for them there can be no other attitude than opposition and fight to the finish (Luxemburg 1951: 370–1).

So while Hobson was definitely a critic of a certain manifestation of British and Western imperialism, he was undoubtedly in favor of a different kind of imperialism that would both effect and secure a more peaceful transition to differential accumulation. In this he was more or less following Cobden in imagining a day when separate and self-governing capitalist nations could coexist peacefully with one another and, through economic competition, continue the work of human progress. Thus, even at the extreme left wing of the liberal tradition we find arguments of Anglo-Saxon superiority connected to practices of primitive accumulation.

However, in addition to internal challenges from below and international rivalry for markets and fields of investment recognized by Hobson and others, Britain was also suffering from massive trade deficits with the United States and continental Europe, deficits that were financed by the large surpluses gained from coercively controlled markets and forceful expropriations in India and China (Davis 2001: 297–8). In other words, the reproduction of liberal order at home meant the denial of certain forms of liberty, property, and autonomy to other peoples (Losurdo 2011). However, as many social scientists have chronicled, liberal imperial rule—as varied as it was at the level of strategy and tactics— meant not only the denial of liberty to different peoples but often the outright rejection of their right to live. Though there are many examples on which to draw, a powerful illustration of this point is offered by Davis's study of famines in the age of empire and the commodification of agriculture. He writes:

> We are not dealing . . . with "lands of famine" becalmed in stagnant backwaters of world history, but with the fate of tropical humanity at the precise moment (1870–1914) when its labor and products were being dynamically conscripted into a London-centered world economy. Millions died, not outside the "modern world system," but in the very process of being forcibly incorporated into its economic and political structures. They died in the golden age of Liberal Capitalism; indeed, many were murdered . . . by the theological application of the sacred principles of Smith, Bentham and Mill (Davis 2001: 9).

What this passage reveals is that not only did liberal government require the forcible suppression of more radical political projects in its infancy at home. The social reproduction and preservation of the domestic liberal order—more often than not justified in the age of empire by the appeal to a biological imperative—required the elimination and transformation of non-capitalist relations of production and social reproduction.

However, if the avoidance of social revolution at home was connected to the imperial practices of differential accumulation and these acts to notions of biological superiority in the colonies, the racial rationalizations and practices of imperialism also contributed to a liberal nationalism that assisted in neutralizing class conflict at home. Scholars of this period have argued that there is little evidence to suggest that the working classes demonstrated any great excitement for imperial adventures and foreign wars (Hobsbawm 2001: 70; Porter 1975: 137). However, as Hobsbawm has argued, this lack of patriotism did not hold for classes one or more rungs up the social hierarchy. Indeed, Hobsbawm has offered the plausible argument that imperialism encouraged the *enfranchised* masses to identify with "the imperial state and nation" (2001: 70). Here, tales of imperial success and victories achieved in foreign wars were celebrated as the national achievements of an "Imperial Race" and served to reinforce sentiments, symbols, and practices of national unity. Though many elites were undoubtedly concerned that the British working class and the poor were a degenerate "race" that could stunt national progress during this period, there were equally other sentiments that suggested it was better to promote national cohesion.

Here both socialists and some liberals argued that this could be achieved through gradual political and economic reform. Perhaps one of the clearest statements of this sentiment was offered by Karl Pearson, an influential socialist of the period. The statement is worth quoting at some length:

> but if the national spirit takes the form of a strong feeling of the importance of organizing the nation as a whole, of making its social and economic conditions such that it is able to do its work in the world and meet its fellows without hesitation in the field and in the market, then it seems to me a wholly good spirit— indeed, one of the highest forms of social, that is, moral instinct. So far from our having too much of this spirit of patriotism, I doubt if we have anything like enough of it. We wait to improve the condition of some class of workers until they themselves cry out or even rebel against their economic condition. We do not better their state because we perceive its relation to the strength and stability of the nation as a whole. Too often it is done as the outcome of a blind class war. The coal owners, the miners, the manufacturers, the mill-hands, the landlords, the farmers, the agricultural laborers, struggle against each other, and, in doing so, against the nation at large, and our statesmen as a rule look on. That was the correct attitude from the standpoint of the old political economy. It is not the correct attitude from the standpoint of science; for science realizes that the nation is an organized whole, in continual struggle with its competitors. You cannot get a strong and effective nation if many of its stomachs are half fed and many of its brains untrained. We, as a nation, cannot survive in the struggle for existence if we allow class distinctions to permanently endow the brainless and to push them into posts of national responsibility. The true statesman has to limit the internal struggle of the community in order to make it stronger for the external struggle (1919: 52–54).

In Pearson's non-Marxist formulation, while the state may have a misguided policy due to the fact that governors have not fully embraced the logic of "science," the state is certainly not conceptualized as an instrument of class domination. Rather, for Pearson, as for other reformers of this period, the state could be used both to protect the race and to improve it over time—what Foucault would later come to call biopower (2003). In the late nineteenth to early twentieth centuries this meant not only encouraging national solidarity but also supporting eugenic policies that promised to create a stronger and fitter race that would compete successfully in the "struggle of race against race and of nation against nation" (Pearson 1919: 52–54).

Thus, in Britain, countering the discourse and practices of class struggle in the latter half of the nineteenth century meant relying on notions of biological and cultural superiority, the practices of imperialism, the often-violent suppression of the working class, and an understanding of an international struggle for existence that encouraged loyalty to an abstraction—the nation— in that it masked class differences. Militant practices—both domestic and international—were not outside, external, or aberrations from the constitution of capitalism's leading imperialist state but integral to it.

NOTES

1 It should be remarked here that relations between and within Indian nations and their relations with the British and American patriots, were complex and fluid during this period.

2 Joseph Townsend (1786) *A Dissertation on the Poor Laws.* http://socserv2. socsci.mcmaster.ca/econ/ugcm/3ll3/townsend/poorlaw.html#N_11_ (5/11/2017).

3 Joseph Townsend (1786) *A Dissertation on the Poor Laws.* http://socserv2. socsci.mcmaster.ca/econ/ugcm/3ll3/townsend/poorlaw.html#N_11_ (5/11/2017).

4 Joseph Townsend (1786) *A Dissertation on the Poor Laws.* http://socserv2. socsci.mcmaster.ca/econ/ugcm/3ll3/townsend/poorlaw.html#N_11_ (5/11/2017).

5 The passage was deleted from later versions due to the controversy it caused.

6 For a critique of this view, see Robbie Shilliam, "Hegemony and the Unfashionable Problematic of 'Primitive Accumulation'," *Millennium: Journal of International Studies*, Vol. 32, No. 1, 2004: 59–88.

7 For a critique of Marx's understanding of modern development at the expense of a fuller international account of multi-linear development, see Robbie Shilliam, "Marx's Path to *Capital*: The International Dimension of an Intellectual Journey," *History of Political Thought*, Vol. XXVII, No. 2, 2006: 349–75.

8 L. S. Stavrianos has argued that "Rhodes's expansionism was accepted and justified by European liberals who insisted on self-determination for subject people in Europe, but conveniently abandoned it when it came to the 'lesser breeds' overseas" (1981: 263).

9 What has to be noted here is that this development was not solely connected to the thought of state authorities but with the practical strategies and tactics of private individuals and joint-stock corporations in their quest to exploit other peoples and accumulate money.

10 It should be noted here that Hobson saw this form of tutelage as benefiting humanity as whole, not just Western civilization.

Act III

The Fossil Fuel Revolution

In this act of our tragedy we move from colonialism and the biopolitical violence of the transatlantic slave trade to the fossil fuel revolution and the emergence of military-industrial complexes. In the first part of the act we are confronted by the close connection between war, money, and energy. The differential accumulation of money through capitalization, the major logic of capitalists, as we have already discussed in the context of colonialism and slavery, is intimately connected up with private and state-led warfare and the source of energy available to those social forces mobilizing for war. In the long history of human warfare at least three eras can be distinguished that can largely, but not exclusively, be divided by an increasing scale of lethality facilitated by the mass exploitation of fossil fuels and what I have previously called the petro-market civilizations they engendered (Di Muzio 2015b; Gill 1995). In the second section of this act we encounter—if not the very first merchants of death—then at least those organized for-profit firms of the industrial era that contributed to the phenomenon of industrialized total war. In the third section of this act we open the curtain on the links between total war and the transition to petroleum usage by military forces. Gasoline, previously a waste product from the production of kerosene used for light, would become vital for the exercise of violent power by the end of the nineteenth century. The struggle of "nation" against "nation" in a competitive international environment for the differential accumulation of money and resources would become tied to a nonrenewable resource: oil. In the penultimate section of Act III, we discuss the atrocities and horrors of World War II and the race to uncover the atomic bomb. While millions of young men lay dead on the battlefields and seas of Europe and the Pacific, the United States, supported by the United Kingdom and Canada, raced to develop the first nuclear weapons in the Manhattan Project (1939–1946). As we will see, both during and after World War II, and despite the knowledge of the power of nuclear weapons to annihilate the species, billions of dollars and thousands of hours of labor were spent on stockpiling an arsenal so large that the capacity to end most human, animal, and natural life on the Earth has been achieved for the first time in human history. No other species on the planet has created such destructive capacity let alone conceived of doing so. If we are indeed unique among the animal kingdom, it may be in this dimension alone where we are exceptional. In the final section we will consider the persistence of militarism in the early stages of the twenty-first century and the massive amounts of money and human resources spent on the ability to destroy life, nature, and infrastructure.

WAR, MONEY, AND ENERGY

We know little of human warfare before the rise of city-states, but since the domestication of agriculture and livestock, scholars have counted just over 3,000 wars since 2000 BCE. The motivations for warfare have varied over human history, but Chaliand argues that most of the wars of antiquity were fought for slaves, land, and generally to plunder the assets of an adversary (Chaliand 2014: 13; Kohn 2007: ix). However, once money represented primarily as gold and silver became more predominant it became impossible to separate organized political violence from money. This is true in at least two senses. First, warfare is generally an expensive enterprise and has to be financed when regents could not pay for war out of the returns from their estates or by selling honorific titles or privileges. The primary way in which this was carried out was through loans from financiers and public taxation. Both mechanisms proved difficult for sovereigns: first in the fact that financiers had to be paid back with hefty interest charges and second in the fact that new or increasing taxes largely attracted the ire, and sometimes revolt of the public. Second, while many lose their lives, livelihoods, and assets in war, warfare can be immensely profitable for the manufacturers and investors of arms firms. If we think of war over roughly the last millennium, Latham argues that we can distinguish three major eras of warfare (2002: 247–60). The first is feudal war, which runs from about the ninth century to the rise of more organized—often called absolutist—states by about the sixteenth century in Europe. Generally speaking, the primary source of wealth during the feudal period was productive labor and land whose products could be coercively appropriated or monetized. In the feudal era, violence was primarily wielded by a specialized class of landed nobles and the means of violence was most often in private hands. The second era of human warfare is modern war or industrialized total war, emerging in the sixteenth century and lasting until the final stages of World War II. One of the chief characteristics of this era was the state's increasing monopoly over the means of violence. The private violence of private individuals that characterized the feudal era was no longer tolerated by centralizing political rulers who were coming to control better defined territories while at the same time consolidating political, military, and fiscal power in their hands. During this period we witness the greater monetization of society and the greater application of science and technology to war-fighting. Whereas feudal wars were limited by the level of technology and relatively primitive sources of energy such as human and animal muscle power and wood, modern war was transformed by the fossil fuel and scientific revolutions, the two, it should be noted, historically coinciding (Jevons 1866: 5). From this point on, warfare became far more lethal and far more devastating. Industrialized modern warfare involved not only the mobilization of conscripts and volunteers to fight on the battlefield but the mobilization of entire societies involved in the mass production of the means of destruction and those goods and services needed to support the war effort of the belligerent ruling classes of Europe. According to Latham we can also conceive of a third era of warfare: postmodern war. Latham places the origins of postmodern war after World War II but argues that it only really started to advance at the end of the Cold War around 1991. This era is characterized by a rapid increase in the means of transport and communication, the re-privatization of violence in some quarters of world order (terrorists, drug cartels, private police squads, privatized military companies), and a less secure "national" identity due to the globalization of culture and technology. Rather than nations fighting over colonies, territory, resources, or greater international power, postmodern war, Latham claims, is likely to be far more about identity politics. However analytically useful Latham's periodization of human warfare over the *longue durée,* he neither emphasizes the greater capitalization of war during the modern period nor does he discuss the role played by fossil fuels in increasing the lethality and destructiveness of war. In our view, both were decisive turning points, crucial for understanding the emergence of military-industrial complexes and the for-profit firms at their core. In other words, since we are concerned with the logic of differential accumulation, it is necessary to reveal how organized violence is capitalized and why there was a turn to nonrenewable fossil fuels as a primary fuel source, not only for domestic heating and manufacture, but for the construction of ever greater means of violence.

Until the modern age, at least in Europe, the financial burden of war rested with the sovereign. As is well documented, most warring regents could never garner enough money to finance war and were constantly in debt to their legally inferior, but financially better off, subjects. Debts were often abrogated to the chagrin of financiers that could do little—at least juridically—to enforce repayment of their initial loans at interest while the sovereign remained the supreme power. And given resistance—both popular and from the noble and merchant classes—to increases in taxation, the warring sovereigns of Europe found themselves in a constant bind. McNeil notes:

> the political authorities found it less and less possible to escape the trammels of finance, and finance depended more and more on the flow of goods to markets which rulers could no longer dominate. They, too, like humbler members of society, were more and more trapped in a cobweb of cash and credit, for spending money proved a more effective way of mobilizing resources and manpower for war and for other public enterprises than any alternative. New forms of management and new modes of political conduct had to be invented to reconcile the initial antipathy between military power and money power; and the society most successful in achieving this act of legerdemain -western Europe- in due season came to dominate the world (1982: 25).

McNeil may be right that it was western Europe that came to dominate the world in due time, but the contradiction between sovereign war and finance was first resolved in England, where the monetary system was far more uniform for centuries than it had been in continental Europe (Davies 2002: 130). As Wennerlind (2011: 17) has chronicled, in the seventeenth century the English were consumed by the problem of a scarcity of money. It was reasoned that the economy could be more productive but the problem identified by those concerned with such matters was a scarcity of money to circulate good and services. Believing real money to be gold and silver coin, some turned to alchemy and the search for the philosopher's stone to no avail (Wennerlind 2011: 48). In the light of these failures a number of proposals were put forward to overcome the scarcity of money problem (Horsefield 1960). Out of dozens of proposals, the new regents of England enthroned in the Glorious Revolution of 1688—William and Mary—accepted that of William Paterson and a coterie of mainly London and Dutch financiers for a Bank of England. Established in 1694, the Bank was to provide a loan of £1,200,000 to the Crown-in-Parliament for war with France (Davies 2002: 260). In return, the Bank was to receive 8 percent interest on the permanent loan and a yearly management fee of £4,000. The 1,509 investors in the Bank were guaranteed an income stream from a new tax, mainly on shipping and alcohol (Davies 2002: 60–61). In effect, investors in the incipient Bank of England were capitalizing the power of the Crown-in-Parliament to tax the English population and punish those who refused to pay up or those who tampered with the coin of the realm. For instance, Sir Isaac Newton led a renewed effort to root out counterfeiters and clippers of the coin and their accomplices. Men found guilty were hanged while women were often burned at the stake

(Wennerlind 2011: 150). In other words, to ensure faith in credit and the value of the coin required an entire policing apparatus to catch those altering or counterfeiting money. But while the Bank was supported by state power, it also had tremendous powers of its own: it could issue bank notes based on a supply of—initially at least—silver coin. Indeed, the Crown-in-Parliament did not receive the loan for war in silver coins but in redeemable paper notes that supposedly represented coin (Desan 2014: 306). The act that created the Bank of England made it clear that the Bank was not to issue loans above its capital unless agreed by Parliament. Little is known with any precision how much coin backed up the new paper notes in circulation. But what is known is that the value of the notes in circulation far exceeded the actual coin at the Bank (Desan 2014: 305–7). Though the Bank's notes never solved the scarcity of money problem in its entirety, it did create "Europe's first widely circulating credit currency" and expanded the money supply, thus helping to facilitate more economic transactions (Wennerlind 2011: 123). But the Bank's owners were not simply directing a stream of income to themselves from the issuance of paper notes. Insofar as the major recipient of new loans was the Crown-in-Parliament, they were also capitalizing the capacity of the state for war. Indeed, over the next centuries, the government would continue to borrow from private social forces, mainly to finance war. As Brewer's analysis notes, "75 per cent and 85 per cent of annual expenditure went either on current spending on the army, navy and ordnance or to service the debts incurred to pay for earlier wars" (1989: 31). It is too easily forgotten by those who make a strict analytical (if not practical) distinction between state and market power that while there were indeed a number of joint-stock companies to invest in at the time, the major capitalized organization of the eighteenth century was the British state:

> Britain was able to shoulder an ever-more ponderous burden of military commitments thanks to a radical increase in taxation, the development of public deficit finance (a national debt) on an unprecedented scale, and the growth of a sizable public administration devoted to organizing the fiscal and military activities of the state. As a result the state cut a substantial figure, becoming the largest single actor in the economy (Brewer 1989: introduction, np).

Even today, as I have pointed out in previous work, the British state—through its national debt—remains the largest capitalized entity relative to its domestically listed firms on the London Stock Exchange (Di Muzio 2015b: 74–76). As a result of mounting debt for ruling class war, a regressive tax apparatus was implemented across the nation so that the middling British became one of the most heavily taxed populations on the planet by the eighteenth century (Braddick 1996; Brewer 1989; O'Brien 1988).

But the expansion of the money supply for war was not the only unique development in England. The debates on the dearth of money also happened to overlap with debates on the shortage of timber—the primary energy source for a much-needed supply of charcoal to fashion iron ore into useful implements for farming and war. Timber was also used in the construction of ships, for heating and cooking and in housing construction. As historians of this era have noted, at least by the seventeenth century (if not before), in many quarters of England there was an energy crisis that more or less impelled the English to turn to coal to solve it (Brinley 1986; Cipolla 1997; Fouquet and Pearson 1998; Goldstone 2002; Malanima 2006; Nef 1997; Podobnik 2006; Smil 1994: 159; Wrigley 2010). Coal had been known in antiquity but was not commonly used as most English who could afford it preferred wood to noxious coal—particularly in heating and cooking. With prices for timber escalating due to a domestic shortage of trees and the protection of royal forests, the English increasingly turned to coal as a major fuel source. The reliance on coal as a primary energy source posed its own set of unique challenges, the most immediate of which was how to access coal seams underground once the surface coal had been exhausted. Miners of both coal and tin confronted the problem of pits filling up with water. Horses and buckets could be used to empty water from the pits but this was incredibly cumbersome and posed problems of its own, not the least of which was the amount of time it would take even to clear a small amount of water. Eventually, an ironmonger solved the quandary by building on the ideas of Thomas Savery and Denis Papin—two Frenchmen largely working in England—who were also interested in the problem of raising water from mines by the use of combusting coal in what eventually became known as a steam engine. Thomas Newcomen (1664–1729) demonstrated the first practical application of the machine for removing water from mines and working under Savery's patent sold just under 2,000 steam engines. The energy-inefficient, though still useful, invention was later improved upon by James Watt (1736–1819). While cotton and textiles certainly contributed to the industrial revolution, the steam engine was the fount and matrix of the new order I have previously called carbon capitalism (Di Muzio 2015b: 72–74). Applying coal-fired steam power across the nation increased the amount of energy available for the manufacture of goods and services. The situation was radically different in Britain than on the continent even by 1840, as Wrigley makes clear:

> Steam engines were more widely employed than elsewhere to provide power in a rapidly widening range of industrial and transport uses. The total of installed steam engine horsepower was far larger than on the continent. In 1840, 75 per cent of the combined total capacity of stationary steam engines in Britain,

France, Prussia, and Belgium was in Britain alone (the other three countries accounted for the great bulk of installed capacity on the continent) (2010: 27).

In other words, Britain was exceptional in the consumption of coal and had thus turned an energy corner at least two centuries before other European powers turned to coal as a primary fuel source. As Thomas has argued, one of the reasons why European powers on the continent did not turn to coal consumption in any comparable amount until much later was due to an abundance rather than a dearth of timber as was the opposite experience in Britain (1993: 118). The same was true for the United States, which did not experience anything like the industrial revolution in Britain until the latter half of the nineteenth century. But recognizing this does not solve the problem of explaining why Britain was more quickly denuded of her forests so that coal came to be employed in ever greater amounts as an energy substitute for wood. Two immediate answers suggest themselves. The area of Britain is only about one-third the size of France, so area or geography may certainly have played a role in Britain's faster consumption of timber. Second, according to the available data, Britain experienced rapid population growth from at least the beginning of the eighteenth century if not before (Wrigley 2010: 155). This too would have likely put pressure on the price of timber and its availability. But while these two immediate answers cannot be overlooked, Thomas has suggested that it was largely Cromwell's strong naval policy combined with the desire for greater tonnage among the merchant class that accelerated the energy crisis and forced Britain to turn to coal within a context of geopolitical competition for the accumulation of money and a social transformation in agrarian relations that dispossessed the peasantry of access to land in waves of enclosures (1993: 100–1). As Thomas states: "The break with the past is seen most clearly in the expenditure on warships. In the years 1650–9 Cromwell's average naval shipbuilding per annum was 3,600 tons; this was over five times greater than the average of 682 tons in the reigns of James I and Charles I (1603–49) and eleven times greater than the average of 333 tons in Queen Elizabeth's time (1558–1603)" (1993: 101). From these figures, there is good reason to agree with Thomas that the Cromwellian revolution that inaugurated a quest for naval supremacy was one of the chief reasons for the diminution of forests, the rising cost of timber, and the greater reliance on coal as a primary energy source for manufacturing the means of violence among additional commercial goods. War and the desire of the ruling class to accumulate more money, it would seem, ushered in the first phase of the fossil fuel revolution and radically transformed Britain into what I have previously called a petro-market civilization—a civilizational order whose social reproduction is wholly contingent on the production and consumption of nonrenewable fossil fuel energy. In this light, for those of us who experience many of the benefits of the industrial revolution today (along with its contradictions), it is worth noting how horrific it was for many of the poor and working classes who fell victim to a new social and economic order premised on greater urbanization, poverty, wage dependence, and industrialization. As Moore does well to recollect, "There is no evidence that the mass of the population anywhere has wanted an industrial society, and plenty of evidence that they did not. At bottom all forms of industrialization so far have been revolutions from above, the work of a ruthless minority" (1974: 506). If industrialization was largely the work of a "ruthless minor- ity," it was a revolution encouraged by the geopolitical competition for money and the necessity of preparing for war. For centuries since the turn to silver and gold as high-powered money that could finance an army and com- mand resources, the organization of political violence remained wedded to limited energy resources. To be sure, human, animal, and renewable energy such as wood were inseparable from war fighting. But Britain made the first radical historical break with low-energy warfare that would eventually make total war a possibility in at least three important respects. First, the surplus energy released from coal allowed for the greater production of steel for guns and ships among other instruments, while the steam engine allowed for the greater propulsion of battleships and trains that connected supply lines and integrated the nascent commercial and international economy of Empire. Second, the use of coal made war far more deadly, particularly for those countries still powered by traditional forms of energy. And while Britain tried its best to keep its technological innovations secret, it was not long before other European nations and a few other countries such as the United States would start to adopt coal as a primary energy source to industrialize their own apparatuses of violence from above (Podobnik 2006: 29). Third, we witness the rise of the first well-organized fiscal-military state where war and the preparation for war were capitalized through an ever mount- ing "national" debt owed primarily to a minority of the investing public (Brewer 1989: 93–94; Ferguson 2006: 195). As I have suggested before, it is important to highlight the fact that massive increases in the magnitude and scale of capitalist accumulation, and thereby the spread of the capitalist mode of power and industrial production, would have been far less—if not impossible—without coal and military spending by the British Empire (Di Muzio 2015b; Di Muzio and Dow 2017). There are two lines of evidence here which strongly suggest war and the preparation for war as the key driver of industrialization, research and development, and capitalist accumulation. First, while historians have argued that textiles (e.g., wool, cotton) were at the heart of the capitalist industrial revolution, it seems highly unlikely that this can be the sole or even main explanation for the amplification of industry and differential accumulation (Thomas 1993: 73). As the British economist John Hicks argued:

> [Early cotton machinery] fits better as an appendage to the evolution of the old industry than in the way it is usually presented as the beginning of the new. . . . There is continuity between the eighteenth-century development of Lancashire and the West Riding and the pre-Industrial Revolution world. There might have been no Crompton and Arkwright, and still there could have been an Industrial Revolution (cited in Cipolla 1977: 211).

As shown previously, the prime mover of the industrial age—the steam engine—was invented by an ironmonger interested in an effective way of removing water from mines, not an inventor interested in spinning and weaving. To put it simply, two activities—spinning and weaving and war and the removal of water from coal and tin mines—led to two different technological innovations and applications, the latter of which spurred on industrial development on a scale never seen before. It was Brewer who captured this difference in at least two dimensions. First, the search for naval supremacy was an enormous undertaking. The British textile industry, to be sure one of the largest sectors of the economy, represented "a mere 18 per cent of the fixed capital required to launch the British navy" (Brewer 1989: 27). Second, no merchant or manufacturer would have had the ability to raise the amount of capital to invest in the British Navy; this required state finance, which also meant a permanent state debt and a redistribution of income to private bondholders (Brewer 1989: 38; see also McNeil 1982: 210–2). For example, from the Nine Years War (1688–1697), public debt increased from £16.7 million to £744 million by 1815, a massive increase of 4,355 percent (Michie 2001: 53). The vast majority of this debt was to pay for war and the preparation for war, particularly the British Navy that controlled the seas by at least the second half of the eighteenth century (Brewer 1989: 31). But while war, coal, steam power, and a burgeoning "national" debt were at the heart of this transformation in local and world order, it was the new discovery of petroleum and the internal combustion engine that would help change the world anew and further entrench militarism and a greater dependence on fossil fuels. How this happened and contributed to a new form of warfare and international violence is the subject of our next section.

TOTAL WAR, OIL, AND THE MERCHANTS OF DEATH

Coal and steam power unleashed the productive forces of society wherever they were used in great quantities. The signs are all around us to today as evidenced by the levels of economic growth of the global political economy over the twentieth century and the OECD's primary reliance on fossil fuels to keep their petro-market civilizations afloat. The development of coal-fired productive forces also contributed to greater urbanization, the monetization of social relations, and a burgeoning sense of nationalism due largely to ruling class propaganda and their desire for social control to stamp out the potential for working-class revolution. As we have seen, the rising nationalism of the late nineteenth century was also rooted in a socio-biological conception of race and the belief among the political and much of the intellectual establishment that international relations and the private accumulation of fortunes were largely about a struggle for survival among separate "races"—with this line of thinking most prevalent in the Anglo-American setting (Carr 2001: 46–48; Füredi 1998: 26). Within this geopolitical context, eventually a new fossil fuel source was found in sufficient quantities in the United States that would profoundly change war-fighting and the fundamental constitution of world order: oil.

Up until the discovery and refining of petroleum, certain whales were hunted to near extinction (e.g., the bowhead and right whales) for their blubber that could be boiled to release oil. Whale oil was marketed as a fuel source for evening light and helped to extend the working day. It was not the only source of evening light at the time—city gas, for instance, was a growing option in urban environments—but it was a leading fuel for light against the dark of night. Though a capitalized, competitive, and profitable industry, whaling started to wane by the beginning of the twentieth century because considerable quantities of ground oil had been found by the Seneca Oil Company in Pennsylvania in 1859 (Black 2000: 16–17; Yergin 1991: 27–29). Early research had demonstrated that petroleum could be refined to make kerosene, a fuel source that could substitute whale oil for evening light. The discovery in Pennsylvania, combined with a commercial application for oil in light and lubrication, set off a rush to find greater quantities of oil throughout the United States and the world. Prospectors, companies, and geologists scoured the earth for any sign of petroleum deposits, a trend that continues today, albeit for different reasons. The reason is different today because, by and large, kerosene is no longer used for light in most urban environments. In 1882, Thomas Edison demonstrated to his financiers that electric light was superior to kerosene and commercially viable given significant investment in the nascent technology (Yergin 1991: 63). The feasibility of electric light threatened the empire of fortunes that had been derived from monetizing kerosene for illumination. With their profitability and capitalization in question, oil companies such as Shell and Standard Oil would need to find a new use for their petroleum stores, not to mention their distribution networks and industrial equipment (Yergin 1991: 79). How this happened is of considerable interest, but this period of history is notoriously murky and so we have to approach an outline with caution (Black 2006; Di Muzio 2015b: 104–5).

The most common explanation for the survival of the early oil companies is simply that a new market for gasoline grew up naturally. In these accounts, the internal combustion engine and the use of gasoline simply arrived on the scene without any violence or power relations to serve them. Yergin provides the leading account: "But just as the invention of the incandescent light bulb seemed to signal the obsolescence of the oil industry, a new era opened with the development of the internal combustion engine powered by gasoline. The oil industry had a new market, and a new civilization was born" (1991: 14). Simple as that. Though an easy quickhanded explanation, it can be severely doubted. Gasoline was largely a waste product in the production of kerosene and hardly thought valuable at all during the era of illuminating kerosene. And while it is true that the invention and spread of the internal combustion engine from the 1880s and the diesel engine from the 1890s did save and ultimately amplify the capitalization of the oil industry, there is little to suggest that the acceptance of gasoline and internal combustion engines "just happened" naturally. We can call this the "smooth transition" hypothesis and it is largely a mainstay of liberal political economy in the same way that today many mainstream thinkers believe we can simply transition from fossil fuels to renewable energy in a straightforward and natural manner due to technological advances, corporate interests, and market signals. But they forget that the social world is constituted by power relations, vested interests, and the logic of differential accumulation at the heart of capitalism (Di Muzio 2012). This means we must entertain an alternative hypothesis that alternatives to the internal combustion engine and gasoline were actively sabotaged by vested interests who understood the threat to their own private accumulation of money. Though the evidence we have is far from overwhelming in historical detail, Black's (2006) investigation suggests that the development of and mass production of electric cars, already a fact by the late eighteenth century, were sabotaged by investors who stood to benefit from gas-powered automobiles. Black relies on evidence from the early twentieth century when Henry Ford and Thomas Edison declared their willingness to jointly produce electric cars, with Ford agreeing to buy a certain amount of new batteries that were being developed by Edison in his laboratory complex in New Jersey. However, on December 9, 1914, Edison's laboratory along with much of his work went up in flames. Black maintains that the fire was highly suspicious in that it spread across a complex of self-contained cement block buildings that were not insured because the buildings were thought to be impervious to fire and Edison kept an on-premise fire brigade. Black also argues that this loss demoralized Edison and paved the way for the internal combustion engine rather than the electric car. Thus, whatever we might think about the rise of private automobility in general (after all it still creates the need for a high-energy environment), a great advance was lost for almost a century until General Motors introduced the EV1 in the mid-1990s only to then subsequently destroy the thousands of cars it produced for highly questionable reasons as chronicled in the 2006 documentary *Who Killed the Electric Car?* Today there is a small resurgence in electric cars, but they continue to make up a relatively insignificant portion of the global fleet of gasoline-powered motor vehicles. Whether the electric car was sabotaged we may never fully know given corporate secrecy, but what is undoubtedly true is that internal combustion not only saved the oil industry but made it one of the most profitable.

But other than sabotage and corporate power plays, it is also possible that marketing along with the greater speed and power of internal combustion engines also played a role in elevating them above electric cars (Yergin 1991: 79). Yergin (1991: 80) also suggests that already by 1905 the manufacturers of internal combustion engines had defeated their steam and electric rivals for commercial viability. This may be so, but obviously Edison and Ford held to the possibility of one day perfecting an electric car that would rival one run on gasoline until the fire of 1914. Another event in 1914 also suggests itself as a predominant reason for the turn to gasoline and internal combustion: World War I. As Yergin has argued, "The battlefields of World War I established the importance of petroleum as an element of national power when the internal combustion machine overtook the horse and the coal-powered locomotive" (1991: 14). Indeed, the orgy of industrial violence wrought upon millions of soldiers throughout the protracted trench warfare of World War I would have been impossible without the energy and inventions released from coal and oil. A new reliance on oil due to its flexibility in transportation and the greater speeds able to be obtained in naval and ground warfare ensured that oil would be a coveted national security resource by any ruling class block anxious to maintain global power and prestige. This not only contributed to the importance of energy to foreign policy agendas among the leading powers who adopted oil, but it also drew national security states into greater alliance with for-profit oil companies scouring the planet for petroleum to monetize. As a result of war, states, structurally forced to borrow from private social forces since the creation of the Bank of England and the international proliferation of this model of banking and finance, would further entrench themselves in permanent debt to the major financiers of war. Two other developments are also important. First, the creation of what Dwight D. Eisenhower would later call a "military-industrial complex" in his presidential farewell address to the United States public in 1961. We will explore this in greater detail in the next section when the paranoia of the Cold War further embedded the merchants of death and their strategies of differential accumulation into the fabric of international society (Engel-brecht and Hanighen 1934). But second, the transition to oil and internal combustion also contributed to the birth of total warfare and an international arms race. Latham captures the essence of the new warfare worth quoting at length:

> During the period of Industrialized Total Warfare (roughly 1914–45), military power rested upon three pillars—mass destruction, mass mobiliza-tion and mass production. On the broad strategic canvas, major war (and the preparation for war) became "total" in both scope and scale as states developed the ability to release the full destructive potential inherent in the nationalization and industrialization of war. During this conjuncture, secular increases in population, coupled with steady improvements in the ability of states to mobilize the human and material resources of the nation, meant that the institution of warfare began to extend itself deep into the social structure just as the industrialization of war meant the means of destruction were becoming increasingly lethal. As a result, for the first time in history, social developments converged with a strictly technical logic of escalating destruc-tiveness to render warfare "total". World War I was an important historical milestone in this process in that it marked the initiation of a shift in the way in which warfare was conceptualized in military, academic and popular circles. It spawned a new cultural framework that would later give rise to terms like "total war" and "mass destruction" as customary descriptors of warfare (2002: 241; see also Shaw 1991).

The belligerent rulers who called for war in the summer of 1914 thought that it would last a few short months (Ham 2013: 81). How wrong they were and how devastating the consequences. Instead of a short war, they bequeathed to the world the total war so effectively described in the previous passage. What came to be known as "The Great War" or the "War to End All Wars" lasted four long and torturous years with soldiers witnessing industrial slaughter on a scale never seen before by *H. sapiens*. Statistics of the casual-ties and deaths during World War I are far from accurate, but it is generally held that at least 38 million people suffered injuries or died during the war. This includes about 8.5 million soldiers and 6.5 million civilians, with the remainder wounded in some capacity.[1] To put the number of casualties in per-spective, consider that the population of Canada in 2017 is roughly 36 million and that of Slovenia in the same year about 2 million for a total of 38 million humans. If an analogy is permitted we can start to understand the magnitude of the casualties and deaths suffered in World War I. It would be as if every Canadian and every Slovenian were either wounded or dead within a four-year period. No doubt the scale of this atrocity is difficult to imagine, but it was facilitated by the merchants of death on government payrolls inventing and developing more effective ways to kill human beings. Ham gives us a glimpse of these developments:

> Artillery presented humankind with the most efficient method of slaughtering itself. Before long-range bombers and nuclear weapons were conceived, huge cannons were invented that could rain shells containing shrapnel (and later, gas) onto the heads of armies. Germany showed the way in the development of artillery and by 1914 had built the most powerful guns on earth. . . . The British Lee-Enfield .303 rifle, with a maximum range of 2.7 kilometers, and the recoilless machine gun ensured an unprecedented number of them would die, or suffer dreadful wounds. The new machine guns could fire 400 rounds a minute. By 1900, military planners had glimpsed the strategic, if not the moral consequences of the recoil-operated Maxim machine gun, which would mow down advancing lines of men like a threshing machine. . . . Hand grenades, mortars, the new French 75-millimetre quick firing field guns and hideous prospect of poisonous gas would send the casualties soaring. Governments would place the first few hundred orders for primitive aircraft in the year before the war, and Zeppelins or airships soon became a familiar sight in the sky. At sea, the ironclad steamship, the turbine propelled destroyer, torpedoes, mines, submarines and the ultimate battleship of the day, the dreadnought, transformed naval warfare (Ham 2014: 16).

Of course the increasing level of lethality had to be financed. One of the ways this was accomplished was through a massive increase in the national debts of the war-fighting powers. For instance, in just two years, from 1917 when President Wilson took a reluctant nation to war, the national debt of the United States increased from US$1.3 billion to US$27 billion by 1919—an increase of 1,976 percent (Sobel 1965: 216). Britain's debt also increased by 924 percent from 1913 to 1918. But the real story was the increase in national debts throughout the so-called Great War. According to J. P. Morgan partner Thomas W. Lamont the debts of the world increased by 475 percent to US$210 billion (Engdahl 2004: 50). To be sure, ordinary citizens of various nations were called on to invest in various war bond schemes throughout this period. But while their contributions were likely a great sum to them, the majority of the war was not financed by the middling sorts or ordinary men and women but by leading banks and major private investors chasing differential returns on their investment in state violence. Thus the capitalization of war, whose embryonic roots we have already uncovered in a struggle for power in Mesopotamia, was not an exception to differential accumulation, but perhaps its very essence. As Sobel reminds us in the case of the United States, the major supplier of the Allies: "With war came prosperity and wealth of almost unimagined scope for American business. Much of this accrued to American corporations that supplied war materials to the Allies, but since those shipments had to be paid for, the primary beneficiaries were the bankers. . . . The gross national product rose from $76.4 billion in 1918 to $84 billion in 1919, and then to $91.5 billion in 1920" (2000: 244). But wealthy American bankers and the owners of corporations furnishing war materials and other goods to the allies were not the only ones to enrich themselves off the war effort. Fearing a changed balance of power in Europe should Britain and France (and Russia up until 1917) lose the war, many Europeans sent their money to the United States where it could be invested in US government securities or in the New York Stock Exchange. But there was also an imperial connection. As Sobel notes, "$200 million of the gold produced in British mines in south and west Africa each year found its way to America" (2000: 245). In other words, far from the resources of gold going to increase the life chances of south and western Africans, the gold was used to finance war. It is likely that the fortunes of many other wealthy Europeans who derived their wealth from colonial exploits also made sure their capital escaped to a more stable and likely more profitable haven in the United States. Thus while men and women were being blown to bits on the battlefields of the war, civilians lay starving and malnourished, limbs were being separated from bodies, soldiers were being shot in the back of the head for refusing to charge the battlefield, and untold psychological trauma was being inflicted on the participants of the industrial slaughter, men—mostly old white men— were safe at home or in their offices niggling over balance sheets and trying to make a profit. Twenty years after the Treaty of Versailles in 1919, the beans would have to be counted again during another industrialized horror show. A passage from McNeil can summarize what was afoot over the centuries since the turn to coal as a primary energy source and later the discovery and application of oil to organized political violence: "War, in short, became well and truly industrialized as industry became no less well and truly militarized" (1982: 357). The seeds of a nascent international military-industrial complex were perhaps sown long before World War I, but they would begin to flourish in this global conflagration and would fully blossom during the carnage of the next great worldwide war.

WORLD WAR II AND THE ANNIHILATION OF THE SPECIES

The Treaty of Versailles, signed by Germany and the Allied Powers in June 1919, blamed Germany for World War I and forced her citizens to pay punitive and ultimately unpayable reparations. John Maynard Keynes, who attended the Paris Peace Conference on behalf of the British Treasury, believed that the reparations would effectively ruin Germany's economy and, frustrated, left the conference. Over two months that summer, Keynes penned *The Economic Consequences of the Peace*, which argued that the punitive stance taken by the Allied powers over Germany's involvement in the war would lay the groundwork for a future European conflict. Twenty years later, a re-militarized Germany under the leadership of Adolf Hitler and the Nazi party would prove Keynes's cautionary warning correct. Using the language of German racial purity and the need for a greater Germany, Hitler's Nazi party abrogated the *Treaty of Versailles*, rearmed the country, and began occupying extra-German territory to provide for German settlers in the east. This vision was inspired by the term *lebensraum* or "living space/habitat" first coined by the German ethnologist and geographer Friedrich Ratzel in 1897. Though Ratzel's concept did not overtly suggest violent colonization, it did instill in the German leadership both before World War I and leading up to World War II a notion that a people is an organism in need of expansion, and therefore in need of greater resources such as land (Ham 2013: 55–57). In this sense, Hitler was not the first to argue for colonization; previous German leaders, steeped in the discourse of social Darwinism, also discussed the need for German imperial expansion. Consider the following passage that surfaced in 1911 by German General Friedrich von Bernhardi: "Without war, inferior or decaying races would easily choke the growth of healthy budding elements, and a universal decadence would follow. . . . Since almost every part of the globe is inhabited, new territory must, as a rule, be obtained at the cost of its possessors—that is today, by conquest, which thus becomes a law of necessity" (cited in Ham 2013: 162).

The main difference with Hitler and previous German leadership was that Hitler believed that *lebensraum* could not be accomplished outside of Europe. Colonization and agricultural settlements for German peasants would have to take place in the east. In his speech in Dusseldorf at the Industry Club on January 27, 1933, Hitler justified the need for German expansion by pointing to how other nations belonging to the "white race" had ruthlessly colonized other peoples by violent means. If an industrial Germany was not to disintegrate into class war, Hitler and the Nazi leadership believed it would have to expand beyond its territorial border in Europe and that this would require the mobilization of the "national instruments of violence" (Arendt 1979: 136). Hitler's rabid anti-communism and fear of class warfare led by communists not only helps to explain his fetish with national unity and racial purity—and all that entailed for political aesthetics—but also why he was appeased for so long by Britain. German Nazism and Russian Communism were to destroy themselves in an orgy of violence while the rest of the world looked on (Engdahl 2004: 81). At first, Hitler and Stalin had other plans. The two nations had agreed to territorially divide much of Eastern Europe to create their own spheres of influence in the region under the Molotov–Ribbentrop Pact of

1939. But Hitler was duplicitous and desired the western part of Russia for the resettlement of German farmers, agricultural riches, the oil of the Caucasus, and a Slavic laboring force to help produce for the war effort (Rich 1973: 204ff). Under Operation Barbarossa, Hitler's war machine invaded the Soviet Union, effectively rescinding the non-aggression pact that had been signed between the two nations in 1939. The Soviet Union would now join Britain and France (who had already declared war after Poland was invaded on September 1, 1939) in fighting the Axis powers. Over the course of the next five years, another tragedy would unfold in the total war of World War II. At least fifty million people would lose their lives by munitions, gas, or starvation, and millions more were wounded and psychologically scared. The total cost of the war, excluding the Soviet Union's, is put at US$400 billion by Michie (2006: 5) or in inflation-adjusted dollars in 2017, about US$5.4 trillion. As in World War I, the war caused national debts to balloon. Differential accumulation during this period, as it had been in the past, was intimately tied to the political violence called forth by rulers in their quest for power. For instance, in the United States, the "national" debt increased from US$41 billion to US$241 billion by the end of the war.[2] In the United Kingdom, the "national" debt went from £7.1 billion in 1939 to £21.1 billion in 1945 (Michie 2006: 209). Once again, the state and its capacity for organized violence was the largest capitalized entity on the planet and, as goes without saying, the debts were unequally owned and owed to the few. But it was spending in another dimension that would profoundly alter the security of the whole world.

In 1939, the world's most famous physicist, Albert Einstein, a German national who immigrated to the United States after Hitler came to power in 1933, was encouraged by his friend and fellow physicist, Leo Szilard, to send a letter to then-president Roosevelt warning him of "extremely powerful bombs of a new type."[3] Though there were precursors leading up to the discovery of nuclear fission, in 1938 two German scientists discovered that a mass burst of energy could be released from uranium. Under the Nazis, German scientists were likely to continue experimenting with uranium with the possibility of building a devastating type of new bomb with the capacity to release a tremendous amount of energy and thus be able to destroy entire city centers. Though hesitant at first, after the Japanese attacked Pearl Harbor on December 7, 1941, Roosevelt decided to put considerable resources into funding the development of nuclear weapons in partnership with the United Kingdom and Canada, the former country already having a fairly developed nuclear program. Dubbed the Manhattan Project, the quest to find the ultimate weapon employed tens of thousands of men and women—most of whom did not know precisely what they were working on—and cost US$27 billion in 2017 inflation-adjusted dollars. By all accounts, the Manhattan Project, under the direction of Major General Leslie Groves of the Army Corps of

Engineers, was one of the largest-scale industrial enterprises in human history. By July 16, 1945, a bomb similar to the one that would be detonated over Nagasaki, Japan, a month later was tested in Jornada del Muerto desert in New Mexico. The test was called Trinity after the sixteenth-century English poet John Donne. The test was a success and its observers realized that the world would never be the same again. It now became theoretically, and later practically possible, to annihilate virtually all life on the earth. Upon being interviewed after the Trinity test, J. Robert Oppenheimer, the nuclear physicist responsible for the bomb's design, somberly quoted the *Bhagavad Gita*'s verse "I am become death, the destroyer of world's." As yet, the "extremely powerful bombs" were not detonated on a human population, but by August 1945 two separate bombs would be dropped on the Japanese cities of Hiroshima (August 6th) and Nagasaki (August 9th).

In the literature, the decision to use nuclear bombs on Japanese cities remains controversial (Ham 2014). Originally, the most common argument was that President Truman decided to use the bomb to save American lives. In this view, without the use of the atomic bomb, American soldiers who would have had to invade mainland Japan to force its surrender from an obstinate Army Group bent on continuing the war were spared a violent death. However, current scholarship views the bombings of Hiroshima and Nagasaki as militarily unnecessary and therefore a political and strategic choice of American leadership at the time. Those who hold to this view argue that the bombing was largely about displaying American power to Soviet Russia, increasing the diplomatic hand of the United States in Europe and the Far East, and ultimately keeping Russia out of Manchuria (Alperovitz et al. 1991–1992: 212). The vast majority of the over hundred thousand killed either in the initial bombing or from radiation poisoning or sickness and starvation in both cities were civilian. Given that the results of the bombings were observed by American scientists, it is also likely that American leadership, was, in part, motivated to drop the bombs on a human population to observe and record their effects. It should be recalled that while human deaths and casualties were certainly anticipated in the bombing of Hiroshima and Nagasaki, up until August 6th and 9th, no nuclear bombs had been detonated on a human society. Hiroshima and Nagasaki gave scientists a chance to see the devastation that could be wrought on humans and their built environments by the new bombs.

Though nuclear weapons have not been used on a human population since 1945, the decimation of populations and cities had a world-changing impact on both the nature of global politics and our understanding of security during what came to be known as the Cold War (1945–1991). Not long after Hiroshima and Nagasaki, the Soviet Union's leadership would advance the need for their own nuclear bomb, arguably for national defense against the capitalist powers of the West. Indeed, the West had tried to crush the Russian Revolution of 1917 in its infancy but, despite the tremendous amount of bloodshed, their intervention was to no avail. As a counterweight to the power of the United States, the unquestionable leading capitalist power after 1945, the Soviets developed their own nuclear weaponry and by August 1949—four years after the Japanese bombings—were testing their first nuclear device: First Lightening. As is well documented in the literature, this not only set off a major arms race between the United States, the Soviet Union, and other peripheral powers but also implicated the world in the possibility of nuclear extinction (Mahnken et al. 2016). To deter this possibility, theoreticians of nuclear war spoke of achieving mutually assured destruction—a situation where both an aggressor and a defender would have the capacity to annihilate each other. Foucault encapsulates this profound change in human affairs: "For millennia, man remained was he was for Aristotle: a living animal with the additional capacity for political existence; modern man is an animal whose politics calls his existence as a living being into question" (1978: 143). The power of American capitalism and differential accumulation versus Soviet communism and central planning was now intimately tied to the most destructive weapons ever invented. Both American capitalism and Soviet communism, by necessity and for different reasons, were evangelical faiths and, like all proselytizing faiths, sacrifices had to be made. But unlike the century's long bloodshed of religious wars, during the Cold War, the entirety of the human race hung in the balance between these two opposed forces.

But while the arms race of the Cold War is largely common knowledge, what might be underappreciated is how the capacity to annihilate the entire species has been capitalized by investors in armament firms. Those purchasing state bonds of the largest militarized countries in the world are certainly capitalizing the power of the state to make war and collect taxes, but we must remember that they also have their counterparts in private industry when firms who receive government contracts for nuclear weapons or their maintenance are capitalized by investors. Consider that while exact figures have never been publicly recorded, one audit of all spending on nuclear weapons, their platforms, maintenance, research and development, and waste disposal amounted to US$9 trillion from 1940 to 1996 (in 2017 dollars) (Shwartz 1998). To the best of our estimates, many more hundreds of billions have been spent since 1996 by both governments and financial institutions in the nuclear industry. What this suggests is that total *international* spending on the nuclear-industrial complex is far higher than a mere look at the United States where we have somewhat reliable figures. While some states (e.g., China and Russia) use state agencies to produce and maintain their nuclear arsenals), in the United States, France, the United Kingdom, and India, publicly listed companies are the main manufacturers and overseers of nuclear bombs and related equipment/facilities. It is impossible to tell exactly how much money is funneled yearly to defense contractors for the explicit purpose of nuclear weapons, but we can be sure a significant portion of public and private finance makes its way into the corporate coffers of defense contractors. For instance, the non governmental organization PAX and the International Campaign to Ban Nuclear Weapons (ICAN) were able to identify twenty-seven companies involved in the production, maintenance, and modernization of nuclear weapons in its 2016 report.[4] Moreover, the report found that "390 banks, insurance companies, pension funds and asset managers from 26 countries were found that invest significantly in the nuclear weapon industry" (PAX and INCAN 2016: 6). From 2013 to 2016 the report found that US$498 billion was invested by these companies who "assisted with share and bond issuances, owned or managed shares and bonds or had outstanding loans to nuclear weapon producing companies" (PAX and INCAN 2016: 6). In comparison, only eighteen financial institutions found in the report preclude investing in the nuclear weapons industry. While the companies listed in the report do not *exclusively* produce, maintain, or modernize nuclear weaponry, insofar as they are receiving government contracts to provide products related to nuclear weapons, their earnings and therefore capitalization depend, at least in part, on the continuing possibility of nuclear conflict and, in some senses, nuclear deterrence. The latter may be true should investors believe that the stockpiling and spread of nuclear weapons is actually a force for peace as has been argued by Kenneth Waltz (1981). Yet to others, such as PAX and INCAN, it seems absurd that more nuclear weapons make us safer as a community of nations. Whatever the truth may turn out to be, it is clear that one of the tragic contradictory legacies of World War II is the capitalization of the ability to annihilate the species when if indeed a nuclear war ever took place, investors would likely have a difficult time collecting their profits.

THE PERSISTENCE OF CAPITALIST MILITARISM

One of the most striking contradictions between the logic of livelihood and the logic of differential accumulation is undoubtedly to be found in the persistence of industrial militarism born in the hothouse of European geopolitics and a thirst for money and empire among the European ruling classes. We have no definite figures of total war spending throughout history, but we can be sure that the figure is in the trillions of US dollars—to use just one standard measure of account. We can only imagine what might have been had that money been used to ameliorate all life on the planet. Here we are reminded of Orwell's claim in *1984* that warfare between the ruling classes of different centralized political communities is primarily about inculcating nationalism and international hatred toward foreigners in order to maintain the hierarchical order that privileges the few at the top of the hierarchy. Orwell presumed that had resources been used for social purposes rather than permanent war and the preparation for war, the masses would be made too comfortable, would therefore have time to reflect on questions of political and social importance, and ultimately come to question the usefulness of a hierarchical social and economic order. To be sure, *1984* is a work of fiction, but there is some considerable truth to Orwell's hypothesis if we think about the fact that nationalist jingoism—often couched in terms of race as we have discussed—was a product of ruling elites and the fact that organized political violence is deployed by political leaders rather than ordinary men and women concerned with a logic of livelihood and social reproduction. Major General Smedley Butler (1881–1940), the most decorated Marine in US history at the time of his death, argued that while the potential for warfare among human groups may not be completely unavoidable, organized political violence could be mitigated. He offered three proposals to lessen the chances of war. First, he suggested that armed forces should primarily be organized for national defense and should avoid provocative maneuvers that would antagonize foreign nations. Second, he argued that the corporate chieftains of the arms industry should earn a salary equivalent to the soldiers risking their lives on the battlefield for the duration of the war. Third, Butler contended that the soldiers who would ultimately fight the war be given the right to vote on its merits. The leadership with a desire to mobilize the armed forces would be asked to present their rationale for war to the rank and file. If the reasons for conflict were found to be insufficient, wrongheaded, or not in the interests of national security, the soldiers could vote to stay put; if the reasons were valid, they would mobilize.[5] To this day Butler's proposals have been ignored and the power to wage war largely remains in the hands of those who are unwilling to risk their lives in battle. Indeed, as the historian Paul Ham has noted in his study of World War I, "wars are decided, usually by small groups of elderly, powerful men, and not by God or Darwin or some sort of 'ism', such as national or patriotism" (2014: 81). This is the great escape of capitalist leadership. Before the emergence of the modern liberal-capitalist state, any sovereign who wanted to declare war not only had to finance their belligerence but also fought in battle, risking their own lives along with the future of their kingdoms. Not so today. Those most often clamoring for war and their intellectual cheerleaders keep their geographical distance from the risk of death on the battlefield. It would seem today that it is much easier to declare war when there is zero chance of putting one's own life on the line. Perhaps Butler should have also suggested that those with the power to declare war should be at the frontlines prepared to die for their belief in violence as a means to resolving conflict. The absentee owners of today's modern corporations have their counterparts in modern-day politics when it comes to war—the absentee politicians—who have the power to declare war and at the same time the power to avoid fighting in them directly.

Before we consider some of the most prominent explanations for the persistence of capitalist militarism it would be good to have an idea of the scale of military spending. The Stockholm International Peace Research Institute, or SIPRI, has kept data since 1949 on world military spending. Although there are gaps in the data for particular countries and for particular years, it is the most comprehensive database we have on military spending. From 1950 to 2016, total worldwide military expenditure was just over US$66 trillion in constant 2015 dollars, an increase of 647 percent. Figure 3.1 charts the overall increase in military spending from 1950 as five-year moving averages. What immediately becomes apparent from the chart is the decline of military spending by 22 percent from 1990 to 2000. The main reason for this downward trend is likely the end of the Cold War. In fact, many commentators throughout the 1990s argued that with the transition to capitalism under way in the former USSR, military spending would give way to a "peace dividend" that would be broadly shared among the populace. From the data in the chart, the events of 9/11 appears to have quashed any notion of a peace dividend as world military spending increased by 59 percent from 2001 to 2016.

During this period of the so-called War on Terror, ushered in by the Bush administration and its allies after the devastation of the attacks on

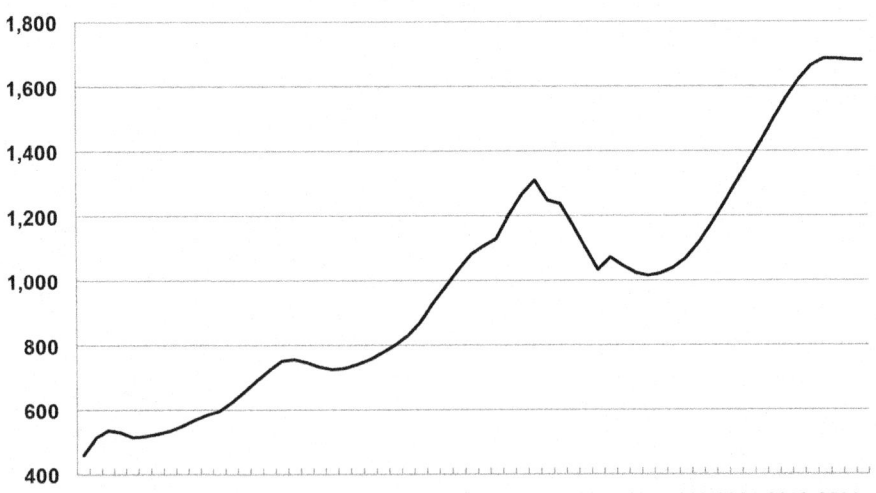

Figure 3.1 World Military Spending 1949–2014 SIPRI

September 11, 2001, total global military spending was just slightly under US$24 trillion in constant 2015 dollars with the United States accounting for just over US$10 trillion of that figure. Over the same period, the profits of the top 100 arms manufacturers tracked by the SIPRI Arms Industry Database also increased tremendously as shown in figure 3.2. Total profit across these companies for the period was US$806 billion. What also stands out from the chart is that even though there was a decline in profitability from 2014 to 2015, from 2002 to 2015, profit increased by 91 percent. If we take the height of profitability in 2012, then the increase for the period is an astounding 276 percent.

According to SIPRI's Arms Transfer Database, the financial value of the arms trade also increased over the so-called War on Terror period. From 2001 to 2014, the financial value of total world arms exports was US$882 billion. Despite some peaks and troughs, the value of arms exports increased by 43 percent over the period with a giant 114 percent increase from 2001 to 2006 during the opening years of the Bush administration's foray into Afghanistan and Iraq. The United States, Russia, France, and the United Kingdom make up the overwhelming majority of the weapons sales to foreign countries.

As a whole, what these figures reveal is the persistence of global militarism. As a species, we have been diverting many of our resources—human, financial, scientific, and technological—to the means of destruction rather than the means of livelihood with the grand perversion being that many of the technological developments that actually enhance life would not have happened without research and development for war. In this light, it behooves us to ask why militarism—rather than war per se—is so persistent. Another way of putting this in an era where we have such destructive potential is the

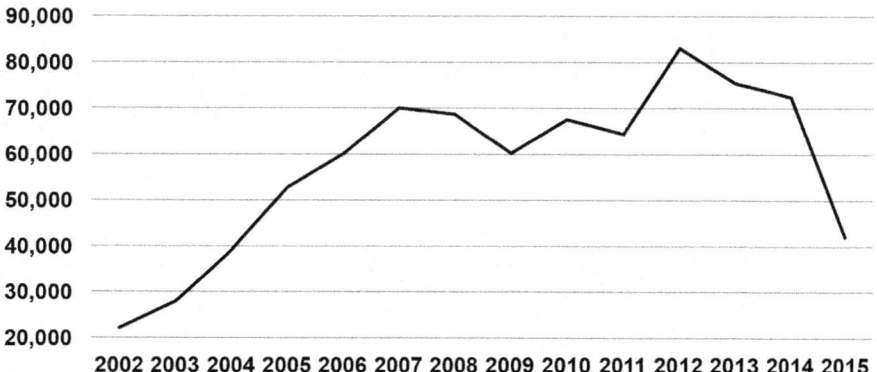

Figure 3.2 Net Profit of the 100 Largest Arms Manufacturers

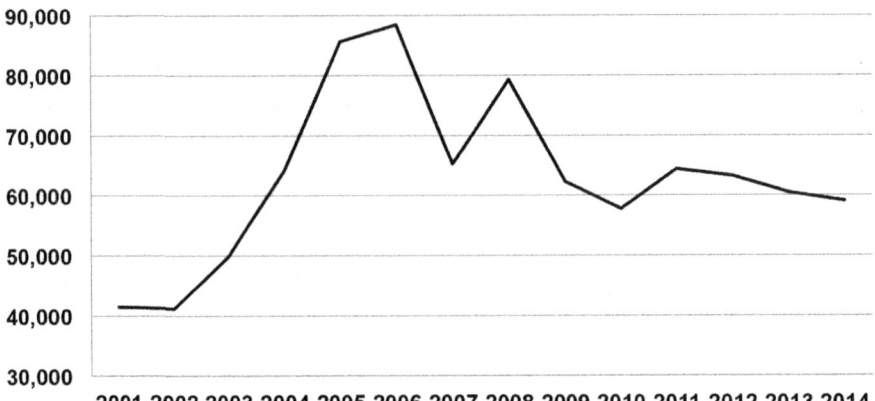

Figure 3.3 Total Value of Global Arms Exports, 2001–2014 (in million US$ constant 2014 prices)

following: "This brings us to one of the central paradoxes of the age. If war is such an unsavory proposition, how can it be that weapons—at once the tools of its prosecution and the prime cause of its present relative futility—retain such a remarkable allure to even the most unlikely nations?" (O'Connell 1989: 4). Three major reasons immediately present themselves. First, the world's territorial division into separate nation states and the entrenched belief among elites and some portion of the public that existential danger exists outside the political community has been put forward by neorealists as the leading cause for war and its preparation (Waltz 1998). Their proposition, endlessly repeated in mainstream international relations theory, is that world order is constituted by anarchy where there is no world government to keep national leaders from going to war if they so please. This is the politics of the constant suspicion and distrust of others rooted in anarchical interpretations of international order. In this existential condition, it would be irresponsible and grossly negligent for national leaders to forgo military preparation since weapons not only allow states to pursue their national interests but they are necessary for national defense. This is the tragedy of the arms race in international relations: the search for security through the militarization of one state leads other national political leaders to militarize their own political communities rendering everyone less secure as more powerful and deadly weapons are produced. If this theory is an accurate assessment of international affairs, then war and the preparation for war can be overcome only by some form of world government that removes the condition of existential anarchy. The major difficulty here, of course, is convincing national leaders—particularly from powerful countries—that a world government is not only feasible but also necessary. And unlike Wendt's (2003) argument that a world state is the next natural progression in human evolution, such a prospect is very far from inevitable.

Another possible reason for the persistence of militarism is institutional path-dependence. As we have seen from the statistics previously, the largest armament firms tracked by SIPRI are for-profit companies whose earnings depend on shaping the terrain of social reproduction in relation to identifying threats, researching and developing new weapons and weapons systems, and garnering public contracts for military hardware, consulting, or military and intelligence services. A world without major threats would mean a world with plummeting earnings for the major arms manufacturers and thus a drastic fall in their overall capitalization. On the other hand, the threat or the perceived threat of future conflict ensures that government contracts continue to be on offer and that corporate earnings are forthcoming. For instance, while the chances of being killed by a terrorist are about the same as being struck by lightning or drowning in a toilet, US government spending on the so-called War on Terror (not total defense spending) from 2001 to 2018 is just over US\$2 trillion (Mueller 2009).[6] And as I have previously demonstrated in *Carbon Capitalism*, the *average* increase in the capitalization of the five leading defense firms by market capitalization in the United States increased by 234 percent—not a bad return considering that the average return on investment for the benchmark S&P 500 was about 7 percent throughout the same period (2001–2014) (Di Muzio 2015b: 136). But if arms companies and their investors have an unmistakable interest in the constancy of militarism, there are two other constituencies that may also be considered to have entrenched self-interests in militarism. The first are political leaders dependent upon local voters. Since armament firms provide jobs for local constituents, disparaging or denigrating the arms corporations providing employment and supporting the local community could be political suicide. Moreover, as is well known in the case of the United States, and likely elsewhere, there is a "revolving door" between those who work in government as legislators or for the military and the corporate universe—arms corporations but also the Institutional major holders of armament firms, lobbyist organizations, and consultancy firms.[7] Workers or unions within the armament industry also have an interest in maintaining the status quo of militarism. According to SIPRI, tens of thousands of people work for what can be called the "defense industry" and their livelihoods are largely contingent on the contracts arms firms obtain from governments—both domestic and foreign. The second constituency is the military bureaucracy, generally interested in new weaponry, winning wars, and for those in strategic positions, obtaining promotions, prestige, and quite often employment in the private sector. If the self-interest of this unholy trinity of corporations (profit), politicians, and workers (getting elected, jobs) and the military bureaucracy (prestige and better weapons and compensation) is the main reason for the persistence of militarism, then it is difficult to see how their self-interest and the path-dependence of their institutional roles can be overcome without significant interruption in the nexus of their relations. The interconnectedness of these three constituencies seems to propel the need for the permanent preparation for war and a waste of resources from the point of view of the logic of livelihood (Duncan and Coyne 2013; Melman 1970, 1974, 1997).

A third reason for the persistence of militarism is for the ruling classes of leading nations to maintain their supremacy over the constitution and reconstitution of world order. In this view, the ability to project overwhelming force is understood to be a good in and of itself. For example, the maintenance of military superiority has been a chief goal of US grand strategy since its inception in the post–World War II era. In NSC-68 (1950), widely interpreted as one of the foundational documents of US grand strategy, its principal author and high-ranking government official, Paul Nitze (1907–2004), argued the need for an accelerated exploitation of scientific potential to expand the technological superiority of the United States and the "free world." This rapid buildup of military force was deemed essential by Nitze to combat the nefarious ambitions of the Kremlin, enforce US foreign policy objectives, and defend allies against potential Soviet invasion. And despite the fact that there is no longer a Soviet or communist threat, military research and development projects since World War II have endured. As Demchak notes, while military modernization was delayed by the Vietnam War, by the late 1970s modernization projects increased dramatically (1991: 41–62). While much of this research and development is classified and hidden in black budgets, the aims are certainly to maintain an unequal balance of lethal force. This original post–World War II position of unparalleled supremacy was reinforced in a US Space Command document called *Vision 2020* that argued for "full spectrum dominance" or the ability of the United States to protect its national interests from land, sea, air, and space as globalization continues to widen the gap between the "have and have nots" (Gill in Gill and Bakker 2003: 214–5). The desire to maintain military supremacy also helps to explain why the US government spends more on "national defense" than its counterparts. For example, in 2017, the government spent US$611 billion, more than the next eight leading military spenders combined: China, Russia, Saudi Arabia, India, France, the United Kingdom, Japan, and Germany—US$595 billion.[8]

While the reasons outlined previously for the persistence of capitalist militarism are not mutually exclusive, and each explanation has some ring of truth to it, what is perhaps most worrisome is that global militarization continues apace in a world where resources could be better spent on social causes. It seems strange that at the same time that global military spending is increasing, the world's leaders have agreed to seventeen Sustainable Development

Goals that, collectively, are supposed to end extreme poverty in the world. The most recent estimate of the financial cost of the goals is US$1.4 trillion a year, about US$200 billion less than current global military spending and about 1.8 percent of the world's gross domestic product.[9] Whether the world will achieve the Sustainable Development Goals is an open question, but that there can be money to do so is not. Should the project fail, there will perhaps be no more stark illustration of the contradiction between the logic of a militarized differential accumulation and the logic of actually improving human lives.

NOTES

1 Mathew White has aggregated and compared the known statistics on the casualties of World War I. http://necrometrics.com/20c5m.htm (accessed 6/21/2017).

2 Matt Phillips 'The Long Story of U.S. Debt, From 1790 to 2011, in 1 Little Chart' The Atlantic, November 13th, 2012. https://www.theatlantic.com/business/archive/2012/11/the-long-story-of-us-debt-from-1790-to-2011-in-1-little-chart/265185/(accessed 6/26/2017).

3 Atomic Heritage Foundation, 'Einstein-Szilard Letter'. http://www.atomicheritage.org/key-documents/einstein-szilard-letter (accessed 6/26/2017).

4 International Campaign to Abolish Nuclear Weapons (2016) Don't Bank of the Bomb: A Global Report on the Financing of Nuclear Weapons Producers. http://www.dontbankonthebomb.com/wp-content/uploads/2016/12/2016_Report_final.pdf (accessed 6/27/2017).

5 Smedley Butler (1935) "War as a Racket." https://www.ratical.org/ratville/CAH/warisaracket.html (accessed 6/21/2017)

6 Kimberly Amadeo 'War on Terror Facts, Costs and Timeline' The Balance, August 10, 2017. https://www.thebalance.com/war-on-terror-facts-costs-timeline-3306300 (accessed 6/22/2017).

7 Center for Responsive Politics, Revolving Door. https://www.opensecrets.org/revolving/ (accessed 6/22/2017).

8 Peter G. Peterson Foundation 'US Defense Spending Compared to Other Countries' June 1, 2017. http://www.pgpf.org/chart-archive/0053_defense-comparison (6/23/2017).

9 Guido Schmidt Traub (2015) 'Investment Needs to Achieve the Sustainable Development Goals' Sustainable Development Solutions Network. http://unsdsn.org/wp-content/uploads/2015/09/151112-SDG-Financing-Needs.pdf (6/23/2017).

Act IV

Corporate Capitalism

In this act, we discuss the socio-legal transformation in ownership structure that developed with the rise of the corporation and the increasing concentration of power and ownership. We will also discuss the capitalization process and how this is related to a firm's ability to exert power over an entire social field to generate greater future earnings—the ultimate aim of capitalism and evidence of broad social power and increasing inequality (Credit Suisse 2015; Nitzan and Bichler 2009). We will see that while capitalization as an act of investment to earn a future flow of income has been part of elite strategies of accumulation for centuries if not millennia, with the rise of the modern corporation, investors confronted the problem of valuation. We will consider two earlier ways of valuing corporations before arriving at the current capitalization model of valuation at the heart of global capitalism. The act then moves to assess the scholarly debates on whether the corporation arose because of greater productivity and the reduction of transaction costs as mainstream economists presume or whether the corporate form arose for reasons of control, power, and profit. Part of this assessment means addressing Veblen's idea of sabotage and an explanation for this process rooted in the cost-plus accounting of capitalism. The curtain then opens up on the very special power of commercial banks to create money as debt owed to its owner/investors. This tremendous power has been vastly understudied, too often ignored, and has important consequences for political possibilities now and in the future. In the penultimate section of Act IV we consider two major routes to differential accumulation: stagflation and mergers and acquisitions. The act concludes by asking whether the analogy between a psychopath and a corporation is convincing, and, if so, how far and in what ways.

ABSENTEE OWNERSHIP AND CAPITALIZATION

The origins of what I have called the "ownership revolution" are notoriously obscure, but in general we could argue that there are two predominant and contradictory theories on the origins of ownership: one based on *tacit consent*, and the other based on *forceful seizure*. The first is best represented by the English philosopher John Locke (1632–1704), who tried to make the argument that private ownership was the result of an isolated individual mixing his labor (itself a property owned by the individual) with the natural world. As long as this individual does not engross too much of the natural world to himself and does not allow property to spoil, Locke argues that the community tacitly consents to the institution of exclusive ownership. But Locke confronts a problem—he has to explain why there is such a disparity of property ownership. His answer is that once money becomes prevalent in an economy and the community agrees to its use as a general medium of circulation, it becomes possible for men to accumulate it disproportionately. Since money represents the power to command goods and services and certain portions of the natural world that have been commodified (e.g., land, mines), the unequal accumulation and ownership of money naturally translates into the unequal ownership of property. At the heart of Locke's explanation for money, then, is tacit consent (Di Muzio 2015a: 166–72). We should recall here that Locke's explanation does not rely on real historical events—however interpreted—but abstract and philosophical suppositions about what "likely happened." Had Locke actually bothered to consult the history of his seventeenth-century England, he would have found conquest more telling for the origin of ownership than consent.

The alternative theory of the origins of ownership is best represented by a more critical tradition of political economy thinking that is perhaps best represented by Thorstein Veblen (1857–1929) and, as we have discussed earlier, Karl Marx (1818–1883). Here I will focus on Veblen because his account of ownership goes deeper than Marx's explanation, which is largely rooted in the English countryside where direct producers are expropriated from their customary tenures in waves of enclosures from at least the fourteenth century and stretches through the international community through colonialism, murder, and dispossession. For Veblen (1964), the origins of ownership lie in the capture and control of women, or the marriage-ownership relation. Veblen argues that the concept of ownership is primarily a relation based on seizure, and it cannot be a relation between an owner and an inanimate object first. This is because physical objects are conceived as an organic extension of an individual's personality, not as something lying outside his or her being. Even in predatory communities, Veblen contends, there was no individual ownership of "durable goods" because a seized booty was either for general or of personal use. In the former, the goods are used and consumed by the group, while in the latter case, the good merely becomes an organic extension of the person using it. The case is different with the seizure of persons. Veblen suggests that the capture of women introduced the concept of ownership to humanity because captive women were perceived as trophies, making it "worthwhile for their captor to trace and keep in evidence his relation to them as their captor" (1964: 47). This relation is not organic, an extension of the individual's personality, but a relation of discretionary power of the use and abuse of another human being. Only then, Veblen speculates, can the institution of ownership be extended to encompass other "consumable goods" (Veblen 1964: 48). Thus, according to Veblen, it is not Lockean individual production that secures property and the right of exclusion but the power and eventually the customary right over the use and abuse of another human being that represents *the nascent stage of ownership*. Whether Veblen's analysis is historically accurate can never be known with precise certainty, but it is a far more plausible theory than Locke's given what we know about the relationship between property ownership, force, and the direct seizure of people and territory in human history. There are countless examples, but let us consider one of the most notorious: the Norman Conquest of England in 1066. In the *Domesday Book*, we have detailed records of how property was expropriated from the English and granted to William and his family, his conquering Normans from France and religious authorities after the Battle of Hastings (Garnett 2009). Though William argued that he was heir to a throne, the Anglo-Saxons and their slaughtered King Harold thought otherwise: William took possession of England by violent conquest. Leading up to and during the English Civil War (1642–1651) this is precisely what a number of subaltern social forces will uphold and argue: that there was indeed a conquest in 1066 and that ever since that time, the common people of England have been oppressed by a sovereign authority that originated from Normandy. The original conquest and the institutional oppression that has occurred since the original colonization became the justification for the rebellion against royal power. The position of sovereign authority mirrored those of its detractors: that indeed there was a conquest but that regents had the right to rule by virtue of their victorious defeat over weaker social forces. In other words, the domination of subjects by the monarchy, its usurpation of property, and its political rule over English territory are justified by the superior violence used in 1066 (Foucault 2003: 100ff). We can continue with examples of property being both made and gained by force, but it may be enough here to simply state that the "might is right" doctrine was deeply entrenched in western European thought as it colonized much of the New World. While the principle of "might is right" may stretch back into the deep human past, by the sixteenth century in Europe the right of conquest was recognized in nascent international law. As noted by Korman, "the right on conquest may be defined as the right of the victor, in virtue of military victory or conquest, to sovereignty over the conquered territory and its inhabitants" (2003: 7). As long as the territory is in the effective possession of the conqueror, title by conquest can be granted. Effective possession meant at least three things according to Korman (2003: 8): (1) "the complete extinction of the political existence of the conquered state," (2) when the conquered state cedes its territory to the conqueror as in a peace treaty, and (3) when the subjugated are unwilling or unable to militarily fight back against a conquering force. As Korman's work makes clear, it was only in the twentieth century when the right of conquest or what is the same—the right to colonization—became the crime of a war of aggression in the Nuremberg Principles adopted by the International Law Commission of the United Nations in 1950. Thus, it would seem that there is far more evidence for ownership and exclusion emerging out of violence and force rather than the tacit consent proposed by John Locke. But while it is interesting to think about the historical origins of the institution of ownership, it is the transformation in the structure of ownership that interests us here.

Before the rise of the modern corporation and absentee ownership, the regulation and supervision of a business concern was largely overseen by sole proprietors or general partnerships with unlimited liability. Under these ownership structures the owners of businesses were legally liable for all debts incurred by the business and courts could seize the personal wealth or assets of the owners in order to settle debts, be they to creditors or suppliers. Moreover, the proprietor or the working business partners of a concern were generally identified with their product within the community and therefore as a rule took pride in their products (shoddy products would bring shame upon the family name), often knew their suppliers and customers personally, and, if they did not produce the commodities or services by their own hands, oversaw and directed the work of hired labor (Veblen 1923: 55). As noticed by Veblen at the turn of the twentieth century, one of the key features of the emergence of the modern corporation is that its owners are mostly absentee in that they have little or nothing to do with the day-to-day running of the business. This does not mean that there are exceptions from time to time, for example Mark Zuckerberg, a cofounder of Facebook and a major holder of Facebook stock, still works as the chief executive officer of the company. But the vast majority of investors in Facebook, from Bono to Jim Breyer, have nothing to do with the daily operations of the company; they are absentee owners. Veblen defined absentee ownership as "the ownership of means in excess of what the owner can make use of, personally and without help" (1923: 12). What this means is that investor or owners are not tied to any one corporation but can come to own or invest in many income-generating firms.

Another way of putting it might be to say that the ownership of corporations now occurs at a distance. But how does absentee ownership come about? Why do owners retreat into the shadows, having little or nothing to do with the daily operations of the firms they, in part, own? Veblen suggested that absentee ownership was a gradual process and corresponds to the growth or extension of the industrial arts. With the extension of industry, Veblen argued that owners must become more calculating in order to turn a profit. In this way, owners must be primarily concerned with accountancy and numbers rather than production per se. The ability to hire workers to fulfill the daily tasks of the firm permits the owner to accomplish this feat of retreat. Eventually, Veblen claims, not only does the owner of the firm retreat from the daily activities of the firm but more to the point—stands outside it and directs it as though it was an instrument wholly and completely utilized to garner profit.

While earlier forms of business ownership mentioned previously are still in existence today, other than states, the most dominant institution in the modern business and social landscape is the modern corporation or what Veblen called "the master institution of civilized life" (1923: 86; see also Korten 2005). Put differently, if nation states can be considered the dominant form of political community in capitalist modernity, the modern corporation with limited liability for its investors is the dominant form of economic arrangement in political modernity. The legal concept of limited liability, first appearing in the United States and the United Kingdom in the nineteenth century, was a crucial invention for the development of the corporate form since it shielded the personal wealth and assets of investors from the claims of creditors, an incredible power for investors whose only risk was their equity stake in the company. We will discuss both mainstream and critical accounts for the rise of the modern corporation and absentee ownership in the next section, but for now we need to focus on some of the accountancy and legal transformations that put capitalization and differential accumulation as a social practice of a minority on a more solid footing.

As we have discussed in the beginning of this book, capitalization can be understood in two interrelated ways: (1) the total market value of a corporation calculated by the value of one share multiplied by all outstanding shares and/or (2) the act of investing by discounting to present value a future flow of income adjusted by some factor of risk. While we know that the practice of investment has a long pedigree, Nitzan and Bichler (2009: 155–6) argue that the "first systematic rules of discounting" were developed by German foresters in the mid-nineteenth century—particularly Martin Faustmann. Faustmann and other foresters were trying to calculate the present value of rotated wooded land and in so doing "developed many of the mathematical formulae of present value" that became the essence of the capitalization formula (Nitzan and Bichler 2009: 156). According to Nitzan and Bichler, it was the

American economist Irving Fisher who would do the most to elevate the process of discounting from an imperfect and localized art to the dominant ritual of modern capitalism. What Fisher was trying to demonstrate in his most famous work was that all income-generating assets implied a discount or what is essentially the same, an interest rate. As Nitzan and Bichler explain:

> In other words, a pecuniary asset, taken in its most general form, is merely *a claim on earnings*. In this sense, bonds, corporate shares, preferred stocks, mortgages, bank accounts, personal loans, or the registered ownership of an apartment block are simply different incarnations of the same thing: they are all income-generating entities. As such, their price is nothing but the present value of the earnings they are expected to generate (2009: 156, emphasis original).

But basing the capitalization of a firm on its *potential future earnings* was originally a tough sell. The modern corporation was such a novel institution that valuing it was highly contested, particularly in the light of earlier models of valuation that were more settled in the minds of investors. As Krier's (2009) research shows, in the late eighteenth and into the nineteenth century, the hard-asset model was the most common way to value what were essentially quasi-public companies largely formed to fulfil infrastructure purposes such as building railroads or canals. This model of valuation saw investors pay for stock in the company at a certain price and the money handed over was recorded as capital in the accounts of the firm. If an investor bought stock worth US$100, this was assumed to be backed by US$100 worth of fixed capital or hard assets. It was also assumed that if corporate bonds were sold to investors—although debt instruments, not equity like stocks—these too were backed by physical assets. Corporations were understood to be fully capitalized if the total value of equity and debt outstanding was equal to the hard physical assets the company purchased and owned with the investments (e.g., property, plant, and equipment). If the value of the total outstanding monetary value of the company's stocks and bonds was over and above the value of the firm's assets, then the company was thought to be overcapitalized since a forced sale of the physical assets would not equal the value of stocks and bonds investors purchased (Krier 2009: 660–2). By the late nineteenth century, with the corporate revolution in full swing and stocks of many business concerns issued, the hard-asset model largely fell out of approval with investors in favor of a dividend pay-out model. In this model, stocks were effectively supposed to work like bonds, providing stockholders with a quarterly yield or dividend. In this model of valuation, investors cared less about corporate earnings per quarter as a going concern and more about the cash on hand at the corporation since available cash meant the ability to pay out regular dividends to stockholders (Krier 2009: 662–3). In this way, the value of the firm's capitalization (its market value) was largely contingent on the ability of corporate managers to pay consistent dividends. Though the capitalization model was gaining steam in the United States in the early twentieth century, by the 1970s, the capitalized earning capacity model began to demonstrate its dominance in the minds of global investors. Little known to the investors that would eventually come around to this model of valuation was that the courts in the United States had radically transformed the meaning of property, paving the path for conceiving of property as an expectation related to future exchange value. As John R. Commons argued in his study of law and the rise of capitalism, for about a century courts in the United States argued that property was title and possession over an object for one's own use within the bounds of the law. This understanding of property was upheld for decades until justices overturned it in the Rate Case of 1890 (*Chicago, Milwaukee & St. Paul Railway Company v. Minnesota*). Commons reflects upon this important majority decision:

> The majority, however, now held . . . that not merely physical things are objects of property, but the *expected earning power* of those things is property; and property is taken from the owners, not merely under the power of eminent domain which takes *title* and *possession*, but also under the police power which takes its *exchange-value*. To deprive the owners of the *exchange-value* of their property is equivalent to depriving them of their property. . . . This, too, is the business man's view of both his property and his capital. When the courts made the transition from ownership of things to ownership of the expected purchasing-power of things, they followed the practices of business. The 'assets and liabilities' of a business firm are but the present estimated exchange-values of its property and debts on expected markets. . . . The stocks and bonds of a corporation are evidences, not of ownership of the physical property, but of residual shares in the expected net income (1959: 16, 158, 169, emphasis original).

What this passage suggests is that while the capitalization model took a while before it was universally adopted, property at least in a juridical sense now meant "expected earning power" or the anticipated money to be received from transacting in the market while using one's property. The justices flew open the door to the capitalized earnings model of valuation. In this model the "estimation of corporate stock value is fundamentally linked to estimation of corporate profits," making the quarterly income statement (or profit and loss statement) of corporations the key document driving the valuation of modern corporations (Krier 2009: 663ff). The consequences of adopting this model of valuation were profound:

> The development of the "capitalized earnings" model of equity valuation was a momentous event that radically affected American capitalism. Unlike the

other two valuation models, the value of an equity security in terms of "future earning power" is nearly limitless. Currently, the highest valued large firms can be valued at more than 400 times their annual earnings. As long as the market believes that earnings will grow in the future, the value can rise without any easily defined limit. The value of equities under the other two valuation models is more limited and exhibits a definite ceiling. The development, implementation and diffusion of this model had a profound impact on financial accounting: the rise of the income statement as the focus of corporate reporting (Krier 2009: 664).

While Krier is right to point out that this model of valuation means that a corporation's market value can be a multiple of its net earnings for the year, it is unlikely that the capitalization of a firm would be 400 times its annual earnings. For example, the monetary value of Apple, the largest firm in the world by market capitalization, was eighteen times its earnings according to the *Financial Times* Global 500—a list of the 500 largest firms in the world by market capitalization. To take another example, Facebook's capitalization, again according to the same data set, is only sixty-two times its net income for 2014.[1] So while the figure of 400 times earnings may be an exaggeration, Krier is right to point out that the market value of firms measured by the total value of their outstanding shares is ultimately dependent upon quarterly corporate earnings and that capitalization is more often than not a greater multiple than earnings. But this model of valuation also has consequences for how firms are run and the workers employed in publicly listed corporations. The chief executives of the world's dominant capital are now partially compensated in highly lucrative stock options, a trend that accelerated in the 1990s. This makes executives far more interested in short-term earnings and cost-cutting than in long-term corporate planning (Henwood 1997: 267–8). As Krier (2009) and others have shown, this can have extremely negative impacts for workers and communities who are dependent on wages and salaries for their livelihoods. One of the costs executives can try to control is the cost of labor but in large industrial firms, this has typically been difficult to accomplish given high rates of unionization and the practice of collective bargaining that was largely the result of a social compact between governments, unions, and corporations after World War II. Automation combined with corporate lobbying to reduce tariff barriers and capital controls—making both capital and commodities more mobile across national borders—was a chief strategy used by corporate executives to discipline the working class, particularly in the heartland of global capitalism. What is more, after the fall of the Soviet Union and the opening of China to global capital flows, 1.3 billion more workers willing (or compelled) to work for low wages were added to the global labor force, putting pressure on higher-waged pockets of labor in advanced capitalist countries. Undoubtedly this contributed to the tragedy of unemployment and underemployment, the deindustrialization of traditional sectors of manufacture, a decline in unionism, urban decay (e.g., the rust belts of the United States, Canada, the United Kingdom, Australia, and Germany), and general social dislocation and a decrease in life opportunities and chances. This transformation in global capitalism corresponds with the change in corporate accounting toward a fetishism with corporate earnings as the chief *raison d'être* for evaluating corporate success. It demonstrates once again how numbers and the way we account for things as a society are never neutral. The shift to the capitalized earnings model not only transformed the spatial terrain of global capitalism but it also enriched corporate chieftains and investors at the expense of workers as data on income and wealth inequality demonstrate (Di Muzio 2015a). From 1990 to 2014, stock market capitalization in the United States alone soared from 58 percent of GDP to 146 percent of GDP, a percentage increase over the period of 152 percent.[2] One could also reasonably argue that this shift opened the door to more extreme forms of right-wing national politics that occlude this history and scapegoat foreigners for taking jobs, failing to assimilate properly, and leeching off the social system. As in the past, this is a worrisome trend since right-wing extremism is generally a politics of fear and bellowing widespread public anxiety can quickly degenerate into hatred and aggression toward groups that are blamed for unfavorable economic or political conditions. How these conditions will fare in the future is largely related to the essential reason for the corporation: efficiency or control?

EFFICIENCY OR CONTROL?

The dominant argument for the emergence of the corporation is that this form of organization is more efficient than its alternatives. This is the idea that the corporate form was somehow "naturally selected" out of the marketplace because its effectiveness prevailed over less efficient forms of organization (Roy 1997: 7). The logic is most forcefully stated by Coase (1937) and later echoed by Chandler (1977), who argued that the corporation exists because it is a technologically superior form of organization capable of reducing a multiplicity of transaction costs by coordinating in-house rather than through the market mechanism. This method of organization has the added benefit of increasing profitability in two main ways—first, by reducing costs, and second, by avoiding the uncertainty inherent in multiple contract making with suppliers. As identified by both Roy (1997) and Nitzan (2001) this argument has a number of flaws. First, as Roy suggests, "efficiency does not operate apart from other social processes like power" (1997: 9). Thus, making the claim that the corporation simply evolved because it is more efficient elides the historical power processes that helped to create the modern firm (Geisst 2000; Josephson 1934; Perrow 2002; Roy 1999). Second, as pointed out by Nitzan (2001: 239), marginal transaction costs are unobservable and therefore this terminology can be used to explain the size of any institution, making the theory irrefutable. In other words, the theory itself seems unverifiable since if a firm is a certain size, or eventually grows, it is by definition efficient since, according to Coase's logic, a firm would not knowingly choose to be smaller if it can increase efficiency by internalizing more transactions through growth or larger if it can turn to the market mechanism when an added transaction would threaten profits. Moreover, as pointed out by Nitzan (2009: 239–40) by Coase's own logic, it would seem that over time, firms would get smaller, not larger, since new technologies in communication and transportation costs have come down over time. Yet the reverse is true. Through waves of mergers and acquisitions, firms have gotten larger and larger. If these critiques were not enough, there is a confusion underlying the mainstream explanation of the rise of the corporation. As Nitzan (2001: 240) argued, what Coase and Chandler both fail to do in their analysis is make a conceptual distinction between a firm (which can own many businesses) and industry (those physical units used in the production of goods and services). Since a corporation is primarily a legal fiction, it can own many industrial units, which means there is no telling how large a firm might become. In the United States, the idea that a corporation could come to own other corporations was a legal decision tinged with power:

> The specific rights, entitlements, and obligations that the state enforces relative to objects is determined by the operation of power and embedded within institutions. Corporate lawyers were able to persuade the New Jersey legislature to change its corporate law to allow corporations to own stock in other corporations, *a right that had been previously denied to both partnerships and corporations and that, once granted, created the legal basis for the corporate revolution at the end of the century.* The New Jersey legislature was more compliant than other states because that state had long enjoyed a profitable relationship with railroad corporations. The choices it faced and the relative payoff of each differed from the situation faced by other states. The relationship among power, institution, and property was very reflexive and historical: early exercise of power institutionalized a set of property relationships that became the context within which power was exercised to embed new property relations within the institutional relations of corporate capital (Roy 1997: 15–16, emphasis added).

What this passage suggests is that far from the search for efficiency as a primary goal, the "corporate revolution" ushered in in the United States, and specifically New Jersey—which became the "home of the trusts"—was a matter of corporate power pushing for a major change in the legal infrastructure that policed property and ownership. The pursuit of power and wealth, not efficiency per se, should be considered the primary reason for the corporate revolution. Writing at the dawn of the modern corporation's rise, Thorstein Veblen was perhaps the most perceptive thinker on this point.

Veblen's social theory of capital accumulation and the absentee ownership of the business enterprise revolves around a dichotomous ontology. For Veblen, the materialist framework of society is divided into two distinct yet interlocking spheres of activity. First, he claimed that modern civilization is characterized by the industrial system, an interdependent sphere of activity that he associated with the machine, technology, creativity, and the community. Left to its own devices, the industrial system, Veblen argued, would be extremely productive and has the capacity to flood the world market with a diversity of goods and services (1904: 27). The livelihood of the community, then, is best served by an uninterrupted and balanced functioning of the industrial process. The second aspect of his binary ontology is the business enterprise, a sphere of activity and traffic that he associated with the *direction* and *control* of industry, monetary accumulation, property, and power (1904: 3).[3] The goal of the modern business enterprise:

> is not productive work, but profitable business. . . . It is a means of making money, not of making goods. The production of goods or services . . . is incidental to the making of money. . . . It is an incorporation of absentee ownership, wholly and obviously. Hence it is necessarily impersonal in all its contacts and dealings, whether with other business concerns or with the workmen employed in industry. It is a business concern only . . . and its aims are confined to results which can be brought into a balance-sheet in terms of net gain (Veblen 1904: 83, 85, 82).

Thus, absentee ownership, the relationship of owners to the firm, is twice removed from the daily operations of the corporation and the needs of the community. The end concern of business is the perpetual generation of money, not the advancement of human well-being and comfort. But in order to accomplish the accumulation of money Veblen argued that the business enterprise must use its organizational and strategic power to sabotage industry as a going concern:

> It is not possible, on sound business grounds, to let the industrial forces of the country go to work and produce what, in the physical sense, the country needs; because a free run of production would, it is believed, be ruinous for business; because it would lower prices and so reduce the net business gain below the danger point. . . . Hence what is conveniently called capitalistic sabotage or businesslike sabotage of industry (1904: 96).

Yet, while Veblen is correct in noting that sabotage is the regular and consistent practice of business, we must ask ourselves, why? For Veblen, "a free run of production" simply lowers prices, hence the logic of curtailing output and promoting unemployment when necessary. But there is a much deeper problem here noticed at length by Marx:

> Modern bourgeois society with its relations of production, of exchange and of property, a society that has conjured up such gigantic means of production and exchange, is like the sorcerer, who is no longer able to control the powers of the nether world whom he has called up by his spells. . . . It is enough to mention the commercial crises that by their periodical return put on its trial, each time more threateningly, the existence of the entire bourgeois society. In these crises a great part not only of the existing products, but also of the previously created productive forces, are periodically destroyed. *In these crises there breaks out an epidemic that, in all earlier epochs would have seemed an absurdity—the epidemic of over-production.* Society suddenly finds itself put back into a state of momentary barbarism; it appears as if a famine, a universal war of devastation had cut off the supply of the very means of subsistence; industry and commerce seem to be destroyed, and why? Because there is too much civilization, too much subsistence, too much industry, too much commerce. The productive forces at the disposal of society no longer tend to further the development of the conditions of bourgeois property; on the contrary, they have become too powerful for these conditions. . . . The conditions of bourgeois society are too narrow to comprise the wealth created by them. And how does the bourgeoisie get over these crises? On the one hand by enforced destruction of a mass of productive forces; on the other, by the conquest of new markets, and by the more thorough exploitation of the old ones (Marx in Morgan 1992: 1197, my emphasis).

Here, Marx argues that industry or the productive forces of society are in fact too productive for the accumulation process to proceed and reproduce itself without some form of calculated management. Too much production, as Veblen would also argue later, leads to a crisis of falling prices and narrower profit margins. But, unlike Veblen, Marx had a deeper understanding of why there must be "periodic crises." For Marx, the accumulation of capital is always undertaken within narrow conditions because of the social relation between capital and labor—*a relation that is differential from the very beginning*. These conditions compel the modern business enterprise to calculate. For Marx, these "narrow conditions" exist in the first instance, because one appropriates a surplus as profit while workers receive a wage. Overproduction for Marx means:

> nothing more than that too much has been produced for the purpose of enrichment, or that too great a part of the product is intended not for consumption as revenue, but for making more money (for accumulation): not to satisfy the personal needs of its owner, but to give him money, abstract social riches and

capital, more power over the labor of others, i.e., to increase this power . . . to produce to the limit set by the productive forces, that is to say, to exploit the maximum amount of labor with the given amount of capital, without any consideration for the actual limits of the market or the needs back by the ability to pay . . . forms the basis of modern over-production (Marx in Tucker: 464–5, 462).

Thus, because capital's weaker counterparts cannot possibly consume enough due to their wages business enterprises are forced to do one of three things according to Marx. Corporations can destroy productive forces or curtail production (sabotage industry), seek out new markets, and/or enhance the exploitation of familiar markets. Marx's observations are certainly prescient but they are not altogether correct for two main reasons. First, Marx never discusses how businesses price their goods in a cost-plus manner. Mathematically, what this means is that there will always be a structural gap between total outstanding purchasing power and total outstanding prices as originally noticed by C. H. Douglas (1922; see also Hutchinson and Burkitt 1997). Figure 4.1 demonstrates this for the case of the United States by comparing the value of all goods and services produced yearly in the United States and tracking this with *all* wages and salaries paid to workers.

If figure 4.1 is not telling of the structural gap, consider the following simplified yet telling example of a firm's cost to do one run of production (Table 4.1).

Suppose the firm is making lighters and during this one run of production it produces 10,000 lighters. The cost per unit would be $0.50. Since

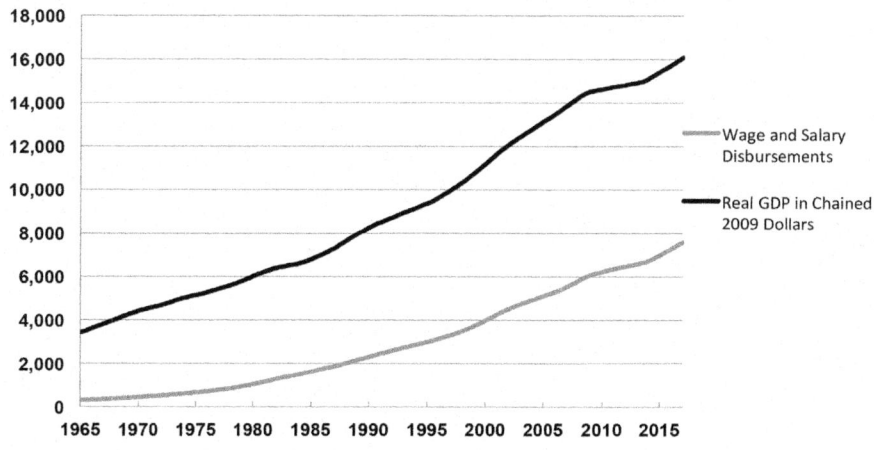

Figure 4.1 GDP and Wage and Salary Disbursements, 1965–2017 (in billion US$)

Table 4.1 ABC Corporation

Electricity/power	$1,000
Raw materials	$1,000
Insurance	$1,000
Interest on debt	$1,000
Labor	**$1,000 (purchasing power)**
Total Cost	$5,000

the goal of the business enterprise is to make a profit, not break even, the company would have to mark up the price of each lighter to reach its markup. In this case, suppose the executives at the ABC Corporation decide to aim for a 10 percent markup or $500. What this means is that each lighter would have to sell for $0.55. Thus, there are 10,000 lighters outstanding on the market at a total price value of $5,500. However, there is only $1,000 of purchasing power in the economy generated by the wages paid to labor (Di Muzio and Noble 2017; Di Muzio and Robbins 2017). Since labor is a cost to the business enterprise, increasing wages cannot solve the structural gap between purchasing power and outstanding prices. As we will discuss in the next section, the only thing that can overcome this gap is credit and, as C. H. Douglas noted, commercial banks have a monopoly over it.

The second reason why Marx's analysis is at best incomplete is because he relied on a labor theory of value to explain prices and accumulation. For Marx, profit or surplus results from the exploitation of labor during the production process. What exploitation means in the Marxist tradition is that workers are not paid for the full value of their labor time during the work day, leaving a surplus for the capitalist to appropriate. In the Marxist framework then, the target profit of $500 in the previous example is the result of failing to pay workers the full value of their labor. But whatever other problems the labor theory of value may have in accounting for the accumulation of money, power, and prices, even if Marx were correct, the structural gap between outstanding purchasing power and outstanding total prices would remain even if the profit of $500 is returned to the workers. So Marx, along with many of his followers, are correct that capitalism is prone to crises of overproduction and underconsumption, but it is not primarily due to the exploitation of labor but the cost-plus accounting of capitalist enterprise and a general shortage of purchasing power. Given this method of accounting, the only thing that can potentially bridge the gap between purchasing power and prices is credit. The control of credit, as it turns out, is a very special power indeed and is explored in the next section.

THE CAPITALIZATION AND OWNERSHIP OF MONEY

The current monetary and fiscal system of modern democracies is neither natural nor neutral but a historical creation that has facilitated the centralization and concentration of wealth (Di Muzio and Robbins 2016, 2017). One of the main reasons for this is that like other corporations producing goods and services, commercial banks are also capitalized but unlike the vast majority of corporations they are capitalized on a very special basis: their ability to create new money. Currently, the banking sector of the global economy is the most heavily capitalized at US$4.8 trillion and it is not difficult to understand why. But to do so we must first dispense with a myth. Most school children are taught that banks take in money from the public as deposits and then use a portion of these deposits to make loans to willing borrowers, who will eventually repay the original amount plus interest over an agreed time period. But this commonplace belief is incorrect. Banks have the special power to create new money when they issue loans to customers and in fact are the major agencies creating the money supply (Werner 2014a, 2014b). Put simply, loans create deposits rather than deposits being the reservoir for loans. What this means is that no saving has to take place as customer deposits in commercial banks before lending by a bank can commence. In fact, deposits are liabilities on a bank's balance sheet, not assets. The balance sheet is different and expands in the case of a bank lending to agreeable borrowers. The loan is recorded as an asset on the bank's balance sheet since customers have agreed to repay the loan with interest. Here it is good to recall that most money in a modern economy is digital (recorded as numbers in a computer) rather than physical notes and coins. While the ratio of digital money to physical cash differs across modern economies, notes and coins represent anywhere from about 3 to 10 percent of the total money supply. States typically have control over the production of notes and coins and generally benefit from their production as the cost to produce notes and coins is less than their total price value. For example, in the United States, the United States Mint is responsible for the production of coins while the Bureau of Engraving and Printing is charged with the production of paper currency. But the overwhelming majority of new money is produced by commercial banks when they make loans to individuals, families, and corporations. It is this power to produce money as debt that investors capitalize when they purchase shares in commercial banks. Of course banks do make money from fees and fines, but the vast majority of their earnings stem from charging interest on loans.

As we have seen, the cost-plus accounting of capitalism creates a gap between purchasing power and the total price value of all goods and services outstanding on the market. As discussed previously, this means that there is

not enough money in the economy to actually purchase the goods and services produced in any given economy. To bridge this gap corporations have
relied on marketing and advertising and international sales, but while these
practices proliferated in the twentieth century they can never bridge the gap
between purchasing power and the total outstanding prices for goods and
services. As it turns out, the sabotage of the money supply by the owners of
the commercial banks and their monopoly over credit virtually guarantees
these owners a perpetual income stream. But commercial banks do not just
profit off loans, fees, and fines, they also have ownership claims over other
large-scale corporations. As three Swiss systems researchers studying the
network of corporate control across the universe of transnational companies
found, there is a hard core of ownership and control by mostly US- and
UK-based financial institutions (Vitali et al. 2011). Specifically, what they
found was that 147 corporations in the core own interlocking stakes in each
other and control 40 percent of the wealth in the aggregate network. Out of a
total network of 43,060 transnational corporations studied, 737 control a full
80 percent of the wealth generated by the network. This is a remarkable finding because it is the first study of its nature. However, the fact that ownership
and control are heavily concentrated may not be too surprising to learn given
that banks have not only organized the floatation of corporate shares but can
also purchase shares in various companies. A longer and more historically
sensitive study than what is allowed for here would have to be undertaken to
flesh out the details, but there are some glimmerings in the financial literature
worth pointing out. For example, Roy's study of the railroad industry in the
United States found that:

> To build or expand a railroad, the services of an investment bank were neces-
> sary, usually a private bank like Prime, Ward & King in the early days, or J.
> P. Morgan & Company at the turn of the century. The investment bank would
> make a study of the properties and individuals involved, draw up a contract for
> selling securities, agreeing to either take the securities on commission, under-
> write them (guarantee their sale), or purchase them outright. If the issue was
> very large, the bank might organize a syndicate of other banks and individuals
> to spread the risk. It would then offer to sell the securities to major investors,
> including commercial banks, insurance companies, and wealthy capitalists, and,
> for a few banks, small investors (1997: 105).

What this suggests is that large-scale business enterprises *en par* with
railroads needed money to operate from social forces in control of the dis-
pensation of credit. In the United States these outside social forces came
to be known as the "Money Trust" and by 1913, with the concentration of
wealth visible to Congress, the Pujo Committee was assembled to investi-
gate the major institutions at the heart of American capitalism. What they

uncovered "was a system of interlocking directorates and other forms of influence centered around six major banks: J.P. Morgan & Co.; First National Bank of New York; the National City Bank of New York; Lee, Higginson & Co.; Kidder Peabody; and Kuhn, Loeb. The bankers' control over credit to the giant enterprises in their orbit gave them control over the commanding heights of the US economy, creating significant barriers to entry for those outside the circle" (Henwood 1997: 260–1). Squarely in the Marxist camp, Rudolf Hilferding (1981) was one of the first to theorize this transformation and he argued that the financial industry, through its ability to extend credit to industry, was coming to control the entire industrial system of corporations. But Hilferding thought that the banks were merely lending out other people's money. In other words, he thought that banks were mere intermediaries who took in deposits—primarily from what he called the "non-productive classes" and industrial and merchant savings—and then either lent the savings of other people to industrial corporations or used some of their deposits to buy shares in industrial firms. As we have discussed, this view is incorrect. Banks did not and do not have to wait for deposits before they issued loans or purchased corporate securities. In previous work with Richard H. Robbins and Leonie Noble I have discussed the consequences of allowing banks to create money, but it is worth reiterating some of the major ones here since they bear on the tragedy of human development and are intertwined with our genealogy of capital as power (Di Muzio and Noble 2017; Di Muzio and Robbins 2016, 2017). First, since most governments only produce a small portion of the money supply—notes and coins—they are structurally forced to go into debt to private social forces if spending priorities are over and above the revenues they receive from taxes, fine and fees. This has led to the near-consistent growth in the "national" debts of the world. Mounting public debt is then used politically to argue for spending cuts and the privatization schedules that sell off public assets to private investors in an effort to raise money. As we will see in the next act, the massive debts accumulated by less developed countries in the 1970s led to privatization waves, cuts in essential services for the most vulnerable, and, in many cases, gross human rights violations (Abouharb and Cingnarelli 2007; George 1982). As of this writing (June 2017), the total outstanding national debts of the world amounts to US$59 trillion and counting. These debts are likely never to be repaid but they do have a political and economic effect: they serve to discipline the fiscal policies of governments while providing a minority of investors with a relatively safe investment vehicle (Hager 2013, 2016; Sinclair 2005). The only way out of this morass is for democratic governments to take control of the money supply and issue their own non-interest-bearing sovereign currency (Huber 2017; Di Muzio and Noble 2017; Di Muzio and Robbins 2017). Second, bank lending is typically tied to assets and income and therefore individuals with higher incomes and greater assets have easier access to credit and have a greater opportunity to amass more wealth. This not only has effects on the scale of economic inequality, but, as Hutchinson and others have argued, it may have also contributed to the centralization and concentration of ownership as small-scale enterprises were often denied necessary credit, creating a pathway for corporate conglomeration and large-scale industry (Hutchinson 1997: 26). Third, since the majority of a country's money supply is issued by banks as debt and there is more debt in the economy than there is the ability to repay due to the fact that banks do not create the amount of interest they will be owed, this creates a perpetual need for economic growth. Moreover, if bank lending slows down or individuals and companies refuse to go into further debt, the inevitable result is recession or depression, greater unemployment, and greater social misery. As Douglas argued, "Banks, through their control of credit facilities, hold the volume of production at all times in the hollow of their hands" (1923: 21). Fourth, since interest is a cost to business and this gets pushed on to consumers, it is inevitable, unless business wants to run at a loss, that as business debt rises so too will the inflation of prices for goods and services. For example, consider the case of the United States where there is over US$13 trillion in non-financial corporate debt. If our hypothesis is correct, we would expect that the amount of interest paid by these firms to banks over time would increase with the consumer price index. As figure 4.2 shows, this is precisely what we find (Di Muzio and Noble 2017). This does not mean that interest on bank credit is the only driver of inflation, but it is

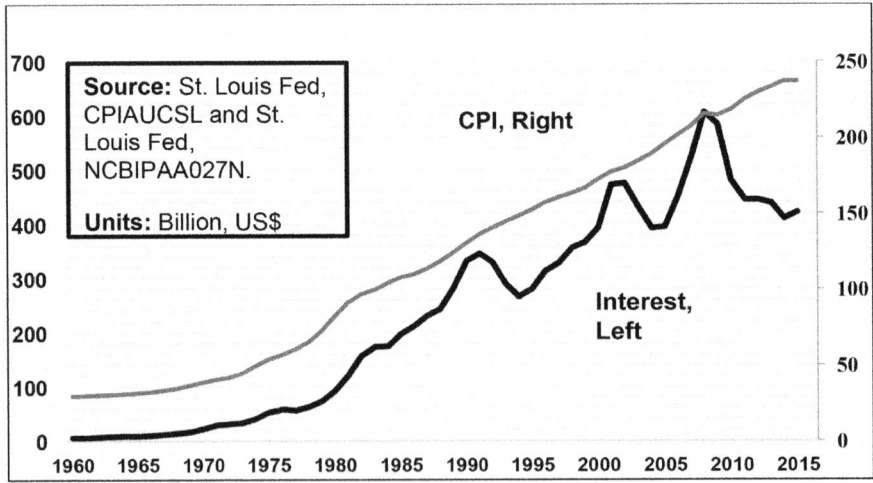

Figure 4.2 United States Non-Financial Interest and CPI, 1960–2005

highly significant since it suggests that one of the key ways to curtail inflation is not to raise interest rates but to abolish them.

The last major consequence of allowing commercial banks to control the money supply is that it enriches the owners of commercial banks based on a fraud. Bankers are not lending other people's money as is commonly presumed; they are creating money when they issue loans to individuals and businesses. In a world with a shortage of money to circulate the goods and services provided by the economy, this is a tremendous power to have ownership over. As we have seen, it has also allowed the banks to come to have ownership claims on non-financial firms. What this suggests, then, is not only do the individuals and families who own the world's major banks profit from a fraud in an environment where credit is necessary, but they also profit from the other corporations they own shares in. Thus one of the greatest tragedies of the rise of capital as power is that the issuance of money—the lifeblood of any economy—has been capitalized for the benefit of the few. As I have argued, this fiscal monetary system, born in the geopolitical crucible of warring feudalism, is neither natural nor inevitable but the result of a political power play that first occurred in Britain with the creation of the Bank of England in 1694. Thus in a world where democratic governments can indeed introduce a non-interest-bearing sovereign currency, let no one ever say that there is "no money" to provide for the goods and services that would facilitate and better a logic of livelihood. The final word on the matter in this section can be given to Douglas:

> A phrase such as "There is no money in the country with which to do such and so" means simply nothing, unless we are also saying "The goods and services required to do this thing do not exist and cannot be produced, therefore it is useless to create the money equivalent of them." For instance, it is simply childish to say that a country has no money for social betterment, or for any other purpose, when it has the skill, the men and the material and plant to create that betterment. The banks or the Treasury can create the money in five minutes, and are doing it every day, and have been doing it for centuries (1923: 9–10).

REGIMES OF DIFFERENTIAL ACCUMULATION AND THE MONEY PROBLEM

It is within the context of a lack of purchasing power in the economy due to the sabotage of money that we can understand four broad strategies of differential accumulation first identified and discussed by Nitzan (2001; see also Nitzan and Bichler 2009: Chapters 15 and 16). As it turns out, due to a lack of purchasing power, corporate executives are working within a structure that puts them in an unenviable position when it comes to generating greater earnings than the average represented by some index like the S&P 500 or the MSCI World Index. As we have discussed, the structural gap between purchasing power and the total outstanding prices of goods and services identified by C. H. Douglas can be mitigated by consumer credit. Indeed, total consumer credit outstanding in the United States currently stands at US$3.8 trillion, a massive increase of 58,689 percent from US$6.5 billion in 1943 when data were first collected.[4] It is worth noting that consumer credit would hardly be needed at all if there were no gap between the value of the goods produced in an economy and the purchasing power available to workers. But while consumer credit can grow over time, this too has limits in the creditworthiness of borrowers, the general level of willingness to borrow among the population, the size of the population, and the commercial bank's willingness to lend for consumption being chief among them. Thus, even if we add the total consumer credit outstanding in the United States (US$3.8 trillion as of March 2017) to the total compensation of employees in wages and salaries (US$8.4 trillion as of May 2017), the structural gap between the monetary value of all the final goods and services produced in the United States over one year (US GDP) and the wages and salaries paid to employees remains at US$4.7 trillion (US$16.9 trillion–US$12.2 trillion). What this suggests is that consumer credit alone cannot bridge the gap created by the cost-plus accounting of firms and the sabotage of money. It is my argument here that the strategies of differential accumulation identified by Nitzan (2001) are largely motivated not just by the drive to accumulate faster than the average but also by the very monetary context in which firms operate.

Nitzan argues that dominant capital—the leading firms by market capitalization—can employ four main avenues to beat the average rate of profit and thus boost their capitalization. The first strategy is greenfield investment, which adds new productive capacity and employment to an economy. But according to Nitzan and Bichler, the willingness of corporate executives to expand production and employees, while perhaps profitable for a time, also runs the long-term danger of excess capacity, particularly when new firms populate the corporate universe and start to cut into an existing firm's market share (2009: 335–6). This strategy is all the more troubling since we already know that the market cannot clear the products of the existing capacity due to a lack of purchasing power. The second avenue that can be followed by dominant capital is cost-cutting to boost profit margins. But Nitzan and Bichler argue that obtaining a reduction in the price of inputs, reducing wages, or bargaining for a reduction in tariff barriers leads to meeting the average rate of return rather than beating it (2009: 363–5). The primary reason for this is that the same cost-cutting strategies will eventually be applied by other competing firms. For example, the International Textile Garment and Leather Workers' Federation identified at least sixty global brands employing sweatshop labor around the world.[5] In other words, it is very difficult, if not impossible, for a company like Adidas to prohibit Nike from using sweatshop labor to lower its costs or vice versa. But cost-cutting is not just the result of corporations vying to beat an average rate of accumulation, but it is also the result of a lack of purchasing power in the economy. The only incentive to using sweatshop labor is that typically human rights are violated as workers are not allowed to organize and collectively bargain for higher compensation and second because using cheap labor can help lower the price of goods for sale to consumers while boosting profit margins. It would make very little sense for a corporation to outsource its labor to a low-wage economy to produce goods if the available purchasing power throughout the economy could clear the goods produced. Since it cannot, cost-cutting remains a strategy of business, but one, as Nitzan and Bichler claim, that may be better at meeting an average rate of return rather than beating it.

The last two strategies are mergers and acquisitions and stagflation. Though there is considerable controversy and debate over how to interpret corporate mergers, that they tend to cluster is beyond dispute (Henwood 1997: 279). In the United States, mergers have come in four major waves (Nitzan 1998: 242). The first wave, dubbed the *monopoly wave*, occurred from 1898 to 1904 and witnessed the emergence of the giant corporation, born of many smaller business organizations from the same industry. The second wave, dubbed the *oligopoly wave* during the 1920s, saw a further consolidation of the business enterprise along similar lines as the monopoly wave. The *conglomerate wave* during the 1950s and 1960s was the third surge of corporate amalgamation and remains unique in some respects. During this period, firms bought other firms whose industrial practices were largely unrelated to each other. The last wave on record, dubbed the *global wave*, began in the 1980s and has continued into the twenty-first century. This period is significant because "conglomerates were broken apart, and combinations between firms in the same or related industries predominated" (Henwoood 1997: 279). Describing these waves, however, is a far cry from understanding and explaining them. There are essentially two mysteries here—the first revolves around why firms merge, and the second has to do with why mergers tend to cluster (Nitzan 2001: 240–1).

In relation to why firms merge, there are two popular answers and one apology. The apology comes from Marshall (1920), who claimed that large-scale business organizations were not only benevolent but also much more efficient. Under this line of reasoning, since all business combinations have the purpose of increasing efficiency, there is no need to think about them any further. Adding to this thesis some years later, Coase (1937) argued that firms merged with one another out of the need to reduce transaction costs. Thus, firms should merge when transaction costs are higher on the open market than they would be if they were internalized within one firm. The last popular argument for why corporations merge is supplied by a string of writers, for example, Manne (1965), Jensen and Ruback (1983), and Jensen (1987), who argued that mergers were a form of disciplinary control over managers who might waver in their commitment to maximizing profits. The threat of a takeover forced managers to increase efficiency and to translate these efficiency gains into increased profits, thereby raising shareholder value (Nitzan 2001: 238–40).

There are but a few problems with these conventional arguments. First, if corporations merge for the sake of greater efficiency then one would assume that the size of firms would get smaller in an era of more efficient technology due to a reduction in transaction costs. Instead, firms have grown larger while the evidence that mergers have increased efficiency remains extremely dubious (Henwood 1997: 279). Second, while one can make a case for mergers being driven by the search for profit, efficiency gains do not necessarily have to enter the picture. Nor is there clear evidence that amalgamated firms are more profitable when they are combined (Nitzan 2001: 240–1). Thus, the conventional wisdom on the motives for corporate mergers does little to solve the question of why corporations combine.

The most convincing answer was advanced by Jonathan Nitzan. For Nitzan, mergers have very little to do with increasing efficiency or seeking a reduction in costs, Rather the purpose of corporate amalgamation is to control efficiency for profitable ends. Specifically, mergers accomplish two main goals. First, by merging instead of creating new capacity (greenfield investment), corporations do not inject any additional capacity into the economy—a necessary requirement if profits are to remain at "reasonable levels." Second, combining increases the power of a particular firm to collect and appropriate additional income streams. The more it merges, the more the corporation has the possibility to collect income streams and increase its power over other elements of dominant capital by virtue of expanding what it can control through ownership. As we have previously discussed, it can do so because the firm is a fictional legal entity identified with business practices and capable of owning a series of industrial plants or facilities. Put differently, corporations merge in order to increase their differential profit by swallowing up their competition or by gaining a new income stream from an unrelated company (Nitzan 2001: 240–1). For instance, Facebook has acquired over sixty-five companies since its incorporation in 2004, while Apple has merged or acquired with at least eighty-seven companies since 1988.[6] But these are just two individual examples at the firm level. Consider that since 1985, the number of worldwide mergers and acquisitions increased by 1,712 percent in 2016 while the value of these transactions increased by 925 percent over the same period. In the three years with the highest dollar value for transactions—1999, 2007, and 2015—mergers and acquisitions

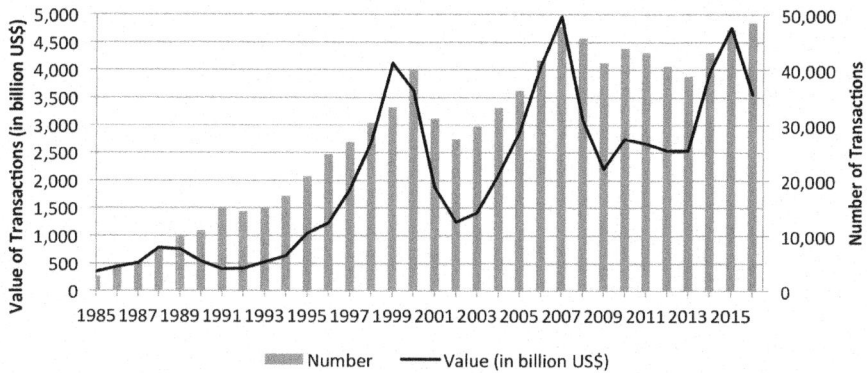

Figure 4.3 Number and Value of Mergers and Acquisitions Worldwide (1985–2016). Source: Institute for Mergers, Acquisitions and Alliances.

were just shy of US\$14 trillion or about the same size as the GDP for the United States in 2005. Thus, taken as a whole the total financial value of all transactions during the period was just over a massive US\$66 trillion for 917,861 transactions or roughly US\$72 million per average transaction. These corporate combinations further consolidate ownership and power in the global economy.[7]

In Nitzan's view, these waves of corporate amalgamation transform the conditions under which future amalgamations may take place. There are three important transformations that should be taken into account. First, a process of amalgamation serves to reduce the number of firms that can be taken over in the future. Thus, at a certain point, merger activity must slow down until the pool of possible targets is replenished. Second, while greenfield investment could serve to replenish the pool of possible takeover targets, it trails mergers "in employment volume and dollar value" because mergers divert capital away from greenfield investment in the first place (Nitzan 2001: 240–1). The result is fewer takeover targets in the immediacy. Last, mergers tend to cause social dislocations as firms reorganize and adapt to their newly created environment. As this process takes time, it would serve to slow down merger activity. However, while this explains why merger activity is not linear over time and tend to cluster, we still must confront why mergers move in cycles (Nitzan 2001: 240–1). The answer is that dominant capital must push its own envelope over space and time, and this appears to be an underlying structural feature of differential accumulation within the context of a dearth of national purchasing power:

> The first, "monopoly" wave marked the emergence of modern big business, with giant corporations forming within their own original *industries*. Once this source of amalgamation was more or less exhausted, further expansion meant

that firms had to move outside their industry boundaries. And indeed, the next "oligopoly" wave saw the formation of vertically integrated combines whose control increasingly spanned entire *sectors*, such as in petroleum, machinery and food products, among others. The next phase opened the whole *US corporate universe* up for grabs, with firms crossing their original boundaries of specialization to form large conglomerates with business lines ranging from raw materials, through manufacturing, to services and finance. Finally, once the national scene has been more or less integrated, the main avenue for further expansion is across international borders, hence the current *global* merger wave (Nitzan 2001: 245, emphasis original).

As we have seen previously, the latest "global wave" is ongoing and at this point there is no telling exactly when it may stop or what the level of concentrated power might become. It could be the case that antitrust regulators concerned with market competition constrain further corporate mergers and acquisitions but it could equally be the case that they oversee and facilitate them. Given the degree of cross-border and national mergers and acquisitions since at least 2000, it looks as though the latter, rather than the former, is the case—at least presently. This trend bodes well for corporations and their investors but is troublesome for consumers because amalgamation provides executives with a chance to more easily pursue the last major road to differential accumulation: stagflation.

The portmanteau of inflation and stagnation—stagflation—was coined by a British politician who used the term in a speech given to the British Parliament in 1965. The term was an attempt to capture the economic reality of rising prices, stagnant or slowing economic output, and high unemployment in the United Kingdom. During the oil crises of the 1970s when prices for a barrel of oil skyrocketed above 400 percent and economies slowed down, the term became more widespread. It is a bizarre term for economists since rising prices are assumed to come on the back of rapid economic growth and high levels of employment. But from the perspective of capital as power, informed by Veblen's critical understanding of the business sabotage of industry, the phenomenon of stagflation is easier to explain. As suggested by Veblen, no free run of production is possible for the business enterprise in pursuit of differential earnings: corporate executives must limit or restrict production up to and including planned and technological obsolescence. When combined with increasing market power—facilitated by mergers and acquisitions—the controlled restriction of output typically coincides with rising prices in the form of a greater markup than would otherwise be the case in "normal" conditions. To be sure, as we have seen in the case of commercial bank interest, increasing differential markups are not the only driver of inflation, but they can and do contribute to rising prices. But since markup inflation is differential, we need to be concerned with its major effect on society, and for Nitzan and

Bichler the major effect is redistribution. As Nitzan and Bichler (2009: 369) have empirically demonstrated, not all firms increase their prices at the same time or at the same rate. This is why we must conceive of inflation as differential with different distributional effects. Not only do Nitzan and Bichler show that inflation is negatively correlated with economic growth (prices tend to decrease when economic growth is heating up), but they also empirically demonstrate that increasing corporate markups tend to redistribute more money from workers to capitalists and from smaller business to dominant capital (2009: 370–4). This redistribution serves to reinforce the power of capital over workers who must pay for the newly higher priced goods or services or forgo consuming them. However, while stagflation can be used as a powerful tool of differential accumulation, particularly by dominant capitalist firms, there are conventional markup practices that are typically followed. What this means is that there are generally upper limits on what a corporation can charge the consumer base if it does not want to threaten earnings.

Thus, as identified by Nitzan and Bichler (2009), there are four major pathways to differential accumulation that can be followed in an economic system with a constant dearth of money: cost-cutting, greenfield investment, mergers and acquisitions, and stagflation. As we have discussed, while the first two are practiced as core business strategies, they tend, over time, to meet, rather than beat, the average rate of accumulation. Mergers and acquisitions as well as stagflation can lead to beating the average rate of profit and thereby boost the capitalization of dominant firms, but these strategies are not without their own political and institutional perils. But, while all these practices are cause for concern in some way, what might be more worrisome is that the institution at the center of the capitalist mode of power behaves in a way that most human beings would find morally abhorrent (Bakan 2003: 28).

THE CORPORATION AS PSYCHOPATH

Over a decade ago, a legal scholar at the University of British Columbia in Canada, Joel Bakan, took a critical look at the corporation and made the argument that while individuals working at a corporation were not necessarily psychopaths (most are not), the institutional and legal structure of the firm causes them to behave in this manner (2003: 56). Using the work of a renowned expert on psychopathy, Dr. Robert Hare, Bakan compared the character traits of a psychopath with the actions of various corporations. Indeed, while there is much fanfare about corporate social responsibility, we must always recall that whatever donations, public relations, or consultations take place between communities and a corporation, the fundamental goal of its executives will be differential profit, not serviceability to the community. This is incredibly worrisome since what Bakan found through a litany of overflowing examples was that the behavior of corporations is remarkably similar to those of a psychopath. According to Bakan, three important legal innovations help us explain the rise of corporations and their peculiar behavior: limited liability, the granting of corporate personhood to a nonphysical entity, and the exclusive focus on profit as the end goal of business. Taken together, Bakan found the modern corporation to display the following psychopathic behaviors: self-interested, manipulative, asocial, self-aggrandizing, unable to accept responsibility for its own actions, and inability to feel remorse. Even a quick perusal through the now defunct *Multinational Monitor*'s website would be enough to substantiate the claim that the most dominant institutions of differential accumulation have been ruthless in the pursuit of corporate earnings. But to provide one recent example, consider that since the global financial crisis of 2007–2009, banks globally have been fined upward of US$300 billion for market manipulation, financing terrorism, and money laundering.[8] Thus, as Bakan claims, while corporations are not going away anytime soon, society should take measures to limit their power.

NOTES

1 Financial Times 500, 2015. https://www.ft.com/ft500?mhq5j=e2 (accessed 6/29/2017).

2 Stock Market Capitalization to GDP for United States. https://fred.stlouisfed.org/series/DDDM01USA156NWDB (7/16/2017).

3 Veblen's ontology here is unmistakable. He clearly identifies the business enterprise with power and agency, while those acting outside this sphere of activity are given a subordinate agency: "As near as it may be said of any human power in modern times, the large business man controls the exigencies of life under which the community lives. Hence, upon him and his fortunes centers the abiding interest of civilized mankind."

4 "Total Consumer Credit Outstanding and Securitized." https://fred.stlouisfed.org/series/TOTALSL (7/4/2017).

5 'Sixty big name brands continuing to use sweatshop labour' The Journal, May 3, 2011. http://www.thejournal.ie/60-big-name-brands-continuing-to-use-sweatshop-labour-130318-May2011/ (7/4/2017).

6 Steve Toth '65 Facebook Acquisitions' Techwyse, October 26, 2016. https://www.techwyse.com/blog/infographics/65-facebook-acquisitions-the-complete-list-infographic/ (7/4/2017).

7 Data are from the Institute for Mergers, Acquisitions and Alliances. https://imaa-institute.org/mergers-and-acquisitions-statistics/ (7/4/2017).

8 Gavin Finch, 'World's Biggest Banks Fined $321 Billion Since Financial Crisis' Bloomberg, March 2, 2017. https://www.bloomberg.com/news/articles/2017-03-02/world-s-biggest-banks-fined-321-billion-since-financial-crisis (7/16/2017).

Act V

Human Development

As I have tried to convey in previous acts, for most of human history since the monetization of social relations, the primary pursuit of the powerful was nothing like building a better or more equal society but maintaining and aggrandizing their power over others. Where we find any evidence of societal improvement (e.g., greater equality in access to resources) or humane developments (e.g., human rights) they are historically exceptional and can be shown to stem from major violent catastrophes or the result of struggles from below pushing up against the ruling order (Scheidel 2017). Though there are multiple contradictions we could identify, the attempt to maintain and aggrandize power meant developing a number of technologies from more lethal weapons to slavery and virulent forms of racism to divide and rule. Philosophies and religious cosmologies that preached natural inequality or compensated their victims by speaking of a world beyond the terrestrial also helped to reinforce radical inequality in opportunities, life chances, and ultimately access to resources. So it would seem somewhat strange that after World War II, the US president Harry S. Truman (in office from 1945 to 1953) openly declared a concern for development in the peripheries of a world order dominated by powerful militarized states, albeit many that were now exhausted from the protracted war. This call, likely half sincere due to the specter of communism and half an exercise in public relations, did not stop the idea of "development" from becoming akin to a global religion (Rist 2008: 20). After centuries of resource exploitation, slavery, and mass murder all in the search for greater money and power, the ruling caste of the capitalist West all of a sudden gave itself the mission to develop the underdeveloped. There are many reasons to be skeptical about this agenda as I will make clear, but I will also argue that it is instructive to compare Truman's announcement with Policy Planning Study 23 authored by George Kennan, Head of the US State Department Policy Planning Staff in 1948, and National Security Council Report 68, authored by a group chaired by Paul Nitze of the US State Department. With this in mind, the act moves to discuss how GDP, a concept that largely solidified as a war-planning tool, became the leading indicator for a nation's well-being and the consequences of this for populations and world order. In the penultimate section of this act we take a closer look at debt as a technology of power and its role in the tragedy of human development and the global political economy of capital as power. The act closes its curtain after discussing the biopolitics of global capitalism and raises the question of whether—in the name of enhancing life—our institutions have actually helped undermine it.

TRUMAN'S POINT FOUR AND POLICY PLANNING STUDY 23

As suggested previously, before President Truman's 1949 inaugural address to the nation, the dynamic between powerful and weaker states was largely one of colonizer and colonized and while "development" or "improvement" had been talked about before, the idea of uplifting the material standards of most of humanity was hardly a topic for conversation in ruling class circles since "improvement" was done for their profit (Rist 2008: 73; Westad 2007: 74). At most there was talk of governing and administering territories, particularly after World War I when the League of Nations Covenant handed over former German and Ottoman territories to the leading victors of the war and their allies. This is why Point Four of Truman's inaugural address is so exceptional: he announced what Rist calls the "development age" by widely circulating the notion that the political economies of a good portion of the globe were "underdeveloped" and thus in need of technical assistance and socio-economic engineering (2008: 71). The first three points of Truman's speech emphasized US support for the United Nations, the reconstruction and development of Europe, and the creation of the North Atlantic Treaty Organization (NATO) as a joint defense organization responsible for checking the power of the Soviet Union (Rist 2008: 70). Point Four of Truman's "program for peace and freedom" reads as follows:

[W]e must embark on a bold new program for making the benefits of our scientific advances and industrial progress available for the improvement and growth of *underdeveloped* areas.

More than half the people of the world are living in conditions approaching misery. Their food is inadequate. They are victims of disease. *Their economic life is primitive and stagnant. Their poverty is a handicap and a threat both to them and to more prosperous areas.* For the first time in history, humanity possesses the knowledge and skill to relieve the suffering of these people. The United States is pre-eminent among nations in the development of industrial and scientific techniques. The material resources which we can afford to use for assistance of other peoples are limited. But our imponderable resources in technical knowledge are constantly growing and are inexhaustible.

I believe that we should make available to peace-loving peoples the benefits of our store of technical knowledge in order to help them realize their aspirations for a better life. And, in cooperation with other nations, we should foster capital investment in areas needing development. Our aim should be to help the free peoples of the world, through their own efforts, to produce more food, more clothing, more materials for housing, and more mechanical power to lighten their burdens.

We invite other countries to pool their technological resources in this undertaking. Their contributions will be warmly welcomed. This should be a cooperative enterprise in which all nations work together through the United Nations and its specialized agencies whenever practicable. It must be a worldwide effort for the achievement of peace, plenty, and freedom.

With the cooperation of business, private capital, agriculture, and labor in this country, this program can greatly increase the industrial activity in other nations and can raise substantially their standards of living. Such new economic developments must be devised and controlled to the benefit of the peoples of the areas in which they are established. Guarantees to the investor must be balanced by guarantees in the interest of the people whose resources and whose labor go into these developments. The old imperialism-exploitation for foreign profit-has no place in our plans. What we envisage is a program of development based on the concepts of democratic fair-dealing.[1]

Thus, only four years after the carnage of World War II, the United States, the world's unrivaled world superpower, looked forward to an era of peace and development. Not only had the war pulled the United States out of the Great Depression but it was plentiful in oil, and other than the attack on Pearl Harbor, had not suffered military bombardment of its massive industrial capacity. Though Rist claims that Point Four of Truman's speech was largely a public relations ploy suggested by a civil servant at the last minute, the statement that the suffering of underdeveloped nations of the world could be alleviated was now communicated to a world audience (2008: 70). But other events were afoot that suggested a far deeper problem than providing technical know-how and assistance to underdeveloped regions of the planet: the fear of communism, the constraints of American fiscal policy, and maintaining the disparity of global wealth. For this reason, I argue that it is instructive to compare Truman's statement with two top-secret post-war planning documents: Policy Planning Study 23 and National Security Council Report 68.

It would be inaccurate to suggest that post-war planners were not concerned about the power of the Soviet Union and the potential spread of communism. But the question is to what degree was the threat exaggerated or even politically useful, particularly when most experts knew that the Soviet Union was devastated after the war and hardly prepared to start a new international conflict. Though going against realist or mainstream thought on the origins of the US post-war military buildup, which generally stress China's communist revolution (1949) and the fact that the Soviet Union had detonated a nuclear bomb (1949), current scholarship argues that the threat of the Soviet Union and the spread of communism were overstated. The primary reason is that those orchestrating post-war planning wanted to provide a justification for a massive military buildup while the United States was not at war. There are two things of note here. First, World War II had taught a generation of planners that deficit military spending could have a "positive" impact on boosting American's GDP (Cardwell 2011; Craig and Logevall 2012: 113–4). Deficit spending of the magnitude required to keep the United States out of recession or depression, however, would be a hard sell to fiscal conservatives in Congress. But if the threat of world communism and the need to provide for "national security" against such an outcome could be heightened to a point of hysteria, Congress would be more apt to accept deficit spending. This was primarily outlined—at least within elite circles—by the now-declassified National Security Council Report 68 which argued that the Kremlin was bent on complete "world domination" through communist infiltration, intimidation, and the Soviet Union's capacity for war.[2] Second, the European Recovery Program (ERP), commonly known as the Marshall Plan, launched in 1947, was reasoned to be insufficient for reconstructing Western Europe—a chief goal stressed in Kennan's 1949 top-secret Policy Planning Study 23. Cardwell (2011) argues that because of the inadequate amount of American dollars reaching European shores from the ERP, ramping up military spending could help overcome the gap in two main ways. First, American dollars could be exchanged abroad for raw materials used in the manufacture of arms and ammunition, and second, under the threat of the spread of communism, new American military bases could be constructed on European and Japanese soil. Countries with a surplus of dollars could then purchase American weapons and manufactures and thus help to keep levels of post-war unemployment to a minimum and American industry in the black. In any case, whether the fear of communism was exaggerated to stimulate the economy and provide American dollars abroad or not, the evidence on the ground is pretty clear. Within three years of both reports (PPS 23 and NSC-68) federal military spending increased by 186 percent and in the following decades by 395 percent while millions of American dollars were spent abroad to the point where the Nixon administration had to abandon the international gold standard by 1971 (Gowan 1999: 19–20).[3] Thus, in an ironic twist of history, the fear of communism may have saved international capitalism by providing American elites with an excuse to run consistent deficits to fund the militarization of the United States and, through its international purchase orders and arms sales, the global economy.

Another reason to be skeptical about the commitment to development can be found in Policy Planning Study 23. The top-secret study is a tour de force of American interests abroad as perceived by its author, George Kennan. In one telling passage he discusses the need to maintain the disparity of global wealth—in particular with Asia:

> We have about 50% of the world's wealth but only 6.3% of its population. This disparity is particularly great as between ourselves and the peoples of Asia. In this situation, we cannot fail to be the object of envy and resentment. Our real task in the coming period is to *devise a pattern of relationships which will permit us to maintain this position of disparity* without positive detriment to our national security. To do so, we will have to dispense with all sentimentality and day-dreaming; and our attention will have to be concentrated everywhere on our immediate national objectives. We need not deceive ourselves that we can afford today the luxury of altruism and world-benefaction. . . . We should dispense with the aspiration to 'be liked' or to be regarded as the repository of a high-minded international altruism. We should stop putting ourselves in the position of being our brothers' keeper and refrain from offering moral and ideological advice. We should cease to talk about vague and—for the Far East— *unreal objectives such as human rights, the raising of the living standards, and democratization.* The day is not far off when we are going to have to deal in straight power concepts. The less we are then hampered by idealistic slogans, the better (Emphasis added).[4]

Thus, just a year before President Truman announced the "age of development," high-ranking officials in the US government were discussing the impossibility of raising the living standards for most of Asia (or half the world's population) and developing arrangements to maintain a global disparity of wealth with the East. While the world has certainly become wealthier since the decades of Kennan's report, the United States currently has 4.6 percent of the global population and by one measure has US$97 trillion of the global wealth pie of US$241 trillion or 38 percent of all global wealth. This means the remaining 95.4 percent of the global population—about 6.7 billion people—is left to divide 62 percent of the world's remaining wealth (Credit Swiss 2013).[5] Overcoming this concentration and disparity of wealth has proven difficult despite decades of "development" fostered by the international business community and international organizations such as the World Bank. The latest estimates on poverty from the World Bank, which defines extreme poverty as living on less than US$1.90 a day, is that 1.1 billion people have moved up the income ladder from 1990, leaving just under a billion people living on less than US$1.90 a day. From a certain angle, this is positive and welcome news. However, we must recall the fact that US$1.90 a day is a somewhat arbitrary cutoff point for extreme poverty and is likely more politically expedient rather than an accurate measure of poverty. Moreover, it is estimated that for everyone to live like a North American we would require about four planets' worth of resources and a level of economic growth that would essentially destroy the biosphere and much life in it. Yet one of the greatest and contradictory tragedies of human development and the pursuit of capitalist accumulation has been the global pursuit of economic growth and our political fixation on the "the world's most powerful number": GDP (Fioramonti 2013: 1).

THE PURSUIT OF GROWTH

As I have previously argued, our current monetary and fiscal system compels us to chase economic growth as a constant concern. Because new money is created as debt and the interest is not created when banks issue loans, combined with a cost-plus system of capitalist accounting and the fact that our governments are structurally forced into ever greater debt, pursuing economic growth is a structural feature of capitalist economies. In the current order of things, a lack of economic growth means more unemployment, debt defaults, bankruptcies, and quite often greater debt and social misery. In fact, what Fioramonti calls the "world's most powerful number" was invented in the United States during the Great Depression of the 1930s and later crystallized into the leading indicator for national welfare during World War II. Gross national product (GNP) was the invention of Simon Kuznets and his associates who were looking to find a single number that would condense "all economic production by individuals, companies and the government" which would rise during times of prosperity and fall during times of stagnation (Fioramonti 2013: 25–26). With its influence after World War II, GNP "became the dominant metric of economic performance across the Western world, and in 1953 the United Nations inaugurated its international standards for national accounts which were largely influenced by the methodology developed by Kuznets and the US Department of Commerce" (Fioramonti 2013: 32). As a leading indicator of productive capacity, focusing on one aggregate number was instrumental in helping the United States coordinate its successful war effort against Japan and Germany. In fact, according to some, tracking GNP was equal in importance to the Manhattan Project. But quantitative indicators have effects for qualitative life and even the inventor of the GNP began to doubt that it could be useful as a measure of national well-being. Since then, critiques of GNP—and from 1991 GDP—have proliferated in popular and academic circles. While critiques differ, what they all have in common is a focus on the fact that measuring economic growth is largely an adding-up exercise. What this means is that socially and environmentally harmful practices *add* rather than subtract from calculations of economic growth. More prisons, nuclear bombs, trash dumps, car accidents, mass deforestation of rainforests, and other undesirable practices all contribute to GDP. For this reason some have suggested that social and environmental harms should be subtracted from GDP if we are to get a realistic sense of national well-being. Others have suggested that a new indicator of societal well-being should guide government policy, though there is no consensus on what that indicator should measure exactly and what means might be employed to gather data. Outside of these conundrums lurks a stronger critique of pursuing economic growth as the end goal of all social activity: that it will end in environmental and societal ruin. For this reason there is a school of thought that argues for a de-growth agenda (D'Alisa et al. 2014; Daly 1997; Hamilton 2004; Jackson 2009; Kempf 2008; Speth 2009; Worldwatch Institute 2012). In this view, advanced countries by GDP are considered to be overworking, overconsuming, and overdeveloped, and ultimately headed toward ecological and societal collapse if they stay the current course:

Ultimately, overdeveloped countries (and overdeveloped populations within developing countries) will need to either proactively pursue a degrowth path or continue down the broken path of growth until coasts flood, farmlands dry up, and other massive ecological changes force them away from growth into a mad dash for societal survival. If overdeveloped populations keep ignoring the looming changes—keeping their proverbial heads buried in the sand—then this transition will be brutal and painful. But if a strategy of degrowth, economic diversification, and support for the informal economy is pursued now, before most of societal energy and capital is focused on reacting to ecological shifts, these overdeveloped populations may discover a series of benefits to their own welfare, to their long-term security, and to Earth's well-being (Assadourian in Worldwatch Institute 2014: 24).

While de-growth activists and scholars differ on what a de-growth agenda should look like, they all emphasize that consuming and working less would increase general societal happiness by allowing people more time for their families, friends, and leisure activities that do not take a toll on the natural environment. In other words, those who advocate for a de-growth agenda think we can live better and more worthwhile lives by consuming and working less (Rist 2008: Chapter 14).

Both pursuits—finding a new indicator (or more likely indicators) for social well-being and de-growth—are admirable but practically and politically difficult. First, sorting out a new indicator or indicators to pursue, while feasible, would require some form of popular consensus on what to measure and how. Second, in the current environment, any major political party that places de-growth on their political agenda would risk their prospects of getting elected. Moreover, a debt-based monetary system such as that of the United States requires growth if debts are to be serviced and economic collapse is to be avoided. What this suggests is that we are in a major structural and political conundrum for a number of reasons. First, economic growth has largely been propelled by the combustion of nonrenewable fossil fuels and is therefore historically exceptional and over time, with the depletion of these energy stores, non-reproducible on the present scale (Di Muzio 2015b; Heinberg 2003, 2007, 2011; Rubin 2009, 2012). As Angus Maddison's work has demonstrated the real takeoff in global economic growth spiked sharply only in the nineteenth century and then, only for countries consuming mass amounts of coal and later oil and gas (2001: 264). As is well known, the combustion of such fuels is a major contributor to runaway global climate change. Second, economic growth is exponential while our natural resources—even if we had unlimited energy—are not inexhaustible. According to the World Bank, the world's GDP in 2016 was just over US$75 trillion.[6] If world growth was to continue at the rate of 3 percent, then the size of the global economy by GDP would be US$199 trillion by 2050 and US$872 trillion by 2100. If we were immodest and used a growth rate of 6 percent, then by 2100 the size of the global economy would be US$9.5 *quadrillion*. Given the evidence of our strains on the natural environment with a GDP of US$75 trillion, it is hard to imagine the levels of devastation that would have to be wrought on future generations and our ecologies even to maintain a world growth rate of 3 percent. In sum, it is not just that the calculation of GDP includes a myriad of practices that are ostensibly socially and environmentally damaging but that the pursuit of economic growth as an end goal for socio-economic policy is in no way sustainable of a finite planet. Chasing growth is ultimately ensnaring us into a trap that will see future generations sacrificed on the altar of material and symbolic accumulation. For all these reasons the most sensible course of action—at least for rich nations—would be one connected to a de-growth agenda. However, as I have suggested, our energy-soaked petro-market civilizations combined with an economic system principally organized around debt and the differential accumulation of power and money makes this an incredibly difficult task to embark upon. In the end, the blind pursuit of growth may prove more powerful than the nuclear bomb for the annihilation of the species. This is no doubt a somber assessment of human affairs, but there is currently little evidence that suggests world leaders are prepared to embark on such a course collectively (Gill 2015). In fact, Klare (2002, 2009) argues that there is a greater possibility for future resource wars than there is for an eco-logical civilization to emerge that takes the limits to growth seriously. What largely propels the quest for resources is the commodification and monetiza-tion of the natural and human world, the prevalence of debt, and corporate accumulation for the 1 percent. It is now time to take a closer look at debt and how it is used as a permanent weapon in the Global South, a permanence that really gained steam during the era of so-called human development.

DEBT AS A TECHNOLOGY OF POWER

Debt has been used as a tool of international power for centuries if not mil-lennia (Graeber 2011). Richard H. Robbins and I have dedicated an entire volume to the topic, arguing that debt is a technology of capitalist power that disproportionality benefits the owners of banks at the expense of everyone else (Di Muzio and Robbins 2016). We have also considered some of the most important effects that the pervasiveness of capitalist debt has on politi-cal possibilities, but here I would like to focus on debt as a technology of power as it was mobilized in the Global South. The story begins with the renewal of the international gold standard under the auspices of the Inter-national Monetary Fund (IMF) after World War II. Originally the IMF was charged with the facilitation of trade by maintaining a system of relatively fixed exchange rates pegged to the US dollar, the strongest currency of the time. In turn, the US dollar was pegged to gold at $35 an ounce. This would mean that countries with surplus dollars could exchange them for gold. Per-haps both a blessing and a curse, as we have already discussed, the United States flooded the world with dollars during the Marshall Plan and its post–World War II spending on foreign bases and the arms industry. By the early 1970s, countries such as France and Switzerland were cashing in US dollars for gold. The Nixon administration and its advisors understood that there was not enough gold to back all the US dollars outstanding and closed the gold window on August 9, 1971. As long as the United States maintained a strong trade surplus with the rest of the world, there would be considerable demand for US dollars (Eichengreen 2008: 127). However, by the second quarter of 1971, the US current account was in deficit, which suggested an overvalued dollar and that the countries of the world were less interested in accumulat-ing surplus dollar reserves. But abandoning the gold standard did not throw the US economy into a tailspin. What Nixon's strategists appeared to under-stand was that even without the backing of gold, foreign nations would still require US dollars for a number of needed and strategic commodities already denominated in US dollars. The most important, at least from the standpoint of modern militarization and industrialism, was oil. Then, two years later, something very strange happened. Despite ample supply and no bottlenecks, Middle Eastern suppliers curtailed production and increased the price of crude oil by an astronomical 400 percent from 1970 to 1974 as demonstrated in figure 5.1 (Adelman 1972: 3).

The most common explanation for the inflation in prices between 1973 and 1974 is the oil embargo against the United States in retaliation for its support for Israel during the post-war peace negotiations after the Arab-Israeli War of 1973. However, this ignores evidence that the Nixon administration was pleading with the Organization of the Petroleum Exporting Countries (OPEC) well before 1973 to raise prices (Gowan 1999: 20ff; Oppenheim 1976: 7). As I have examined in greater detail elsewhere, this only seems strange if viewed from the perspective of methodological nationalism, that is: that high-ranking officials act in the best interests of the nation as a whole rather than subgroups of dominant capital such as the oil and arms industry (Di Muzio 2015b: 124ff). But viewed from the perspective of differential accumulation, the policy of increasing oil prices had considerable advantages, albeit for a few. First, it increased the profits of oil firms, helping them to service debts to creditors and facilitating the search and development of more risky oil sinks such as those in the North Sea and Prudhoe Bay. Second, surplus profits in oil-producing countries—particularly in the Middle East—were used to purchase military hardware, which was more profitable for arms companies than domestic sales in the United States (Nitzan and Bichler 2002: 214). The US government helped facilitate these sales and justified them as indispensable for fighting communism. Third, since the financial systems of

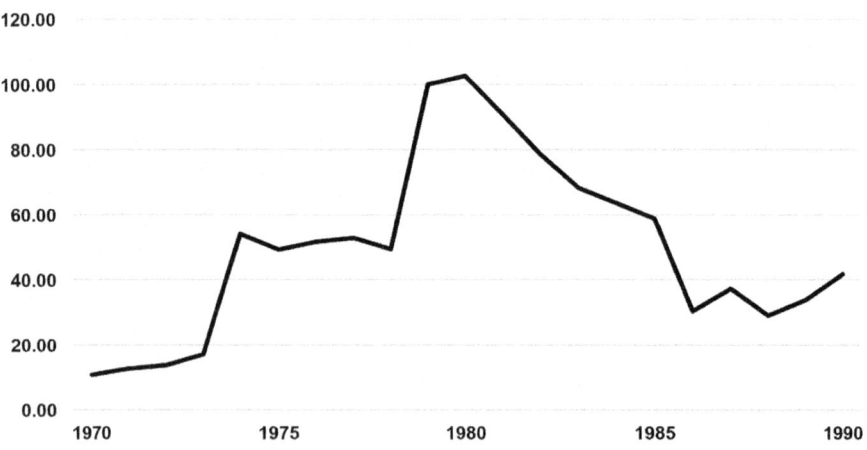

Figure 5.1 Crude Oil Price, 1970–1990, Source: BP Statistical Review (2012 US$)

the oil-producing companies could not absorb the record-breaking profits derived from the sale of oil, money was mainly deposited in US and UK banks and parked in US and UK government securities, thus helping them to finance their deficit spending (Spiro 1999; US Senate 1975: 4). Fourth, the increasing cost of oil made oil imports more expensive for non-oil-producing developing countries, thereby increasing their need for greater loans in US dollars, the currency of world petroleum. Last, the deposits in US and UK banks likely put pressure on the banks to find profitable channels for making loans. Throughout the 1970s, charging low but variable interest rates, commercial banks from the United States and the United Kingdom made billions of dollars in loans to countries and companies in what is today referred to as the "Global South" (the former Third World) (George 1988; Henry 2003).

While official data from the World Bank's international debt statistics on total external debt of developing countries only extend back to 1970, Stavrianos puts the figure of developing countries' debt at US$19 billion in 1960 (1981: 448). As an aggregate, what this suggests is that the total external debt of developing countries has increased from 1960 to 2013 by 6,136 percent (figure 5.2). What the chart also indicates is that external debts appear to be permanent and increasing in the aggregate. One of the major contributors to this trend was the Volcker shocks of 1981 when the federal funds rate was increased by 272 percent from an average low of 4.4 percent in 1982 to an average high of 16.4 percent in 1981. Since foreign borrowing was at variable rates in American dollars, interest rates skyrocketed overnight. This did not reduce inflation in the United States—the main "official" purpose of the interest rate hikes—but it did have a differential effect for American financial power. The Volcker shocks compounded the debt of the global

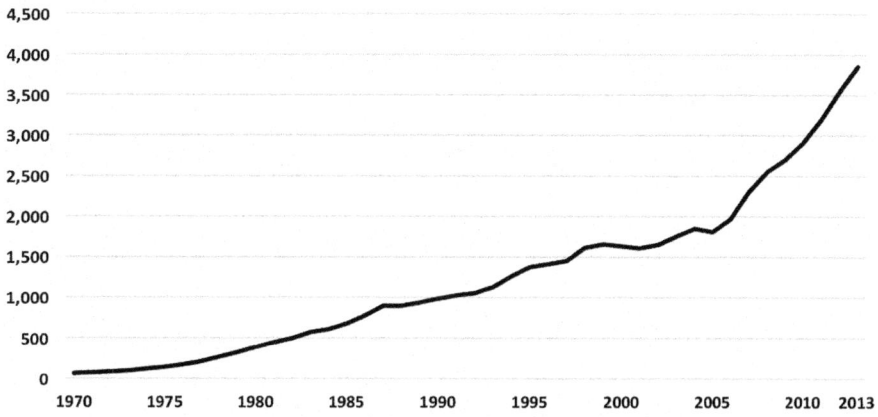

Figure 5.2 Developing Country External Debt Stocks, World Bank, series DT.DOD. DLXF.CD, (US$ Billion)

South, opening the door to greater neoliberal reforms. Such reforms largely recalibrate an economy as a debt repayment machine to foreign creditors. The consequences of debt for peoples of the Global South has been better covered in detail elsewhere, but our concern is with the overall effect of the process: the reconfiguration of political economies for *global* differential accumulation (Abouharband Cingranelli 2007; Chossudovsky 2003; Di Muzio and Robbins 2016; George 1998; Llyod and Weissmen 2002; Perkins 2004). Organized chiefly through the IMF representing a consortium of US and UK banks, new loans were issued to service the interest payments on old debts, further consolidating what can only be called a capitalist debt trap. Consider that 129 countries are accountable to the World Bank's Debt Reporting System and you will have some sense of the magnitude of this trap. Since the bulk of external loans have to be serviced in US dollars rather than the local currency, if leaders in the Global South want future access to credit without suffering punitive interest rates, this forces indebted states to produce for the world market to earn dollars to service loans. Neoliberal reforms also help to liberalize the capital account, facilitating the practice of cross-border global mergers and acquisitions mentioned in Act IV and helping to concentrate the power of corporate ownership. Last, one cornerstone of neoliberal reforms is the privatization of state assets, which increases the structural power of capital vis-à-vis the state and more often than not leads to no greater efficiencies, layoffs, and increased prices for goods and services for the public. But lest we think that debt as a technology of power is something wholly new and only wrapped up with the Grand Strategy of the United States, it is worth recalling that during the era of European imperialism, it was very well known among elites that debt traps could lead to recalibrating political economies to serve an imperial center:

> When a country which has contracted a debt is unable, on account of the slenderness of its income, to offer sufficient guarantee for the punctual payment of interest, what happens? Sometimes an out-and-out conquest of the debtor country follows. Thus France's attempted conquest of Mexico during the second empire was undertaken solely with the view of guaranteeing the interest of French citizens holding Mexican securities. But more frequently the insufficient guarantee of an international loan gives rise to *the appointment of a financial commission by the creditor countries* in order to protect their rights and guard the fate of their invested capital. The appointment of such a commission literally amounts in the end, however, to a veritable conquest. We have examples of this in Egypt, which has to all practical purposes become a British province, and in Tunis, which has in like manner become a dependency of France, who supplied the greater part of the loan. The Egyptian revolt against the foreign domination issuing from the debt came to nothing, as it met with invariable opposition from capitalistic combinations, and Tel-el-Kebir's success bought with money, was

the most brilliant victory wealth has ever obtained on the field of battle (Loria in Hobson 1901: 54–55, emphasis added).

Entire countries have been, and can be, taken over by force, but the real advance of global capitalism may show itself in this: that the nation states of the world are now taken over by debt and instead of an ad hoc "financial commission" thrown together during a temporary debt crisis, there are permanent institutions such as the IMF and World Bank to monitor and manage a permanent crisis of debt for the benefit of foreign creditors.

THE BIOPOLITICS OF GLOBAL CAPITALISM

After examining disciplinary power, the French social theorist Michel Foucault suggested that there was a new power that was not specifically targeted at this or that particular individual, but one that operated at the level of the population or segments of it. He called this "biopower" and he associated it with the management and control of social order by governing authorities. What helped make the exercise of biopower possible was greater and growing statistical knowledge on populations and their regularities. Foucault argued that whatever the actual effects of power, the purpose of it as a social technology was to enhance or improve human life. In other words, interventions or regulatory measures became—at least in discourse and not without several contradictions—geared toward improving life, prolonging its duration, improving its chances of survival, and compensating for failings (Foucault 2003: 254). We can see this clearly reflected in the charters of many international organizations concerned with development and at the level of national welfare states. Foucault argued that this power is fundamentally different from the old power of the sovereign and his right "to take life or let live" (Foucault 1978: 135). Unlike sovereign power represented primarily by the sword, biopower is not exercised to repress, exact, and dominate but to make life flourish in all its dimensions. But is this a completely accurate assessment of human affairs? At first glance it might seem so. Take for example the World Bank Group, by whose own admission it is "one of the world's largest sources of funding and knowledge for developing countries."[7] The mission of the World Bank Group is to reduce extreme poverty (note it does not say end it) and promote a shared prosperity by increasing the incomes of the poorest 40 percent in every country. Why is this so? Because poverty gnaws at life, it destroys its opportunities, it saps its energies, and it spoils life potentials. In this sense, we would suspect the World Bank to be concerned with what I have called the logic of livelihood. But contradictions immediately appear when we examine the method it employs to accomplish its goals.

At base, the goal of the World Bank is similar to the one Adam Smith artic-
ulated in 1776—to increase the "wealth of nations" or in their own words:
"With rising populations, economic growth is the only sustainable mechanism for increasing a society's standard of living" (World Bank 2005: 2).
Knowing this to be the case, the World Bank then identifies the agent responsible for economic growth—the private firm:

> Driven by the quest for profits, [private firms] invest in new ideas and new
> facilities that strengthen the foundation of economic growth and prosperity.
> They provide more than 90 percent of jobs, creating opportunities for people
> to apply their talents and improve their situations. They provide the goods and
> services needed to sustain life and improve living standards. They are also the
> main source of tax revenues, contributing to public funding for health, educa-
> tion, and other services. Firms are thus critical actors in the quest for growth and
> poverty reduction (World Bank 2005: 1).

Since firms are the "critical actors" that have a unique ability to generate growth and thereby reduce poverty, the World Bank argues that it is its
desire—albeit within limits—that governors must pay particular attention to.
What governors must pay particular attention to is the investment climate—
a series of economic, political, and social phenomena that either encourage
investment or prevent it. The aim here is not simply to define, monitor, and
protect market freedoms, but to adjust or alter variables so that rational-
economic actors can make decisions in a safe, transparent, and relatively pre-
dictable business environment. Creating an environment that will attract and
maintain investors is considered a *constant process* and involves much more
than settling contractual disputes and protecting property. It involves a series
of manipulations to create "the right disposition of things" so that firms will
unleash their creative potential, spur growth, and thereby raise the standard of
living. The question then becomes, what is "the right disposition of things"?

According to the Bank, this will vary depending on time and place as well
as the capacity and resources of governors. Yet despite this variance, there is
a bare minimum of underlying initiatives in "four core areas" that governors
may wish to undertake to improve their investment climates: (1) stability
and security, (2) regulation and taxation, (3) finance and infrastructure, (4)
workers and labor markets. Evidence signaling a *stable and secure* environment involves a low crime rate, efficient and reliable contract enforcement,
the provision of more secure rights to property in land and other property,
and ending the practice of expropriation without compensation. In regard
to *regulation and taxation*, "the right disposition of things" involves fostering a competitive environment, fighting corruption, the simplification of tax
structures, and improving customs administration. Interventions at the level

of *finance and infrastructure* include better bank regulation, the creation of credit bureaus to provide lenders with information on borrowers, the strengthening of shareholder and creditor rights, and the better management of public resources. As far as *workers and labor markets* are concerned, the Bank suggests that governors enhance their human capital through education and skills training, that they ensure the flexibility of both the formal and informal workforce, and introduce some scheme of insurance for displaced workers (World Bank 2005: 11–15). These are just some of the minimum requirements deemed necessary to improve the investment climate and reduce, but evidently not end, extreme poverty. And since creating a favorable investment climate is conceived of as a never-ending process, there are always more interventions to make.

Thus, while entire populations are implicated in this project, it is through the private for-profit firm, an artificial member of this population insofar as it is a legal fiction, that life will be saved, that life expectancies will improve, that life's chances will be bettered. Life must not be properly arranged and put in order for life's sake, but for the sake of the private firm that then has the power to grant life to others as long as it is profitable. Biopower is to work through differential accumulation, a strange proposition since the very goal of differential accumulation is to make income, wealth, and life chances more unequal. We could touch upon a number of examples but one of the direst that demonstrates the contradiction between the logic of livelihood and the biopolitical logic of differential accumulation is the heartbreaking wave of farmer suicides in India. Due to indebtedness and crop failures over 200,000 farmers have committed suicide since the World Bank imposed reforms on India that altered the nature of its rural agriculture and the life chances of its farmers. As Shiva reports:

In 1998, the World Bank's structural adjustment policies forced India to open up its seed sector to global corporations like Cargill, Monsanto and Syngenta. The global corporations changed the input economy overnight. Farm saved seeds were replaced by corporate seeds, which need fertilizers and pesticides and cannot be saved. Corporations prevent seed savings through patents and by engineering seeds with non-renewable traits. As a result, poor peasants have to buy new seeds for every planting season and what was traditionally a free resource, available by putting aside a small portion of the crop, becomes a commodity. This new expense increases poverty and leads to indebtedness. The shift from saved seed to corporate monopoly of the seed supply also represents a shift from biodiversity to monoculture in agriculture. The district of Warangal in Andhra Pradesh used to grow diverse legumes, millets, and oilseeds. Now the imposition of cotton monocultures has led to the loss of the wealth of farmer's breeding and nature's evolution.[8]

Thus one of the central contradictions of the tragedy of human development and capital as power is that the earnings of multinational corporations
and the profits of their owners/investors are privileged over and above the
lives of Indian farmers. But then again, this is just one example of many
that demonstrates the contradictions between the logic of livelihood and the
differential accumulation of money and power. Perhaps there is no better
example than our inability to effectively deal with global climate change,
already a direct threat to livelihoods around the world, mostly those of the
poor and vulnerable. The sad truth is that combating climate change in any
serious way runs up against the logic of growth and differential accumulation
that is almost fully based on our production and consumption of fossil fuels.
In the end, as Gore suggested, we might just end up being a naked ape playing
with matches on a petrol dump (Di Muzio 2015b: 171).

NOTES

1   Harry S. Truman Library and Museum 'Truman's Inaugural Address, January
20, 1949'. https://www.trumanlibrary.org/whistlestop/50yr_archive/inagural20jan
1949.htm (accessed 7/7/2017, emphasis added).

2   NSC 68: United States Objectives and Programs for National Security. April 14,
1950. http://www.fas.org/irp/offdocs/nsc-hst/nsc-68-9.htm (accessed 7/8/2017).

3   Federal Government: National Defense Consumption Expenditures and Gross
Investment. https://fred.stlouisfed.org/series/FDEFX (accessed 7/7/2015).

4   Memo by George Kennan, Head of the US State Department Policy Plan-
ning Staff. Written February 28, 1948, Declassified June 17, 1974. George Kennan,
"Review of Current Trends, U.S. Foreign Policy, Policy Planning Staff," PPS No. 23.
Top Secret. Included in the U.S. Department of State, Foreign Relations of the United
States, 1948, volume 1, part 2 " (Washington DC, Government Printing Office, 1976),
509–29.

5   Calculations are based on an American population of 323 million with an adult
population of 282 million (above eighteen years old) and a global population of seven
billion. Average global wealth per adult in the United States is US$345,000, accord-
ing to Credit Swiss Global Wealth Databook, 2016.

6   World Bank, Gross Domestic Product, 2016. http://databank.worldbank.org/
data/download/GDP.pdf (accessed 7/10/2017).

7   The World Bank, Who we Are. http://www.worldbank.org/en/who-we-are
(accessed 7/12/2017).

8   Vandana Shiva (nd) 'From Seeds of Suicide to Seeds of Hope: Why Are Indian
Farmers Committing Suicide and How Can We Stop This Tragedy?' HuffPost. http://
www.huffingtonpost.com/vandana-shiva/from-seeds-of-suicide-to_b_192419.html
(accessed 7/12/17).

Epilogue

SATURN AND WORLD CIVILIZATION

Hanging in the Museo del Prado in Madrid is one of Goya's most notorious and gruesome black paintings: *Saturn Devouring His Son*. The painting is an allegory about the perpetuation of power. Saturn, upon hearing that one day one of his children will dethrone him, devours his children as they are born so as to guarantee his rule in perpetuity. In this imagery, I like to think of Saturn as a metaphor for the logic of differential accumulation since it is primarily about chasing money and power at the vast expense of most of humanity and future generations. As we have discussed this drive has a long lineage with the main difference between our own time and the distant past being that the logic of differential accumulation is now embedded in the capitalized state and giant inter owned corporations that shape and reshape the social reproduction of an uneven global petro-market civilization. As I have tried to show, the incessant drive to accumulate money and power is the root of many of our social problems from Indian farmer suicides to the militarization of global order and from the increasing inequality of wealth, income, and life chances to the threats of global climate change, racist discourses, and environmental collapse. As I have suggested in previous works (Di Muzio 2015a, 2015b), it is not as if we lack solutions to many of these harmful practices but the fact that a few actually benefit from current arrangements and they are the ones most likely to be "last to starve" while reaping rewards en route to the demolition of the natural environment and, with some considerable plausibility, the end of *Homo sapiens* (Diamond 2005). All of this may seem far-fetched until you consider the previous collapse of civilizational orders and that many of the world's worst atrocities were not anticipated. It is true that I have chosen not to dwell on developments that we might consider achievements in many parts of the world: clean water, democracy, the respect for human rights, humanitarian aid, the eradication of disease, medical discoveries, and cleaner energy, just to name a few. For some, this will be considered a major shortcoming of the present work, but I believe there are sufficient—mainly uncritical—accounts of human development that can satisfy my critics who prefer to view human history with more rose-colored glasses. Moreover, it should be said that I did not stress our achievements because most of the advances we might point to are largely in spite of the logic of differential accumulation and have more to do with the logic of livelihood—the logic that makes life worth living. As I have tried to demonstrate, this latter logic is too often controlled, undermined, and snuffed out by the compulsion to gain more money and power by a few. In the end, given the multiple crises we face from extreme poverty, the environmental consequences inherent in our continued use of fossil fuels, the mass pollution of factory farming, and the multiple threats posed by a warming planet, we may make the plausible argument that those with the greatest capitalization are those who have harmed society and the environment the most (Di Muzio 2015c; Kempf 2008). This will likely seem counterintuitive to some readers since the wealthy of our societies are generally revered, held in high esteem, or both. A longer study may indeed bear the level of this sabotage out, but if we consider the owners of armament firms, the extractive industry (oil, gas, and mining), and the owners of the banks that invest in them, we might start to get a picture of how this thesis might be substantiated in greater detail than I have been permitted here or that Kempf has discussed in a previous work.

What the future holds for the tragedy of human development no one can predict with certainty. But to borrow a term from computing, it should be clear that our main operating system is geared toward differential capitalization and the accumulation of social power rather than the enhancement of life and the protection of our environments that sustain it. For those who care about the future of the planet and future generations, our task is to find a new operating system with new indicators for life. Like the Sword of Damocles, our fate as an intelligent species may hang in the balance.

References

Abouharb, M. Rodwan, and David Cingranelli (2007) *Structural Adjustment and Human Rights*. (Cambridge, UK: Cambridge University Press).

Abramsky, Kolya ed. (2010) *Sparking a Worldwide Energy Revolution*. (Oakland, CA: AK Press).

Alkhateeb, Firas (2014) *Lost Islamic History: Reclaiming Muslim Civilization from the Past*. (London: Hurst Publishers).

Alpern, Stanley B. (1995) "What Africans Got for Their Slaves: A Master List of European Trade Goods," *History in Africa,* Vol. 22: 5–43.

Alperovitz, Gar, Robert L. Messer, and Barton J. Bernstein (1991–2) "Marshall, Truman, and the Decision to Drop the Bomb," *International Security*, Vol. 16, No. 3: 204–221.

Alperovitz, Gar, and Lew Daly (2008) *Unjust Deserts: How the Rich are Taking our Common Inheritance and Why We Should Take It Back*. (New York: The New Press).

Amhed, Nafeez Mosaddeq (2010) *A User's Guide to the Crisis of Civilization: And How to Save It*. (London: Pluto Press).

Amin, Samir (2011) *Global History: A View from the South*. (Cape Town, South Africa: Pambazuka Press).

Anderson, Perry (2013a) *Passages from Antiquity to Feudalism*. (London: Verso Books).

Anderson, Perry (2013b) *Lineages of the Absolutist State*. (London: Verso Books).

Appenzeller, Tim (2012) "Human Migrations: Eastern Odyssey," *Nature*, Vol. 485: 24–26.

Arendt, Hannah (1979) *The Origins of Totalitarianism*. (San Diego: Harcourt Brace Jovanovich).

Armitage, Simon J., Sabah A. Jasim, Anthony E. Marks, Adrian G. Parker, Vitaly I. Usik, Hans-Peter Uerpmann (2011) "The Southern Route 'Out of Africa': Evidence for an Early Expansion of Modern Humans into Arabia," *Science*, Vol. 331, I. 6016: 453–6.

Auyang, Sunny (2014) *The Dragon and the Eagle: The Rise and Fall of Chinese and Roman Empires*. (London: Routledge).

Bakan, Joel (2005) *The Corporation: The Pathological Pursuit of Profit and Power*. (New York: Free Press).

Bakker, Isabella, and Stephen Gill (2003) *Power, Production and Social Reproduction: Human In/Security in the Global Political Economy*. (Basingstoke, UK: Palgrave Macmillan).

Banner, Stuart (2005) *How the Indians Lost Their Land: Law and Power on the Frontier*. (Cambridge, MA: Belknap Press).

Barker, Graeme (2009) *Agricultural Revolution in Prehistory: Why Did Foragers Become Farmers?* (Oxford, UK: Oxford University Press).

Barry, John (2012) *The Politics of Actually Existing Unsustainability: Human Flourishing in a Climate-Changed, Carbon Constrained World*. (Oxford, UK: Oxford University Press).

Bartlett, Robert (1994) *The Making of Europe: Conquest, Colonization and Cultural Change, 950–1350*. (Princeton, NJ: Princeton University Press).

Bell, Stephanie, and John F. Henry (2001) "Hospitality versus Exchange: the Limits of Monetary Economies," *Review of Social Economy*, Vol. LIX, No 1: 203–226.

Bellwood, Peter (2005) *First Farmers: The Origins of Agricultural Societies*. (Hoboken, NJ: Wiley-Blackwell).

Benjamin, Walter (1968) *Illuminations*. Ed. Hannah Arendt. (New York: Harcourt, Brace & World).

Berger, Mark T., and Heloise Weber (2014) *Rethinking the Third World: International Development and World Politics*. (Basingstoke, UK: Palgrave Macmillan).

Berlin, Ira (1998) *Many Thousands Gone: The First Two Centuries of Slavery in America*. (Cambridge, MA: Belknap Press).

Black, Brian (2000) *Petrolia: Creating the North American Landscape*. (Baltimore: Johns Hopkins University Press).

Black, Edwin (2006) *Internal Combustion: How Corporations and Government Addicted the World to Oil and Derailed the Alternatives* (New York: St. Martin's Press).

Blackburn, Robin (2010) *The Making of New World Slavery: From the Baroque to the Modern, 1492–1800*. (London: Verso Books).

Blackburn, Robin (2011) *The Overthrow of Colonial Slavery, 1776–1848*. (London: Verso Books).

Bloch, Marc (1962) *Feudal Society Vol. 1: The Growth of Ties of Dependence*. Trans. L. A. Manyon. (London: Routledge).

Boehm, Christopher (2001) *Hierarchy in the Forest: The Evolution of Egalitarian Behavior*. (Cambridge, MA: Harvard University Press).

Borstelmann, Thomas (2001) *The Cold War and the Color Line*. (Cambridge, MA: Harvard University Press).

Bowden, Brett (2009) *The Empire of Civilization: The Evolution of an Imperial Idea*. (Chicago: University of Chicago Press).

Braddick, Michael J. (1996) *The Nerves of State: Taxation and the Financing of the English State, 1558–1714*. (Manchester, UK: Manchester University Press).

Braudel, Fernand (1983) *The Wheels of Commerce: Civilization and Capitalism 15th to 18th Century.* Trans. Sian Reynolds. (London: William Collins, Sons & Co. Ltd).

Brecht, Bertolt (1986) "Theatre for Pleasure or Theatre for Instruction," *Brecht on Theatre: The Development of an Aesthetic.* Ed. and Trans. John Willett. (New York: Schocken Books).

Brewer, John (1989) *The Sinews of Power: War, Money and the English State: 1688–1783.* (London: Unwin Hyman).

Burke, Peter, Ed. (1991) *New Perspectives on Historical Writing.* (Cambridge, UK: Polity Press).

Burnett, Andrew (1987) *Coinage in the Roman World.* (London: Seaby).

Cain, P. J., and A. G. Hopkins (1993) *British Imperialism: Innovation and Expansion.* (New York: Longman Publishing).

Capgemini and RBC (2015) *World Wealth Report 2015.* https://www.worldwealthreport.com/.

Cardwell, Curt (2011) *NSC 68 and the Political Economy of the Early Cold War.* (Cambridge, UK: Cambridge University Press).

Carney, Sean (2005) *Brecht and Critical Theory.* (London: Routledge).

Carr, E. H. (1981) *The Twenty Years' Crisis, 1919–1939.* (Basingstoke, UK: Palgrave Macmillan).

Carswell, John (1960) *The South Sea Bubble.* (London: Cresset Press).

Chadwick, Robert (2005) *First Civilizations: Ancient Mesopotamia and Ancient Egypt.* (London: Equinox Publishing Ltd).

Chaliand, Gérard (2014) *A Global History of War: From Assyria to the Twenty-First Century.* Trans. Michèle Mangin-Woods and David Woods (Oakland, CA: University of California Press).

Chandler, Alfred D., Jr. (1977) *The Visible Hand: The Managerial Revolution in American Business.* (Cambridge, MA: Harvard University Press).

Chatfield, Michael, and Richard Vangermeersch. Eds. (1996) *The History of Accounting: An International Encyclopedia.* (New York: Garland Publishing).

Chomsky, Noam (2004) *Hegemony or Survival: America's Quest for Global Dominance.* (New York: Holt).

Chossudovsky, Michel (2003) *The Globalization of Poverty and the New World Order.* (Pincourt, Canada: Global Research).

Claeys, Gregory (2000) "The 'Survival of the Fittest' and the Origins of Social Darwinism," *Journal of the History of Ideas*, Vol. 61, No. 2: 223–240.

Clay, C. G. A. (1984) *Economic Expansion and Social Change: England 1500–1700, Vol. 1: People, land and towns.* (Cambridge, UK: Cambridge University Press).

Coase, Ronald H. (1937) "The Nature of the Firm," *Economica*, Vol. 4: 386–405.

Commons, John R. (1959) *Legal Foundations of Capitalism.* (Madison, WI: University of Wisconsin Press).

Copeland, Morris A. (1974) "Concerning the Origin of a Money Economy," *The American Journal of Economics and Sociology*, Vol. 33, No. 1: 1–18.

Cox, Robert W. (1981) "Social Forces, States and World Orders," *Millennium: Journal of International Studies*, Vol. 10, No. 2: 126–155.

Craig, Campbell, and Frederik Logevall (2012) *America's Cold War: The Politics of Insecurity.* (Cambridge, MA: Belknap Press).

Credit Suisse (2015) *Global Wealth Report 2015.* https://publications.credit-suisse. com/tasks/render/file/?fileID=F2425415-DCA7-80B8-EAD989AF9341D47E.

Daryaee, Touraj (2013) *Sasasian Persian: The Rise and Fall of an Empire.* (London: I. B. Taurus).

Davies, Glyn (2002) *A History of Money: From Ancient Times to the Present Day.* (Cardiff, UK: University of Wales Press).

Davies, Stephen (2003) *Empiricism and History.* (Basingstoke, UK: Palgrave Macmillan).

Davis, David Brion (2006) *Inhuman Bondage: The Rise and Fall of Slavery in the New World.* (Oxford, UK: Oxford University Press).

Davis, Mike (2001) *Late Victorian Holocausts: El Niño Famines and the Making of the Third World.* (London: Verso Books).

Debeir, Jean-Claude, Jean-Paul Deléage, and Daniel Hémery (1991) *In the Servitude of Power: Energy and Civilization through the Ages.* (London: Zed Books).

de las Casas, Bartolomé (1993) *Witness: Writing of Bartolomé de las Casas.* Ed. and Trans. George Sanderlin (Maryknoll, NY: Orbis Books).

de las Casas, Bartolomé (2007) *A Brief Account of the Destruction of the Indies.* (London: R. Hewson).

Demchak, Chris C. (1991) *Military Organizations, Complex Machines: Modernization in the US Armed Services.* (Ithaca, NY: Cornell University Press).

Diamond, Jared (2005) *Collapse: How Societies Choose to Fail or Succeed.* (New York: Penguin Books).

Dickson, P. G. M. (1967) *The Financial Revolution in England: A Study in the Development of Public Credit, 1688–1756.* (New York: St. Martin's Press).

Di Muzio, Tim (2011) "The Liberal Renaissance and the Ends of History," *Journal of International Relations and Development*, Vol. 15, I. 2: 158–176.

Di Muzio, Tim (2012) "Capitalizing a Future Unsustainable: Finance, Energy and the Fate of Market Civilization," *Review of International Political Economy*, Vol. 19, I. 3: 363–388.

Di Muzio, Tim, Ed. (2014) *The Capitalist Mode of Power: Engagements with the Power Theory of Value.* (London and New York: Routledge).

Di Muzio, Tim (2015a) *The 1% and the Rest of Us: A Political Economy of Dominant Ownership.* (London: Zed Press).

Di Muzio, Tim (2015b) *Carbon Capitalism: Energy, Social Reproduction and World Order.* (London: Rowman & Littlefield International).

Di Muzio, Tim, and Leonie Noble (2017) "The Coming Revolution in Political Economy: Money, Mankiw and Misguided Macroeconomics," *Real World Economic Review*, Vol. 80: 85–108.

Di Muzio, Tim, and Richard H. Robbins (2016) *Debt as Power.* (New York: Oxford University Press).

Di Muzio, Tim, and Richard H. Robbins (2017) *An Anthropology of Money: A Critical Introduction.* (New York: Routledge).

Douglas, C. H. (1922) *The Control and Distribution of Production.* (London: Cecil Palmer).

Draper, Nicholas (2010) *The Price of Emancipation: Slave-Ownership, Compensation and British Society at the End of Slavery.* (Cambridge, UK: Cambridge University Press).

Drescher, Seymour, and Stanley Engerman (1998) *A Historical Guide to World Slavery*. (Oxford, UK: Oxford University Press).

Duncan, T. K., and Christopher J. Coyne (2013) "The Origins of the Permanent War Economy," *The Independent Review*, Vol. 18, No. 2: 219–240.

Duncan-Jones, Richard (1998) *Money and Government in the Roman Empire*. (Cambridge, UK: Cambridge University Press).

Edgell, Stephen, and Jules Townshend (1992) "John Hobson, Thorstein Veblen and the Phenomenon of Imperialism: Finance Capital, Patriotism and War," *American Journal of Economics and Sociology*, Vol. 51, No. 4: 401–420.

Engdahl, William (2004) *A Century of War: Anglo-American Oil Politics and the New World Order*. (London: Pluto Press).

Engelbrecht, H. C., and F. C. Hanighen (1934) *Merchants of Death: A Study of the International Armaments Industry*. (New York: Dodd, Mead and Company).

Ezzamel, Mahmoud (2009) "Order and Accounting as a Performative Ritual: Evidence from Ancient Egypt," *Accounting, Organizations and Society*, Vol. 34, No. 3–4: 348–380.

Ezzamel, Mahmoud, and Keith Hoskin (2002) "Retheorizing Accounting, Writing and Money with Evidence from Mesopotamia and Ancient Egypt," *Critical Perspectives on Accounting*, Vol. 13, No. 3: 333–367.

Ferguson, Niall (2006) *The Cash Nexus: Money and Power in the Modern World, 1700–2000*. (New York: Basic Books).

Ferro, March (1997) *Colonization: A Global History*. (London: Routledge).

Fioramonti, Lorenzo (2013) *Gross Domestic Problem: The Politics Behind the World's Most Powerful Number*. (London: Zed Books).

Flannery, Kent, and Joyce Marcus (2012) *The Creation of Inequality: How Our Prehistoric Ancestors Set the Stage for Monarchy, Slavery, and Empire*. (Cambridge, MA: Harvard University Press).

Foucault, Michel (1978) *History of Sexuality, Volume 1: The Will to Knowledge*. (New York: Pantheon).

Foucault, Michel (2003) *"Society Must be Defended" Lectures at the Collège de France, 1975–1976*. Ed. Mauro Bertani and Alessandro Fontana. Trans. David Macey. (New York: Picador)

Fouquet, Roger, and Peter J. G. Pearson (1998) "A Thousand Years of Energy Use in the United Kingdom," *The Energy Journal*, Vol. 19, No. 4: 1–41.

Friedenberg, Daniel M. (1992) *Life, Liberty and the Pursuit of Land: The Plunder of Early America*. (Buffalo, NY: Prometheus Books).

Fukuyama, Francis (1989) "The End of History?" *The National Interest*, Summer: 3–35.

Füredi, Frank (1998) *The Silent War: Imperialism and the Changing Perceptions of Race*. (London: Pluto Press).

Gale, Barry G. (1972) "Darwin and the Concept of a Struggle for Existence: A Study in the Extrascientific Origins of Scientific Ideas," *Isis*, Vol. 63, No. 3: 321–344.

Garnett, George (2009) *The Norman Conquest: A Very Short Introduction*. (Oxford, UK: Oxford University Press).

George, Susan (1988) *A Fate Worse than Debt*. (London: Penguin).

Gerratana, Valentino (1973) "Marx and Darwin," *New Left Review*, Vol. 82: 60–82.

Gibbon, Edward (2000) *The History of the Decline and Fall of the Roman Empire.* (London: Penguin).

Gilje, Paul A. (1996) "The Rise of Capitalism in the Early Republic," *Journal of the Early Republic*, Vol. 16. No. 2: 159–181.

Gill, Stephen, and Isabella Bakker (2003) *Power, Production and Social Reproduction.* (Basingsoke, UK: Palgrave MacMillan).

Gleeson-White, Jane (2011) *Double Entry: How the Merchants of Venice Created Modern Finance.* (New York: W.W. Norton & Company).

Goldstone, Jack A. (2002) "Efflorescences and Economic Growth in World History: Rethinking the 'Rise of the West' and the Industrial Revolution," *Journal of World History*, Vol. 13, No. 2: 323–89.

Goldsworthy, Adrian (2010) *How Rome Fell.* (New Haven, CT: Yale University Press).

Gwatkin H. M., and J. P. Whitney (1911) *The Cambridge Medieval History.* (New York: Macmillan).

Hager, Sandy Brian (2013) "What Happened to the Bondholding Class? Public Debt, Power and the Top One Per Cent," *New Political Economy*, Vol. 19, No. 2: 155–182.

Hager, Sandy Brian (2016) *Public Debt, Inequality and Power: The Making of a Modern Debt State.* (Oakland, CA: University of California Press).

Hall, Charles A. S., and Kent A. Klitgaard (2012) *Energy and the Wealth of Nations: Understanding the Biophysical Economy.* (New York: Springer).

Ham, Paul (2014) *1914: The Year the World Ended.* (Sydney: Random House).

Ham, Paul (2014) *Hiroshima, Nagasaki: The Real Story of the Atomic Bombings and Their Aftermath.* (New York: Thomas Dunne Books).

Hansen, James, Makiko Sato, Gary Russell, and Pushker Kharecha (2013) "Climate Sensitivity, Sea Level and Atmospheric Carbon Dioxide," *Philosophical Transactions of the Royal Society Association*, Vol. 371: 1–31.

Hawkins, Mike (1997) *Social Darwinism in European and American Thought, 1860–1945: Nature as Model and Nature as Threat.* (Cambridge, UK: Cambridge University Press).

Heinberg, Richard (2003) *The Party's Over: Oil, War and the Fate of Industrial Societies.* (Gabriola Island, Canada: New Society Publishers).

Heinberg, Richard (2007) *Peak Everything: Waking up to a Century of Declines.* (Gabriola Island, Canada: New Society Publishers).

Heinberg, Richard (2011) *The End of Growth: Adapting to our New Economic Reality.* (Gabriola Island, Canada: New Society Publishers).

Heuman, Gad, and Trevor Burnard (2011) *Routledge History of Slavery.* (London: Routlege).

Hilferding, Rudolf (1981) *Finance Capital: A Study of the Latest Phase of Capitalist Development.* Ed. Tom Bottomore. (London: Routledge & Kegan Paul).

Hill, Christopher (1991) *The World Turned Upside Down: Radical Ideas During the English Revolution.* (New York: Penguin Books).

Hilton, Rodney (1990) *Class Conflict and the Crisis of Feudalism.* (London: Verso Books).

Hobsbawm, Eric (1972) *Primitive Rebels: Studies in Archaic Forms of Social Movement in the 19th and 20th Centuries.* (New York: W. W. Norton & Company).

Hobsbawm, Eric (2001) *The Age of Empire: 1875–1914.* (London: Abacus).

Hobson, J. A. (1972) *Imperialism.* (Ann Arbor, MI: University of Michigan Press).

Hogendorn, Jan, and Marion Johnson (1986) *The Shell Money of the Slave Trade.* (New York: Cambridge University Press).

Hollander, David B. (2007) *Money is the Late Roman Republic.* (Leiden, Netherlands: Brill).

Holton, Woody (1999) *Forced Founders: Indians, Debtors, Slaves and the Making of the American Revolution in Virginia* (Chapel Hill, NC: University of North Carolina Press).

Horsefield, Keith, J. (1960) *British Monetary Experiments, 1650–1710.* (Cambridge, MA: Harvard University Press).

Horsman, Reginald (1961) "American Indian Policy in the Old Northwest, 1783–1812," *The William and Mary Quarterly*, Vol. 18, No. 1: 35–53.

Horsman, Reginald (1981) *Race and Manifest Destiny: The Origins of American Racial Anglo-Saxonism.* (Cambridge, MA: Harvard University Press).

Houldcroft, C. J., and S. J. Underdown (2016) "Neanderthal Genomics suggests a Pleistocene Time Frame for the First Epidemiologic Transition," *American Journal of Physical Anthropology*, Vol. 160: 379–388.

Huber, Joseph (2017) *Sovereign Money.* (Basingstoke, UK: Palgrave Macmillan).

Hudson, Michael (2000) "Mesopotamia and Classical Antiquity," *American Journal of Economics & Sociology*, Vol. 59, No. 5: 3–26.

Hutchinson, Frances, and Brian Burkitt (1997) *The Political Economy of Social Credit and Guild Socialism.* (London: Routledge).

Ikenberry, G. John (2011) *Liberal Leviathan: The Origins, Crisis, and Transformation of the American World Order.* (Princeton, NJ: Princeton University Press).

Ingham, Geoffrey (2004) *The Nature of Money.* (Cambridge, UK: Polity Press).

Jackson, Tim (2009) *Prosperity without Growth: Economics for a Finite Planet.* (London: Earthscan).

Jahn, Beate (2013) *Liberal Internationalism.* (Basingstoke, UK: Palgrave Macmillan).

Jenkins, Keith (2003) *Rethinking History*, 2nd ed. (London: Routledge).

Jevons, William Stanley (1866) *The Coal Question: An Inquiry Concerning the Progress of the Nation, and the Probable Exhaustion of Our Coal-Mines.* (London: Macmillan.)

Kats, P. (1930) "A Surmise regarding the Origin of Bookkeeping by Double Entry," *The Accounting Review*, Vol. 5, I. 4: 311–316.

Keely, Lawrence H. (1996) *War before Civilization: The Myth of the Peaceful Savage.* (Oxford, UK: Oxford University Press).

Keister, Orville R. (1963) "Commercial Record-Keeping in Ancient Mesopotamia," *The Accounting Review*, April: 371–376.

Kilbourne, Richard Holcombe (1995) *Debt, Investment, Slaves: Credit Relations in East Feliciana Parish, Louisiana, 1825–1885.* (Tuscaloosa, AL: University of Alabama Press).

Klein, Naomi (2014) *This Changes Everything: Capitalism vs. the Climate.* (New York: Simon & Shuster).

Kohn, George Childs (2007) *A Dictionary of Wars*. (New York: Facts on File).

Korman, Sharon (2003) *The Right of Conquest: The Acquisition of Territory by Force in International Law and Practice*. (Oxford, UK: Oxford University Press).

Korten, David C. (2001) *When Corporations Rule the World*. 2nd ed. (Bloomfield, CT: Kumarian Press).

Krier, Dan (2009) "Speculative Profit Fetishism in the Age of Financial Capital," *Critical Sociology*, Vol. 35, No. 5: 657–675.

Latham, Andrew (2002) "Warfare Transformed: A Braudelian Perspective on the 'Revolution in Military Affairs'," *European Journal of International Relations*, Vol. 8(2): 231–266.

Lewis, Mark Edward, and Timothy Brook (2010) *The Early Chinese Empires: Qin and Han*. (Cambridge, MA: Harvard University Press).

Linebaugh, Peter (2006) *The London Hanged: Crime and Civil Society in the Eighteenth Century*. (London: Verso Books).

Linebaugh, Peter, and Marcus Rediker (2000) *The Many-Headed Hydra: Sailors, Slaves, Commoners, and the Hidden History of the Revolutionary Atlantic*. (Boston: Beacon Press).

Lineweaver, Charles H. (2008) "Paleontological Tests: Human-Like Intelligence is not a Convergent Feature of Evolution," Ed. J. Seckbach and M. Walsh. *From Fossils to Astrobiology*. (New York: Springer): 353–369.

Liu, Wu, María Martinón-Torres, Yan-jun Cai, Song Xing, Hao-wen Tong, Shu-wen Pei, Mark Jan Sier, Xiao-hong Wu, R. Lawrence Edwards, Hai Cheng, Yi-yuan Li, Xiong-xin Yang, José María Bermúdez de Castro, and Xiu-jie Wu (2015) "The Earliest Unequivocally Modern Humans in Southern China," *Nature*, Vol. 526, No. 7575: 696–699.

Lloyd, Moya, and Andrew Thacker, Eds. (1997) *The Impact of Michel Foucault on the Social Sciences and Humanities*. (Basingstoke, UK: Palgrave Macmillan).

Loewe, Michael, and Edward L. Shaughnessy (1999) *The Cambridge History of Ancient China: From the Origins of Civilization to 221 BC*. (Cambridge, UK: Cambridge University Press).

Loewen, James W. (1996) *Lies My Teacher Told Me: Everything Your American History Textbook Got Wrong*. (New York: Simon & Schuster).

Lorenz, Chris (1998) "Can Histories be True? Narrativism, Positivism, and the Metaphorical Turn," *History and Theory*, Vol. 37, I. 3: 309–29.

Luxemburg, Rosa (1951) *The Accumulation of Capital*. Trans. Agnes Schwarzschild. (London: Routledge).

Malanima, Paolo (2006) "Energy Crisis and Growth 1650–1850: The European Deviation in a Compartive Perspective," *Journal of Global History*, Vol. 1: 101–121.

Malthus, Thomas Robert (1992) *An Essay on the Principle of Population*. Ed. David Winch. (Cambridge, UK: Cambridge University Press).

Manning, Richard (2004) "The Oil We Eat," *Harper's*. February: 37–45.

Manning, Richard (2005) *Against the Grain: How Agriculture Has Hijacked Civilization*. (New York: North Point Press).

Marx, Karl (1887) *Capital: A Critique of Political Economy Volume 1*. Trans. Samuel Moore and Edward Aveling. (Moscow: Progress Publishers).

Marx, Karl (1990) *Capital: A Critique of Political Economy, Volume One*. Trans. Ben Fowkes. (London: Penguin Books).

McLeay, Michael, Amar Radia, and Ryland Thomas (2014) "Money Creation in the Modern Economy," *Quarterly Bulletin Q1*. (London: Bank of England).

McNeill, William H. (1982) *The Pursuit of Power: Technology, Armed Force, and Society since A.D. 1000*. (Chicago: University of Chicago Press).

Mellars, Paul (2006) "Why did Modern Human Populations Disperse from Africa ca. 60,000 Years Ago – a New Model," *Proceedings of the National Academy of Sciences USA*, Vol. 103, No. 25: 9381–9386.

Melman, Seymour (1970) *Pentagon Capitalism: The Political Economy of War*. (New York: McGraw-Hill).

Melman, Seymour (1974) *The Permanent War Economy: American Capitalism in Decline*. (New York: Simon & Schuster).

Melman, Seymour (1997) "From Private to State Capitalism: How the Permanent War Economy Transformed the Institutions of American Capitalism," *Journal of Economic Issues*, Vol. 31, No. 2: 311–330.

Moore, Barrington Jr. (1974) *The Social Origins of Dictatorship and Democracy: Lord and Peasant in the Making of the Modern World*. (New York: Penguin University Books).

Morgan, Michael L., Ed. (1992) *Classics of Moral and Political Philosophy*. (Indianapolis: Hackett Publishing Company).

Morris, Ian, and Walter Scheidel, Eds. (2010) *The Dynamics of Ancient Empires: State Power from Assyria to Byzantium*. (Oxford, UK: Oxford University Press).

Morris, Ian (2014) *War! What Is It Good For?: Conflict and the Progress of Civilization from Primates to Robots*. (New York: Farrar, Strauss and Giroux).

Morton, Adam David (2005) "The 'Failed State' of International Relations," *New Political Economy*, Vol. 10, No. 3: 371–379.

Mueller, John (1999) *Overblown: How Politicians and the Terrorism Industry Inflate National Security Threats, and Why We Believe Them*. (New York: Free Press).

Mumford, Lewis (1934) *Technics and Civilization*. (London: Routledge).

Nef, John U. (1966) [1932] *The Rise of the British Coal Industry, Volumes I–II*. (Abingdon, UK: Frank Cass).

Nef, John U. (1977) "An Early Energy Crisis and its Consequences," *Scientific American*. November: 140–150.

Nikiforuk, Andrew (2012) *The Energy of Slaves: Oil and the New Servitude*. (Vancouver, Canada: Greystone Books).

Nitzan, Jonathan (1998) "Differential Accumulation: Toward a New Political Economy of Capital," *Review of International Political Economy*, Vol. 5, No. 2: 169–217.

Nitzan, Jonathan (2001) "Regimes of Differential Accumulation: Mergers, Stagflation and the Logic of Globalization," *Review of International Political Economy*. Vol. 8, No. 2: 226–274.

Nitzan, Jonathan, and Shimshon Bichler (2002) *The Global Political Economy of Israel*. (London: Pluto Press).

Nitzan, Jonathan, and Shimshon Bichler (2009) *Capital as Power: A Study of Order and Creorder*. (London: Routledge).

NSC 68: United States Objectives and Programs for National Security. April 14, 1950. Internet accessible: (6/23/2017) http://www.fas.org/irp/offdocs/nsc-hst/nsc-68-9.htm.

O'Brien, Patrick K. (1988) "The Political Economy of British Taxation, 1660–1815," *The Economic History Review*, Vol. 41, No. 1: 1–32.

O'Connor, James (1979) *The Fiscal Crisis of the State.* (New Brunswick, NJ: Transaction Publishers).

Oppenheimer, Stephen (2003) *The Real Eve: Modern Man's Journey Out of Africa.* (New York: Basic Books).

Orwell, George (1990) *Nineteen Eighty-Four.* (New York: Penguin).

Pakenham, Thomas (2009) *The Scramble for Africa.* (London: Abacus).

Palgrave, Inglis R.H. (1894) *Dictionary of Political Economy.* (London: Palgrave Macmillan).

Peacock, Mark S. (2006) "The Origins of Money in Ancient Greece: the Political Economy of Coinage and Exchange," *Cambridge Journal of Economics*, Vol. 30: 637–650.

Pearson, Karl (1919) *National Life from the Standpoint of Science*, 2nd Ed. (Cambridge, UK: Cambridge University Press)

Perelman, Michael (2000) *The Invention of Capitalism: Classical Political Economy and the Secret History of Primitive Accumulation.* (Durham, NC: Duke University Press).

Perry, Matt (2002) *Marxism and History.* (Basingstoke, UK: Palgrave Macmillan).

Pettifor, Ann (2017) *The Production of Money: How to Break the Power of Bankers.* (London: Verso Books).

Pinker, Steven (2011) *The Better Angels of Our Nature: Why Violence Has Declined.* (New York: Viking).

Piterberg, Gabriel, and Lorenzo Veracini (2015) "Wakefield, Marx and the World Turned Inside Out," *Journal of Global History*, Vol. 10: 457–478.

Podobnik, Bruce (2006) *Global Energy Shifts: Fostering Sustainability in a Turbulent Age.* (Philadelphia: Temple University Press).

Porter, Bernard (1975) *A Short History of British Imperialism 1850–1970.* (New York: Longman).

Powell, Marvin A. (1996) "Money is Mesopotamia," *Journal of the Economic and Social History of the Orient,* Vol. 39, No. 3: 224–242.

Price, T. Douglas (1995) "Social Inequality at the Origins of Agriculture," *Foundations of Social Inequality.* Ed. Gary M. Feinman and T. Douglas Price. (London: Plenum Press): 129–151.

Quigley, Carroll (1979) *The Evolution of Civilizations.* (New York: Liberty Fund).

Randers, Jorgen (2008) "Global Collapse – Fact or Fiction?" *Futures*, Vol. 40: 853–864.

Raphael, Ray (2002) *A People's History of the American Revolution: How Common People Shaped the Fight for Independence.* (New York: HarperPerennial).

Rich, Norman (1973) *Hitler's War Aims Ideology: The Nazi State and the Course of Expansion.* (New York: W.W. Norton & Company).

Rist, Gilbert (2008) *The History of Development*, 3rd ed. (London: Zed Books).

Roberts, J. M. (2007) *The New Penguin History of the World*. (New York: Penguin).

Rockström, Johan et al. (2009) "A Safe Operating Space for Humanity," *Nature*, Vol. 461: 472–5.

Rodney, Walter (1973) *How Europe Underdeveloped Africa*. (London: Bogle-L'Ouverture Publications).

Rowbotham, Michael (1998) *The Grip of Death: A Study of Modern Money, Debt Slavery and Destructive Economics*. (Charlbury, UK: Jon Carpenter Publishing).

Roy, William G. (1997) *Socializing Capital: The Rise of the Industrial Corporation in America*. (Princeton, NJ: Princeton University Press).

Rudé, George (1959) *The Crowd in the French Revolution*. (Oxford, UK: Oxford University Press).

Runciman, W. G. (1983) "Capitalism without Classes: The Case of Classical Rome," *The British Journal of Sociology*, Vol. 34, No. 2: 157–181.

Savranskaya, Svetlana V. (2005) "New Sources on the Role of Soviet Submarines in the Cuban Missile Crisis," *Journal Of Strategic Studies*, Vol. 28, No. 2: 233–259.

Sayer, Andrew (2015) *Why We Can't Afford the Rich*. (Bristol, UK: Policy Press).

Schaps, David M. (2007) *The Invention of Coinage and the Monetization of Ancient Greece*. (Ann Arbor, MI: University of Michigan Press).

Scheidel, Walter (2015) *State Power in Ancient China and Rome*. (Oxford, UK: Oxford University Press).

Scheidel, Walter (2017) *The Great Leveler: Violence and the History of Inequality from the Stone Age to the Twenty-First Century*. (Princeton, NJ: Princeton University Press).

Schwartz, Stephen (1998) *Atomic Audit: The Costs and Consequences of US Nuclear Weapons Since 1940*. (Washington, D.C.: Brookings Institution Press).

Shaw, Martin (1991) *Post-Military Society: Militarism, Demilitarization and War at the End of the Twentieth Century*. (Philadelphia: Temple University Press).

Sherwood, Marika (2004) "Britain, the Slave Trade and Slavery, 1808–1843," *Race & Class*, Vol. 46, No. 2: 54–77.

Sinclair, Timothy (2005) *The New Masters of Capital: American Bond Rating Agencies and the Politics of Creditworthiness*. (Ithaca, NY: Cornell University Press).

Smil, Vaclav (1994) *Energy in World History*. (Boulder, CO: Westview Press).

Smith, Michael S. (2005) "Anti-Radicalism and Popular Politics in an Age of Revolution," *Parliamentary History*, Vol. 24, I. s1: 71–92.

Sobel, Robert (1965) *A History of the New York Stock Market*. (New York: Free Press).

Sobel, Robert (2000) *The Pursuit of Wealth*. (New York: McGraw-Hill).

Sosin, Jack M. (1964) "Imperial Regulation of Colonial Paper Money, 1764–1773," *Pennsylvania Magazine of History and Biography*, Vol. 88, No. 2: 174–198.

Spufford, Peter (1988) *Money and Its Uses in the Middle Ages*. (Cambridge, UK: Cambridge University Press).

Stavrianos, L.S. (1981) *The Global Rift: The Third World Comes of Age*. (New York: William Morrow and Company).

Strayer, Joseph R. (2005) *On the Medieval Origins of the Modern State*. (Princeton, NJ: Princeton University Press).

Thomas, Brinley (1986) "Was There an Energy Crisis in Great Britain in the 17th Century," *Explorations in Economic History*, Vol. 23: 124–152.

Thomas, Brinley (1993) *The Industrial Revolution and the Atlantic Economy*. (London: Routledge).

Thompson, E. P. (1991) *The Making of the English Working Class*. (New York: Penguin Books).

Thorpe, Rebecca U. (2014) *The American Warfare State: The Domestic Politics of Military Spending*. (Chicago: University of Chicago Press).

Trouillot, Michel-Rolph (1995) *Silencing the Past: Power and the Production of History*. (Boston: Beacon Press).

Tucker, Robert C., Ed. *The Marx-Engels Reader*, 2nd Ed. (New York: W.W. Norton & Company).

Tyerman, Christopher (2007) *God's War: A New History of the Crusades*. (New York: Belknap Press).

Veblen, Thorstein (1904) *Theory of the Business Enterprise*. (New York: Transaction Publishers).

Veblen, Thorstein (1923) *Absentee Ownership: Business Enterprise in Recent Times: The Case of America*. (New York: Transaction Publishers).

Veblen, Thorstein (1964) *Essays in Our Changing Order*. (New York: Transaction Publishers).

Vitali, Stefania, James B. Glattfelder, and Stefano Battiston (2011) "The Network of Global Corporate Control," *PLoS ONE*, Vol. 6, No. 10: 1–36.

Vogel, Jeffrey (1996) "The Tragedy of History," *New Left Review*, I. 200: 36–61.

Wade, Nicholas (2007) *Before the Dawn: Recovering the Lost History of Our Ancestors*. (New York: Penguin).

Wainstock, Dennis D. (1996) *The Decision to Drop the Atomic Bomb*. (New York: Praeger).

Waltz, Kenneth N. (1981) "The Spread of Nuclear Weapons: More May Better," *Adelphi Papers*, No. 171. (London: International Institute for Strategic Studies).

Waltz, Kenneth N. (1988) "The Origins of War in Neorealist Theory," *Journal of Interdisciplinary History*, Vol. 18, No. 4: 615–628.

Weatherford, Jack (1997) *The History of Money*. (New York: Crown Business).

Weaver, John C. (2003) *The Great Land Rush and the Making of the Modern World, 1650–1900*. (Montreal: McGill-Queen's University Press).

Wells, Spencer (2004) *The Journey of Man: A Genetic Odyssey*. (New York: Random House).

Wells, Spencer (2010) *Pandora's Seed: The Unforeseen Cost of Civilization*. (New York: Random House).

Wendt, Alexander (2003) "Why A World State Is Inevitable," *European Journal of International Relations*, Vol. 9, I. 4: 491–542.

Wennerlind, Carl (2011) *Casualties of Credit: The English Financial Revolution, 1620–1720*. (Cambridge, MA: Harvard University Press).

Werner, Richard A. (2014) "Can Banks Individually Create Money out of Nothing? – The Theories and the Empirical Evidence," *International Review of Financial Analysis*, Vol. 36: 1–19.

Wesseling, H.L. (1996) *Divide and Rule: The Partition of Africa, 1880–1914*. (New York: Praeger).

West, Delno (1992) "Christopher Columbus and His Enterprise to the Indies: Scholarship of the Last Quarter Century," *The William and Mary Quarterly*, Third Series, Vol. 49, No. 2: 254–277.

Williams, Eric (1984) *From Columbus to Castro: The History of the Caribbean 1492–1969*. (New York: Random House).

Wilson, Carter (1996) *Racism: From Slavery to Advanced Capitalism*. (London: Sage Publications).

Wilson, Edward O. (2013) *The Social Conquest of the Earth*. (New York: Liveright).

Wolf, Eric R. (2010) *Europe and the Peoples Without History*. (Berkeley, CA: University of California Press).

Wolfe, Patrick (2006) "Settler Colonialism and the Elimination of the Native," *Journal of Genocide Research,* Vol. 8, I. 4: 387–409.

Wolfe, Patrick (2016) *Traces of History: Elementary Structures of Race*. (London: Verso Books).

Wood, Ellen Meiksins (2002) *The Origin of Capitalism*: A Longer View. (London: Verso Books).

Wray, Randall, Ed. (2004) *Credit and State Theories of Money: The Contributions of A. Mitchell Innes*. (Cheltenham, UK: Edward Elgar).

Wrigley, E. A. (2010) *Energy and the English Industrial Revolution*. (Cambridge, UK: Cambridge University Press).

Yergin, Daniel (1991) *The Prize: The Epic Quest for Oil, Money and Power*. (New York: Free Press).

Young, Alfred F., Ed. (1976) *The American Revolution: Explorations in the History of American Radicalism*. (DeKalb, IL: Northern Illinois University Press).

Young, Robert M. (1969) "Malthus and the Evolutionists: The Common Context of Biological and Social Theory," *Past and Present*, No. 43: 109–145.

Zinn, Howard (1995) *A People's History of the United States 1492-Present*. (New York: Harper Perennial).

Zizek, Slavoj (2011) *Living in the End Times*. (London: Verso Books).

Zook, Gorge Frederick (1919) "The Company of Royal Adventurers of England Trading into Africa, 1660–1672," *The Journal of Negro History*, Vol. 4, No. 2: 134–231.

Index

About the Author

Tim Di Muzio is senior lecturer in politics and international studies at the University of Wollongong. He is the author of *The 1% and the Rest of Us*, *Carbon Capitalism*, and, with Richard Robbins, *Debt as Power* and *An Anthropology of Money*, among other works.

Lightning Source UK Ltd.
Milton Keynes UK
UKOW04f0730291217
315181UK00001B/84/P

9 781783 487141